SETTING THE FOUNDATIONS

*A guide to the study of the life
and teaching of Jesus Christ as
presented in the first three Gospels*

Rosalyn Kendrick
*Head of Religious Education
Bilton Grange High School, Hull*

Advisory Editor
Rev. John Pridmore
*Head of Religious Education
King Edward's School, Witley*

HULTON EDUCATIONAL

ACKNOWLEDGEMENTS

Photos are reproduced by kind permission of the following:
J. C. Allen 16, 23, 35, 163, 215
Sonia Halliday/Jane Taylor 160, 203, 239

Maps and illustrations: Roy Jones
Editorial: Peter Ford
Cover Design: Anthony Short

First published in Great Britain 1983
by Hulton Educational Publications Ltd
Raans Road, Amersham, Bucks HP6 6JJ

ISBN 0 7175 1156 1

Printed in Great Britain by
Richard Clay (The Chaucer Press) Ltd, Bungay, Suffolk.

For Danny and Frances

Contents

PALESTINE in the time of CHRIST

The Great Sea

Sidon

Zarephath

Damascus

Mt. Hermon

Tyre

PHŒNICIA

Cæsarea Philippi

GALILEE

Ptolemais

Chorazin

Capernaum

Bethsaida

Magdala

Sea of Galilee

Cana

Gergesa

Tiberias

Mt. Carmel

Nazareth

Nain

DECAPOLIS

Cæsarea

SAMARIA

River Jordan

Samaria

Sychar

PERÆA

Shechem

Joppa

Arimathea

Lydda

Bethel

Ephraim

Bethabara

Jericho

Emmaus

Jerusalem

Bethany

Azotus

Bethlehem

JUDEA

Hebron

Dead Sea

Gaza

Wilderness of Judea

N

Introduction

It is assumed that the reader of this book is intending to begin a study of religious education. He may be a student, hoping to pass an examination in the subject, or he may simply be a seeker with an inquiring mind and a willingness to work – for there is much work to be done!

This course is designed for all who wish to have a firm grounding in the knowledge of Jesus as presented in the first three gospels (Mark, Matthew and Luke), and leads specifically to the 'O' level qualification in that subject.

The person tackling this course needs to have:

1. A good working Bible, preferably the Revised Standard Version, or any version which includes the Old Testament and footnotes for cross-reference at the bottom of the page.
2. A good commentary on the text of the Gospels. I would suggest work by Guy, Peake, MacNeile, Luce or Campbell.
3. Finally, notebook and pencil, peace and quiet, and a determination to 'win' – and to remember that 'the way is not easy and the gate is narrow' that leads to success. A plodder may certainly arrive in the end, but the faint-hearted will give up as soon as the way gets tough.

Chin up! Firm resolve – and forward!

THE EVENTS IN THE NEW TESTAMENT

PALESTINE	CHRISTIANITY	ROME	ERA
37. Herod became King			B.C.
		30. Augustus First Emperor	
	6. Birth of Christ (?)		
4. Death of Herod Accession of Archelaus Antipas and Phillip			
6. Archelaus deposed Judaea under Procurators		6. Coponius First Procurator	A.D.
6-7. Revolt of Judas of Gamala, the Zealot			
15. Annas deposed		14. Tiberius made Emperor	
18-36. Caiaphas as High Priest	26-27. Mission of John the Baptist (?)	26. Pontius Pilate made 6th Procurator	
	29. Crucifixion (?)		
	33. Conversion of Saul		
		36. Pontius Pilate deposed	
		37. Caligula made Emperor	
41. Agrippa I made King of Trachonitis, Galilee and Judaea		41. Claudius made Emperor	
44. Death of Agrippa Procurators resumed Felix			
	47-48. Paul's 1st journey		
	49. Council of Jerusalem		
	49-50. Paul's 2nd journey		
	52-56. Paul's 3rd journey	54. Nero made Emperor	
58. Festus succeeds Felix			
	64-5. Martyrdom of Peter and Paul	64. Fire of Rome	
		66. Civil Wars, Vespasian made Emperor	
67. Revolt of Palestine	67. Christians flee to Pella		
78. Destruction of Jerusalem by Titus		79. Titus made Emperor	
132. Bar-Cochbar's Revolt			
135. Jerusalem refounded as Aelia Capitolina			

1

THE MASTER'S VOICE

Those of you with aged parents or the tendency to pick up an assortment of old rubbish at jumble sales, will probably have seen – if not listened to – old gramophone records. Many of these used to have a picture of a little dog listening in amazement to his master's voice coming, as if by magic, out of an enormous trumpet.

There is no record or cassette, of course, of the voice of Jesus, but there is no reason why we should not make a selection of things that he said, that give us a mental picture of what Jesus was really like, what he was getting at.

Here is a selection of such passages through which one can get to know a little of the character of the Master.

Luke

Chapter 4, verses 16–21
Chapter 4, verses 32, 36–37
Chapter 4, verses 42–44
Chapter 5, verses 29–32
Chapter 6, verses 20–23
Chapter 6, verses 27–31
Chapter 6, verse 35
Chapter 7, verses 41–43
Chapter 8, verses 43–48
Chapter 9, verses 23–27
Chapter 9, verses 46–48

Matthew

Chapter 18, verses 10, 14

Luke

Chapter 10, verses 25–28

Chapter 11, verses 9–10
Chapter 12, verses 4–7
Chapter 12, verses 11–12
Chapter 12, verses 22–24
Chapter 13, verses 6–9
Chapter 14, verses 12–14
Chapter 15, verses 4–7

Matthew

Chapter 18, verses 21–22

Luke

Chapter 17, verses 20–21
Chapter 18, verses 10–11, 13–14
Chapter 18, verses 15–17

Matthew

Chapter 18, verses 19–20

Luke

Chapter 18, verses 29–30
Chapter 21, verses 1–4

Matthew

Chapter 26, verses 26–29

Luke

Chapter 22, verse 42

Chapter 23, verses 33–34
Chapter 23, verses 46–47
Chapter 24, verses 15–16,
                           25, 27
Chapter 24, verses 30–31
Chapter 24, verses 36–43

Matthew

Chapter 28, verses 19–20

Work suggestions

1. Read the passages round the class as a 'spoken anthology'.
2. An alternative: copy the passages out on to file paper, and make them into a little booklet. Give it the title 'The Master's Voice'. The title page could then be given a suitable design or illustration.

2
WHO WAS JESUS?

Jesus, the founder of the Christian religion, was born in Palestine, one of the provinces of the Roman Empire, some 2,000 years ago. No one knows the exact date – our date of 25 December in the year 1 was worked out by a Roman monk, Dionysius Exiguus, in the sixth century, and we now know that he made a mistake of several years. December the 25th was picked because it was thought to be the birthday of the Sun. The most likely year for Jesus' birth was 6 B.C., two years before the death of Herod the Great.

He was born in a cattle-shed, possibly in a cave, in the town of Bethlehem, near the capital city of Jerusalem. His parents, who were members of the family of David, a famous past king, had gone there to be enrolled during a population census. From there the family fled to Egypt because the ruler of Palestine, Herod the Great, had heard from some astrologers that a king had been born, and he tried to destroy his possible rival. When Herod died they returned, and settled in Nazareth, a town in Galilee.

Only one incident of Jesus' childhood is recorded: his visit to the Temple at the age of twelve, when he was found arguing with the rabbis like an expert.

When he was about thirty, his cousin John, son of the priest Zechariah, appeared near the River Jordan declaring that God was about to send the long-awaited deliverer, known as the Messiah, and he called on the nation to get ready for him by giving up their sins and being baptised. Jesus also went to him, and as he was baptised certain signs from heaven were seen that revealed that *he* was the Messiah of Israel. He withdrew into the solitude of the wilderness for six weeks to prepare for his mission. He refused the temptations to win the people over by magic or turn the Romans out by force, and chose instead a ministry of teaching and healing.

He chose Capernaum, by the Sea of Galilee, as his main centre of activity, and immediately became very popular. He chose twelve men from the crowds that followed him to become his chief helpers. His popularity stemmed from his miracles of compassion (his anxiety to relieve suffering whenever he found it), his superb teachings, and his ability to bring forgiveness and happiness and hope to those who met him.

But while the common people heard him gladly, many of the leaders of the Jews rejected him. Jesus could see that although some of the leaders certainly lived very careful and religious lives, in his opinion they had missed the point about what the teachings of God really meant and he tried to correct their ideas. Some of these leaders accused him of blasphemy (claiming to be as important as God), living with the wrong sort of company, and even using the power of the Devil. Jesus decided to meet the authorities in Jerusalem, knowing that this might well bring about his death.

He rode into Jerusalem on an ass, in fulfilment of one of the things said about the Messiah in the Old Testament, and defied the authority of the priests in their own Temple by clearing it of the people who looked after the business side of the sacrifices – those who changed Roman money into Temple money, and those who sold animals and birds to be killed on the altar.

Before he was arrested he gave his disciples a farewell meal, in which the breaking and eating of bread and the drinking of wine represented the sacrifice of his own body and blood.

One of his disciples, Judas Iscariot, plotted with the priests to betray him, and Jesus was arrested while praying in the Garden of Gethsemane. The disciples escaped. Jesus was put on trial before Caiaphas the High Priest, Herod Antipas the ruler of Galilee, and Pontius Pilate, the Roman Governor of Judaea. Pilate sentenced him to be scourged and then crucified. Between nine in the morning and three in the afternoon on a Friday, he slowly died, forgiving his enemies as he did so.

He was laid in the garden tomb of a rich man, which was sealed with a heavy stone in front of witnesses. Guards were placed on his tomb because there was already a rumour that Jesus had hinted that he would not stay dead. The Jews didn't believe this, but they thought that the disciples might sneak his body away and pretend he had come back to life. However, early on the Sunday morning his women disciples went to the tomb and discovered that the body had indeed gone.

The story was dismissed until the disciples themselves met Jesus, spoke to him, touched him, and even watched him eat. For forty days he appeared at various times, then these appearances ceased. Ten days after his disappearance, the disciples received wonderful miraculous powers, and the Christian Church was born.

Questions

1. What year has been suggested for the birth of Jesus?
2. Where was Jesus born?
3. *Why* was Jesus born there?
4. Who was the ruler of Palestine at that time?
5. In which town did the family of Jesus finally settle?
6. Who 'prepared the way' for Jesus?
7. What sort of ministry did Jesus choose?
8. How many chief helpers did Jesus have?
9. Why was Jesus so popular with the people?
10. Why did many of the religious leaders reject him?
11. How did Jesus defy the authority of the priests?
12. Who betrayed Jesus?
13. Where was Jesus arrested?
14. Who put Jesus on trial?
15. What was the sentence passed on Jesus?
16. Who actually sentenced Jesus to death?
17. On which day of the week did Jesus die?
18. What was the amazing discovery on the Sunday morning?
19. For how long did Jesus make appearances to his friends?
20. When did the disciples receive the Holy Spirit and its powers?

Creative Writing

If Jesus had not risen from the dead, would there have been anything particular about his life that would have made him a better man than, say, Gandhi or St Francis or Pope John Paul II?

3
THE POLITICAL BACKGROUND

At the birth of Jesus the whole known world was governed by a **Roman Emperor** called Octavian **Augustus** and his wife Livia. After the Battle of Actium in 31 B.C., in which Augustus defeated Mark Antony and his Egyptian queen Cleopatra, he gradually brought the Roman Empire into a state of peace. He overhauled the administration of all the countries in the Empire, and did a great deal to rid it of corrupt practices. Every province was subjected to a regular population census, so that the amount of tax the Romans would take from them would not be too much for the people to bear. St Luke's Gospel suggests that Jesus was born in the same year as one of these taxation censuses.

Each individual country in the Empire was governed by a Roman senator, but Palestine had the special privilege of its own king, **Herod the Great**, who had been an officer in the Roman army in his youth, and a great friend of Mark Antony. When Antony and Cleopatra committed suicide, he changed his allegiance to the triumphant Augustus. Herod's sister, Salome, had been a close friend of the empress Livia, and several of Herod's children were educated in Rome, including the prince Archelaus.

When Herod died in 4 B.C., Archelaus became the ruler of Judaea and Samaria. Augustus said that he could be made a king later, if he proved himself worthy. He was eighteen years old, and when he made his first public appearance in Jerusalem the people demanded the abolition of purchase tax, a general reduction in other taxes, and the release of certain political prisoners. Archelaus agreed to these demands, and the crowd sensed that he was weak and immediately clamoured for more. Old Herod had recently executed some men for pulling down a golden eagle he had set up over a temple gate, and the crowd started to chant slogans. Archelaus tried to make peace, but his officers were stoned by the people, a riot started, the troopers were sent in, and about 3,000 were killed!

Meanwhile, his brother, **Herod Antipas** – who had been Herod's sole heir before he changed his will – was seething with fury because Herod's last will had reduced his claim. He set off for Rome to press his case. Archelaus followed him hastily, and, seizing the opportunity, bandits and desperadoes took up arms all over the country, ransacking and looting.

Augustus was asked to settle the terms of the will, and finally Archelaus was made Ethnarch of Judaea, Samaria and Idumaea; Antipas was made Tetrarch of Galilee and the Peraea; and **Philip**, another brother, was made the Tetrarch of the Hauran territory at the foot of Mount Hermon. (An Ethnarch was a governor of a province, while a Tetrarch was a governor of part of a province.)

Philip reigned until the year A.D. 34, married his niece Salome, and died childless. Archelaus, after his shaky start, proceeded to upset the Jews further by marrying the princess Glaphyra, who had previously been married to one of his other brothers. In A.D. 6 he was denounced to Augustus, who banished him to Vienne on the Rhône, where he died eight years later. His territories were taken over by a Roman **Procurator**, or governor.

At the time of Christ's death, the Roman governor was **Pontius Pilate**, and the Emperor was called **Tiberius**. Tiberius was a brooding, unhappy man, whose life had been wrecked by politics and his political marriage to Augustus' daughter Julia, whom he hated. In the year 26 he retired to the island of Capri, leaving the running of the Empire in the hands of his cruel minister, **Sejanus**. Pilate, who took up his appointment in Judaea in 26, was presumably one of the officials picked by Sejanus, who particularly despised the Jews. Certainly Pilate did not seem able to understand how to handle the various Jewish problems that arose during his time of office.

Certain people, the **Herodians**, hated having Roman governors, and were loyal to the family of Herod, and wished to have them in sole command again, instead of the Romans. Many of the rich and influential people were Herodians.

Another group of people hated the Herodians almost as much as they hated the Romans. These were the underground resistance fighters known as the **Zealots**. Their slogan was 'No friend but the Zealot, no king but God.' They were keenly awaiting the arrival of the Messiah, who would be a battle-leader to rid them of the Roman overlords, and who would also be the rightful king of the Jews because he would be a descendant of the great king of the Old Testament, David.

The Zealots were actively involved in assassinating Roman soldiers whenever they got the chance. Some of them were expert knife-throwers, known as **sicarii** or 'dagger-men'. (It has been suggested that the betrayer of Jesus, Judas Iscariot, may have had his name derived from Ish-Sicarii, literally 'dagger-man'. A deliberate

Herod's Forum, Samaria *Herod the Great was famous for his magnificent cities and lavish buildings. Samaria was one of the cities that benefited from his ambitious schemes.*

pun may have been intended, as he was the one who 'put the dagger in' for Jesus, so to speak.)

One of Jesus' other disciples, Simon the Zealot, was connected with the movement. A famous Zealot leader who was released at the very Passover feast when Jesus was killed was Jesus Bar-Abbas – not so much a murderer as a national hero, and very much what a lot of the Jews would have liked Jesus to be.

The main enemies of the ordinary folk were the **Publicans**, or tax-collectors. These were officials of Rome who counted the population and made sure that the tax-money found its way safely to the Senate in Rome. They were often crooked, always hated, and very often spies and informers. Jesus surprisingly chose at least one of them (Matthew, or Levi) to be among the Twelve Apostles, and we know that he had other friends who were tax-collectors, people who changed their ways after they had met him (for example, Zacchaeus). In fact, Jesus was constantly disliked by the respectable Pharisees for having anything to do with publicans at all!

Samaritans were the people of the area Samaria, whose capital city was also called Samaria, built on the hill Samaria. These were the descendants of the northern tribesmen of Israel who had inter-married with the invading Assyrian soldiers and the people they brought there many years before the time of Jesus, in the seventh century B.C. When the pure Jews of the south returned from their exile in Babylon, they would have nothing to do with the Samaritans, and refused all their offers of assistance.

The Samaritans had been much dismayed by the hostile attitude of the exiled Jews. They maintained that their own worship was pure, and that they had always remained faithful to the Jewish Law. In fact, the brother of the Jewish High Priest felt so sympathetic towards them that he became *their* High Priest. This rivalry did not help matters, and when the Jews refused to let the Samaritans help in the rebuilding of the ruined Temple at Jerusalem, the Samaritans established a temple of their own on Mount Gerizim.

It is an interesting fact that the Samaritan version of the Ten Commandments is different from that of the Jews. According to the Samaritans, the true tenth commandment was an order that Mount Gerizim should be recognised as the holy mountain, and not Mount Zion, on which the Jerusalem Temple was built. The Jews, of course, claimed that the Samaritans had altered the Law to suit their own purpose. The Samaritans denied this vehemently, claiming that their Law was written on a scroll by the great-grandson of Moses. The scroll, which still exists today (although tourists only see copies of it), was written on the skins of sheep sacrificed at Passover.

Over the centuries, the ill-feeling between Jews and Samaritans gradually grew worse, especially as the Samaritans claimed that their own High Priest was the true one, and that the shrine and priests in Jerusalem were false. Just before one Feast of the Passover, matters came to a head when a Samaritan threw human bones all over the Jerusalem Temple courtyard, thus making it unclean. From that time on, although Gentiles could enter the outer court, Samaritans were no longer allowed in the Temple at all.

In fact, Jews would not let a Samaritan even touch them, if they could help it. They thought that even the shadow of a Samaritan could make a person unclean, so much did they hate and despise them. Jews travelling from Galilee to Judaea crossed over the River Jordan rather than pass through their territory.

Questions

1. Which nation ruled the whole of the known world?
2. Name the Emperors (a) at the birth, and (b) at the death, of Jesus.
3. How was the kingdom of Palestine split up after the death of Herod the Great?
4. Which of Herod the Great's sons was deposed?
5. Which of Herod the Great's sons would have been the ruler of Jesus, who lived at Nazareth in Galilee?
6. What was a procurator?
7. Which Roman procurator executed Jesus?
8. What was a Herodian?
9. What were the resistance fighters called?
10. Name one of Jesus' disciples who was a resistance fighter.
11. Who was set free at the time Jesus was crucified?
12. Which of Jesus' disciples was a tax-collector?
13. Why were tax-collectors so despised by the people?
14. What was a Samaritan?
15. Why had the Samaritans been banned from the Temple?
16. How did travelling Jews avoid their territory?
17. What was the attitude of Jesus to tax-collectors and Samaritans?

Creative Writing

Try to imagine you are living in an occupied country. You have possibly seen films or programmes showing what life was like for countries occupied by the Nazis in the Second World War. The Romans, although well organised and good builders, were cruel and ruthless conquerors. When Jesus was a boy, he would have heard of or even seen himself the mass crucifixion of 6,000 followers of a leader of the resistance movement.

A Samaritan Priest *The Samaritans were regarded as rivals and enemies by the Jews. Jesus taught that this enmity was wrong.*

Either: Write an essay as if you were a Galilean boy watching the Roman troops pass through your village.

Or: Make a list of what you think might have been the advantages or disadvantages of the civilised Roman occupation of the rather wild territory of Palestine.

4
THE RELIGIOUS AUTHORITIES

At the time of Jesus, there were five main different sorts of religious people: the priests, Sadducees, Pharisees, Scribes and Essenes.

1. The Priests

These were the men who ran the Temple at Jerusalem. They were the only ones allowed by Jewish Law to make animal sacrifices, and the enormous number of sacrifices brought to the Temple made this a full-time job. On the big festivals, thousands of animals were slaughtered, according to a very ancient ritual, and it was believed that God enjoyed this kind of offering. Many people in Old Testament times had pointed out that God preferred righteous living and kindness towards other people; but nevertheless the old sacrificial system carried on.

Animals for sacrifice could be bought in the outer courtyard of the Temple, after one had first changed one's money into the special Temple coins, which didn't have Caesar's head on them! They objected strongly to Caesar's head, as Caesar was supposed to be a god himself, and it would be most insulting to their True God to fetch in a rival's image.

Being a priest was passed down in families only. One could not just decide to become one. In order to qualiify one had to be born into the tribe of Levi. The total number of priests was divided into twenty-four sections or 'houses', which went on duty in turn throughout the year. Certain duties were much more important than others, for example, burning the incense near the curtain that veiled the innermost room of the Temple. This duty was cast for by lot, and a person could only do it once in a lifetime. (John the Baptist's father, Zechariah, was performing this duty when he saw the angel Gabriel.)

The chief priest was a cunning man called **Caiaphas**, who had taken over when his father-in-law Annas had been deposed by the Romans for being too nationalistic. Priests were helped by **Levites**, other members of the priestly tribe, who did all the general household tasks at the Temple and also made up the choir and the police force there. No one but a priest could ever go in certain areas of the Temple, and therefore all the building repairs, cleaning and so on had to be done by priests.

Since Herod the Great had come to the throne, the High Priest had been chosen from four main families: those of Annas, Boethus, Phiabi and Qamhit. They had to pay an enormous amount of money to gain the position, so this record indicates just how rich those families were. The Boethusians were related to Herod's family, as he had married the daughter of one High Priest, and their son Herod Philip Boethus lived as a gentleman in Rome. (He was married to the lady Herodias who is mentioned in the gospels as demanding the head of John the Baptist.)

2. The Scribes

These were the teachers of the Law. They were experts at reading, writing and giving opinions on the Old Testament scriptures. They were also known as **Rabbis** or **Lawyers**, although this did not mean that they were like our judges. They were the ones who worked out what the various old sayings really meant, and handed down their teachings to the rabbis who came after them. By the time of Jesus, there was an enormous amount of material to be learnt before one could be called a rabbi, and they were beginning to specialise in the different sections, instead of trying to learn it all – an impossible task for one man.

The Pharisaic scribes were famous for their wisdom and humanity, and tried hard to change the existing cruel laws for more merciful ones. For example, a man could only be beaten for thirty-nine strokes and no more – unlike the Roman law which allowed a man to be beaten to death. Famous scribes included Shammai, who had once been the only man to dare to speak out against Herod the Great, and Hillel, who seems to have influenced Jesus by his merciful teachings. Another famous scribe was Gamaliel, the teacher of St Paul.

3. Sadducees

These were members of a small, rich, aristocratic party, many of them priests. The High Priest himself, Caiaphas, was a Sadducee. They claimed descent from the chief priest of King David in the Old Testament, who was called Zadok – the Righteous One. They controlled the Temple, the Treasury, and had a two-thirds majority on the ruling council known as the **Sanhedrin**. They favoured 'modern' Greek culture and education, but resisted any change in the written

Law of the Jews – the first five books of the Old Testament. They completely rejected the ideas of the Pharisees. They were very powerful and very unpopular.

4. Pharisees

These were vast numbers of very devout, educated men who were not satisfied with the way the Sadducees ruled the religious affairs of the Jews. They did not believe that God had fixed His rules once and for all – they thought that, as times changed, the laws ought to be reinterpreted to fit each new situation. They should show signs of progress, and not just stand still. Therefore they were completely opposed to the Sadducees, and worked out many added rules and regulations that they felt would help people to keep the Law properly in their daily lives. These extra rules were known as the Oral Tradition (because they were not written down, but passed on from teacher to teacher) or the Tradition of the Elders. For example, they went into detail about what could and could not be done on the sabbath day. Work was not allowed, and therefore one could not drag a chair across a sandy floor as this would make a furrow, and that would be ploughing! They even used to argue whether or not it would be correct to eat an egg that had been laid on the sabbath!

They also held exciting ideas about life after death. They knew that God must be kind and just, yet they knew that very often the innocent *did* suffer, and the good *did* die young. This suggested that either God was unfair or He didn't care what happened to His worshippers, or even worse, that maybe He didn't exist at all. The only acceptable alternative was that God was fair and did care, but the injustices of this world were put right somewhere else, in another life! They thought there would be a time of judgement for everyone, followed by either **Paradise**, the Persian word for a beautiful garden, or **Gehenna**, a place where all the evil would be burnt up and cease to exist. The name Gehenna was taken from the Valley of Hinnom where one of the Old Testament kings had worshipped the fire-god Moloch and sacrificed babies to him. After his death, the Jews reacted with horror to this place, and it was used as a rubbish dump, which was perpetually kept burning to prevent the spread of disease. (The flames of hell were not supposed to be an everlasting punishment, but a means of getting rid of the evil, once and for all.) They also believed in the possibility of messengers from this other world making contact with the living, either as **Angels** or **Demons**.

Only one third of the Sanhedrin was Pharisaic, so they were usually overruled by the Sadducees, who argued with them continuously over their beliefs. The Pharisees were reformers, but the Sadducees wanted to keep things as they had always been, and in their control.

Pharisees were very influential and popular, however, in the villages and around the country. They were generally very outspoken against anything Greek or Roman, were pious and devout, kindly and charitable, and ran the local synagogues. They were also fervently waiting for the Messiah to come. Jesus was probably closely connected with the Pharisees, and was treated as a Pharisaic rabbi when he taught in the synagogues. He was often entertained by Pharisees, although he spoke up loudly against those who were hypocrites.

Much of the gospel mention of the Pharisees is of a critical nature, as Jesus certainly disapproved of their slavish devotion to the tradition they had built up, which was often in direct opposition to the spirit of the original Law. Nevertheless, one should bear in mind that, on the whole, the Pharisees were much admired and loved.

5. The Essenes

Not enough is known about this group of people to do them justice, since discoveries about them really date from the finding of the

Qumran *The Essene monks who lived by the Dead Sea, and who may have brought up John the Baptist after the death of his parents, hid their precious scrolls in these caves.*

23

Dead Sea Scrolls in the 1940s, and scholarly argument is still going on. However, we do know that they were a very devout sect of religious extremists who lived in communes, one of which has been discovered near the Dead Sea. They appear to have had other groups around the country. They were total pacifists, loathed riches, held all property in common, studied herbal medicine, and were generally involved in the fight against evil in the world. They were particularly opposed to the rich and corrupt Temple priesthood, and regarded themselves as the pure priesthood. They looked forward to a time when Jerusalem and the Temple would be handed over to them.

Some scholars think Jesus may have had connections with them, and that John the Baptist may even have been adopted by them when his aged parents died. He certainly conducted his mission not very far from their encampment, so he must have had some contact with them. They practised baptism, ate a communal meal, worked in bands of twelve – a few obvious parallels with Jesus' ministry. However, it is also true to say that they did not welcome outcasts and sinners into their number, and their three-year training programme before being accepted into the order seems to be the very opposite of the open way in which Jesus dealt with people.

Questions

1. Who were the only people allowed to sacrifice animals?
2. How did a person become a priest?
3. How many 'houses' of priests were there?
4. What duty was only performed once in a lifetime?
5. Who was the chief priest?
6. What were the Temple cleaners and labourers called?
7. What were the names of the four main priestly families?
8. What was a scribe?
9. Name three famous scribes.
10. Which scribe may have influenced Jesus?
11. Which party did Caiaphas belong to?
12. What was the Sanhedrin?
13. Which party opposed the Sadducees with their beliefs?
14. What was the Oral Tradition?
15. Give one example of the Oral Tradition.
16. Why did the Pharisees believe in life after death?
17. What were the two places called, that a person could go to in the after-life?
18. Why did Jesus sometimes disagree with the Pharisees?
19. Give three facts about the Essenes.

20. What features of Jesus' ministry seem to be similar to things the Essenes did?

Creative Writing

It has often been thought, quite wrongly, that the Pharisees were all over-pious hypocrites – men who needed criticising and correcting for their wrong opinions. The gospels reveal that Jesus often did criticise certain Pharisees, but also that he would have agreed considerably with them.

Read through the section on the Pharisees and state what things *you* would have admired or agreed with, and which things you would not have agreed with.

5
THE EXPECTED MESSIAH

The Jews were a very special race of people, in several ways quite different from all the other nations of the world. The most important thing about them that made them different was their firm belief that there was only one God, and that He had been able to speak to certain people. The whole of their nation's history and literature over at least a thousand years was concerned with the gradual revelation of God's Person and His relationships with men.

They believed that God had created the universe, but that the people in it had sometimes chosen to do evil and selfish things rather than good. When people did do wrong it had far-reaching effects on themselves and on those around them, and this was seen as a kind of punishment from God that they were inevitably bringing on themselves. This, of course, was not what God intended at all – indeed, it caused Him a great deal of distress, and He longed to put things right. However, He would not force people to believe in Him, or make them live in the particular way He chose for them, because that would be to make them into robots.

Instead he managed to show certain people the way that He thought they ought to live, so that others could hear their teachings and follow their examples. These people were the famous leaders of the Old Testament stories – people like Abraham and Joseph and Moses; and the prophets – like Jeremiah and Isaiah and Ezekiel. Each of these discovered something about the nature of God, and was able to pass the information on.

Right from the very beginning, the Jews felt that they were special to God. They were His 'chosen people'. Jewish history began with a Sumerian worshipper of the moon called Abraham, who became so convinced that he could hear a voice calling to him that he left his land and his family in obedience to it. He travelled to a new land that he believed had been 'promised' to him and his descendants. His cowardly, cheating grandson Jacob was also suddenly made aware of God's existence in a vision which changed his life. His son, Joseph, would have died a slave in Egypt had he not been given the gift of reading the future from dreams. Their descendant,

Moses, changed from being a runaway murderer to the deliverer of the Jewish slaves when he, too, was confronted by that same God who had disturbed the lives of his ancestors.

Moses formed the Jews into a nation, and the Law which formed the whole basis of the future Jewish religion was believed to have been given by God to Moses. The most famous part of that Law is known as the Ten Commandments. From that time on, the Jews were bound to a Covenant, a kind of contract, in which God agreed to guide them and care for them and regard them as His special people, so long as they obeyed his laws. They were to love God, and honour him with all their heart, soul, mind and strength. If they did, then God would never fail them or desert them.

In the years that followed, before the nation had kings, various individuals were 'chosen' as leaders in times of necessity, following the direct guidance of God as given by the prophets – people who were in 'communion' with the Divine Voice – or through the sacred lots used by the priests, the Urim and Thummin, a procedure in which God apparently made lights shine from the letters of the alphabet stitched in the High Priest's breastplate, to spell out words and messages (cf. Josephus, *Antiquities*, 3:217; Yoma, 73b).

Even when a monarchy was finally established, the king was not considered to be above the authority of the man who spoke the oracles of God, that is, the prophet. Throughout the remainder of Jewish history, there continued to be a group of people who considered that monarchy in itself was wrong. God was the True Monarch, and His guidance alone was sufficient. But as long as the King acted as if he were God's regent on earth, the prophets were reasonably satisfied. The second, and greatest king – David – was thought of as the ideal friend of God.

Sadly, power corrupts, and the prophets were not always so happy with their kings. The Jewish nation was supposed to be the bride of God, but the bride was not always faithful! The events that brought about the ill-fortune of the nation were seen to be the deserved results of a people that had rejected its true leader. The prophet Hosea, who himself had a very unhappy marriage when the bride he dearly loved ran way from him, was one at least who realised how much God was actually hurt and distressed when His people turned their backs on Him.

Prophets began to look foward to the time when a Chosen One would receive the power, or spirit, of God – and lead the nation back to a new holiness. Foreign nations, with their evil influences, would be beaten back, and a new kingdom of God set up on earth.

People who believed in God longed for Him to take action just as He had for Moses, and to prove beyond doubt that He *was* God, and powerful, and able to help them out of their distress. The people waiting to be gathered into the kingdom were like sheep waiting for a shepherd, like a harvest waiting to be reaped.

The word **Messiah** means 'Anointed One'. To be anointed means to be set apart from other people and marked with holy oil. The person chosen was not picked by his fellow-men, but by God. He would be quite unmistakable, because he would have certain talents or powers. The prophets, with their special gifts, had even worked out specific details about the birth and life of this Chosen One.

By the time that Jesus was born, the expectation that the Messiah would appear at any moment had reached fever-pitch. They searched the Old Testament prophecies for clues that would help them know the Messiah when he came – and plenty of clues were there to be found.

Questions

1. In what sense were the Jews a special nation?
2. Why was God disappointed with the human race?
3. Why did God not force people to believe in Him?
4. Name three people who had discovered something about the nature of God.
5. How did awareness of God change the lives of (a) Abraham, and (b) Moses?
6. What is the most famous part of the Jewish Law called?
7. Look up Deuteronomy 5:6–21. Choose one of the commandments and write it out.
8. What was a prophet?
9. Which was the more important – a prophet or a king?
10. What does the name 'Messiah' mean?
11. Turn to the index in your Bible. Count up the number of books there are in (a) the Old Testament, and (b) the New Testament.

Research

These passages are a selection from the Old Testament prophecies that you can look up for yourself, and see what they have to say about the expected Messiah. When we have seen what they tell us, we must try to find out whether or not Jesus really fitted those expectations.

1. Numbers 24:16–17. What could Balaam the prophet 'see'?
2. Psalm 91:11–12. What was special about the way the Messiah would be treated?
3. Isaiah 9:6–7. What titles would the Messiah be given? Which throne would he rule from?
4. Isaiah 11:1–2. What would the 'spirit' give the Messiah?

5. Isaiah 35: 5–7, 10. Would the Messiah bring happiness or sorrow? In what ways?
6. Micah 5:2. Where would the Messiah come from?
7. Jeremiah 23: 5. Whose descendant would the Messiah be? What would he do?
8. Ezekiel 34: 11–16. What would the Messiah be like? Copy out verse 16.
9. Isaiah 40:10–11. Write out this passage.
10. Isaiah 61:1–2. What was the Messiah going to do?
11. Zechariah 9:9. How would the Messiah arrive in Jerusalem?
12. Zechariah 12:10. What would happen to him?
13. Malachi 3:1. How would the people know when the Messiah was coming?
14. Isaiah 53. Read the whole chapter. Many Jews did not think that this passage referred to the Messiah, but to Israel the nation. However, the Christian Church saw how closely this and other 'suffering' passages fitted our Lord. Under the title 'The servant chosen to suffer', write out verses 3–5, 9.
15. Psalm 22:1–2, 7–8, 16–20. What did the writer see happening on this occasion?

Now let us see whether or not Jesus fitted those requirements. It is certainly true that many of the Jews of his time did *not* think he was the Messiah, and the modern Jews still don't. (Many of those Jews would have accepted him as Messiah if he had started an army to fight the Romans.) To make up our minds properly about who Jesus was, we must study all we can of his life and teaching. But let us start with a few facts.

1. Matthew 1: 2–16. Was Jesus descended from David?
2. Matthew 11:1–6. What did Jesus say about himself when John asked him if he was the Messiah?
3. Matthew 21:1–11. How did Jesus enter Jerusalem?
4. Mark 15:20, 24–25. Which of these details are similar to Psalm 22?
5. John 19:32–42. Was Jesus pierced? Did a rich man bury him?

One important reason why the Jews did not recognise Jesus as the Messiah was that they were fully expecting someone who would lead them in battle and drive out the Roman occupation. Jesus did not do this. Find Mark 12:13–17, Matthew 5:38–42, Luke 7:1–10. What was the general attitude of Jesus to the Romans?

Nevertheless, the Messiah *was* engaged in a fight, and we have to face the same enemy ourselves. Find Ephesians 6:10–13. Who was he fighting?

Creative Writing

What things would you consider it to be worthwhile fighting for? Some people talk about peace at any price, and others could only accept peace with honour. Are there some unpleasant fights that a Christian would have to take on, if he was still to call himself a Christian?

6
THE BIRTH OF JESUS

The birth narratives are the accounts that we have of the actual birth of Jesus (called the **Nativity**), and the events that happened then. If you read the opening chapters of our four gospels carefully, you will notice that only two of them, Matthew and Luke, have any mention of the birth of Jesus at all, and the details given in these two vary considerably. St John's Gospel begins with a prologue revealing Christ's nature as the Word of God and the Light of the World; and St Mark's Gospel begins with the ministry of John the Baptist. They miss out completely the stories of Jesus as a baby.

Other gospels besides our four were written that *did* mention the birth of Jesus, but these gospels included some very extraordinary stories and were not thought to be very reliable, so they were not included in our Bible.

St Luke's Gospel opens with a passage addressed to Theophilus, an unknown person whose name means 'lover of God'. This may have been a real person, or it may have been just an expression like 'dear reader'.

Luke then gave the account of the occasion when the priest Zechariah saw a vision of the angel Gabriel in the Temple; Gabriel told him that his barren wife, Elizabeth, would bear the child that was to be the forerunner of the Messiah. Shortly after Zechariah's vision, the angel Gabriel visited a young girl of the house of David whose name was Mary. He announced that she had been chosen by God to bear a child who would be the saviour of his people, and, possibly to convince her that all this was not just her imagination, told her as proof that her cousin Elizabeth, the wife of Zechariah, was pregnant. When Mary visited her cousin she found that it was indeed so, and realised that the angel must have been telling the truth about herself also. She stayed with Elizabeth until just before the birth of her son, John the Baptist. The whole story was told from Mary's point of view, and it may be that St Luke got his information from Mary herself, or from one of the women followers of Jesus whom he mentioned in his gospel.

St Matthew's Gospel, on the other hand, gives Joseph's point of

The Church of the Nativity, Bethlehem
This early church was built over the cave-stable of the Bethlehem inn where Jesus was born. It was the only inn in Bethlehem, and the site was unintentionally preserved when a pagan Roman Emperor tried to discourage Christianity by building a pagan shrine over it.

view. The gospel begins with a family tree in three groups of fourteen names (that is 7 + 7 × 3; three and seven are very significant holy numbers), showing Jesus' descent from David, and through him from Abraham. Actually, our version of Matthew – which was translated from a Greek script – only gives thirteen names in the third part of the list. A scholar, Dr Hugh Schonfield, has supplied the missing name – Abner – from between Abiud and Eliakim, from an old Hebrew manuscript of the gospel.*

Then Joseph discovered that Mary was pregnant. He considered releasing her from her promise to him, knowing that the child was not his. The Jewish penalty for adultery was death by stoning, but Joseph was a kind man and did not want this to happen. He was going to send her away quietly when an unnamed angel appeared to him in a vivid dream, and told him that the child would be God's own son. Joseph trusted his dream and did not send Mary away.

St Luke then went on to tell of a population census for taxation purposes in which it was required that every person should go to be registered at his ancestral home. As Mary and Joseph were of the family of King David, they had to travel from Nazareth in Galilee where they lived, to Bethlehem in the province of Judaea,

* Hugh Schonfield, *Saints Against Caesar*, Macdonald, London, p. 154.

which had been David's city. Owing to the many travellers there, they could not find proper accommodation, and spent the night in a stable. There, Mary gave birth to a child. This was not so cruel as it sounds, for Mary would most certainly have wanted the privacy of the stable in which to give birth to her child rather than a stuffy room in an inn crowded with about thirty people.

Some shepherds in a field on night watch had a vision of angels telling of the birth of a saviour, and where they might find him. They went to look, and found the mother and child, and told them what they had seen.

After eight days Jesus was unwrapped from his swaddling bands (the customary strips of bandaging used very widely until this century to keep new-born babies feeling warm and secure, and also to try to stop the deformities of rickets), and was circumcised and named according to the Jewish Law. Then, after a further thirty-three days, during which time Mary was ritually unclean, the family went to the Temple where a sacrifice of two doves was made. This was the 'poor man's offering', as opposed to a lamb – but this is no proof that Joseph was poor, as has often been suggested. He may have been short of funds because of the long time of his presumably unexpected delay in Bethlehem. No doubt, with the terrible unemployment of that time, a carpenter was a comparatively wealthy citizen.

In the Temple, Jesus was recognised as being no ordinary child by two people inspired by the Holy Spirit – an old man named Simeon, who had been told that he would not die until he had seen the Messiah; and the ancient prophetess Anna. Then, when all the laws had been satisfactorily dealt with, Mary and Joseph travelled home to Nazareth.

St Matthew's Gospel, however, gives a very different picture. There is no mention of the journey from Galilee for the census, or the birth of Jesus in a stable, or the visit of the shepherds. Instead, he tells of Magi, or astrologers, who had seen some strange occurrence in the sky, and had travelled (perhaps from Babylonia or Persia) to the court of Herod the Great to find a new king and give him presents. The explanation of this star is difficult, but astronomers of the present day, following discoveries made by Johannes Kepler in 1606, have suggested that what they were looking at was a conjunction of the two planets Jupiter and Saturn, which would certainly have been noted by the astrologers. In fact, a cuneiform tablet found at the ancient Babylonian school of astrology at Sippar has furnished us with the very proof that they *did* know of it.

In 7 B.C. this conjunction happened three times, once in the spring, once in the autumn, and a third time in December. This triple conjunction happens once every 120 years. The Greek phrase in Matthew 2:2 which reads 'in the East' is more accurately translated as 'in the first rays of dawn', and would refer to the first sighting by the Magi in the spring. When they arrived in Jerusalem, at the time of the third sighting, the conjunction would have been clearly visible as one looked from Jerusalem down the road to Bethlehem. So this theory seems to fit the facts – even the fact that apparently Herod himself and the rest of the population did *not* see the star. They did not know what to look for. The Christmas card idea of the huge, brilliant jewel in the sky is something of an exaggeration. It would have been about as bright as the planet Venus.

It is also known, incidentally, that there were comets around in March 5 B.C., and April 4 B.C., but the comet theory does not seem so satisfactory as the Jupiter–Saturn one.

Herod knew, obviously, that there was no new baby in his family, and assumed that all this had some reference to the long-awaited Messiah. He found out from the priests where the Messiah was to be born according to the prophecies, and from the Magi how long the 'star' had been in the sky. Then the Magi found Jesus – not in a stable, but a house – and after giving him their gifts had a dream warning them not to return to Herod but to go home another way. Joseph was also warned of the danger in a dream, and he fled with the baby to Egypt in time to escape the slaughter of all the baby boys in Bethlehem up to the age of two.

When Herod died, Joseph again had a prophetic dream announcing that it was safe to return, but on realising that Herod's cruel son Archelaus had now been made ruler of Judaea, he took his family to Nazareth in Herod Antipas' province, the first time that Nazareth is mentioned in this account.

These facts are rather disturbing to someone brought up on the old traditional picture of the nativity scene, complete with wise men and shepherds all crammed in together and set amid snow and little lambs. And from this survey of the two accounts, we can see that either:

(a) Matthew is correct and Luke is wrong; or
(b) Luke is correct and Matthew is wrong; or
(c) They are both wrong; or
(d) They are both right, and there is an explanation for the differences in their versions.

It is possible that the last of these is, in fact, the correct option, since the two gospels do seem to be referring to completely different events. Only St Luke mentions the actual birth of Christ, and the events which would follow the birth of any ordinary Jewish boy

The Cave of the Nativity *The star on the floor of the cave marks the spot which tradition claims is the place where Jesus was born.*

according to the Law. In St Matthew's account, Herod killed not new-born babies, but toddlers up to the age of two, so presumably the Magi told him of the earlier appearance of the conjunction they had witnessed. It is fair to mention here that there is no official record of this visit or of the slaughter of the babies that followed it, but the act was quite in keeping with Herod's character and methods – he had already killed three of his own sons for suspected plotting to gain his throne!

The Holy Family would certainly not have been still camping in a stable two years after the birth of Jesus, but may well have been staying in a house in Bethlehem, where they quite possibly had relatives. If we could actually date the census held while Quirinius was Legate of Syria, we would know much more. It is known that there was a census in the year A.D. 6 after the deposition of Archelaus, and that the Romans tended to hold enrolments every fourteen years or so. When St Luke says that 'this was the *first* enrolment' made by Quirinius, he may have known that the one in A.D. 6 was his second, which would suggest that the first would have been in about 7 B.C. This would give us a lapse of three years between the census and Herod's death in 4 B.C. If this could be proved, it would solve one of the Bible's most intriguing problems.

Whatever the case, it is to be noted that the portrayals of the shepherds and wise men arriving together at the stable are quite incorrect. The suggestion that these Magi were three kings did not arise until the sixth century, and little lame shepherds with gifts are quite mythical.

The Three Gifts

The three gifts that the Magi brought to the infant Jesus were very important symbols. Gold represented kingship, wealth and temporal power. Frankincense represented worship, the life of prayer and meditation, and spiritual power. Myrrh was a precious and sweet-smelling ointment often used during burials, and also as a painkiller. It is significant that Christ's own works of healing, and, of course, his death and burial, were highly important signs of his Messiahship.

Questions and Research

1. Find Matthew 1:18 to 2:23.
(a) What was Joseph's reaction when he found out Mary was pregnant?
(b) Why didn't he 'divorce' her?
(c) What had the wise men seen that brought them to Herod?

(d) What did Herod find out from the priests?
(e) How many wise men were mentioned?
(f) What instructions did Herod give to the wise men?
(g) What did Herod find out from the wise men?
(h) Does it say that they found Jesus in a stable?
(i) Where did they find Jesus?
(j) What did they give to him?
(k) What did these three gifts represent?
(l) Why did the wise men go home another way?
(m) Where did Joseph and his family go, and why?
(n) What did Herod do? Why do you think he made the deadline the age of two?
(o) When did Joseph bring his family back from Egypt?
(p) Who was the new ruler of Judaea?
(q) Where did the family go and settle?

2. Find Luke 1:26–38.
(a) What details do we learn of Jesus' parents in verses 26–27?
(b) Who visited Mary?
(c) Where had 'he' made a previous appearance?
(d) How did Mary react to the vision?
(e) What was the message she was given?
(f) What was suggested about the fatherhood of the child?
(g) What indication was she given that this was not just a dream (something that she did not know which she could go and check up)?

3. Find Luke 1:39–56.
(a) Where did Mary go, and what happened when she got there?
(b) Verses 46–55 are known as the 'Magnificat'. What were Mary's main feelings as expressed in it?
(c) How long did Mary stay with Elizabeth?

4. Find Luke 2:1–40.
(a) Who was Caesar Augustus?
(b) Who was Quirinius?
(c) What had Caesar just ordered?
(d) Why did Joseph and Mary go to Bethlehem?
(e) What happened when they got there?
(f) Had Joseph made any arrangements for Mary's confinement?
(g) Where did she have her baby?
(h) What did she do with her new-born son?
(i) What were swaddling bands?
(j) What is a manger? (Look it up.)
(k) Verses 8–14. What happened out in the countryside?
(l) How many shepherds were there? Lame boys? Snow and ice?

(m) What was the shepherds' reaction to the vision? What did they do?

(n) What was done to Jesus on the eighth day?

5. Find Leviticus 12 in the Old Testament. How long was a mother unclean after bearing a son? And a daughter? What were the normal offerings made after childbirth?

6. Find Luke 2:22–40.
(a) What was offered for Jesus?
(b) Where was this sacrifice made?
(c) Who saw Jesus in the Temple? What had God promised him?
(d) Why was his speech so moving?
(e) What did he prophesy for Mary?
(f) Who else saw Jesus, and what did she have to say?
(g) What happened after the sacrifice?

7. By now it should be obvious that we have two very different accounts of the birth of Jesus. Let us note the differences carefully.
(a) Whose story do we have in Luke, and whose in Matthew?
(b) How did Joseph get his message, and how did Mary get hers?
(c) Who visited the baby in Luke, and who in Matthew?
(d) What presents does the baby get in Matthew, and in Luke?
(e) Which ruler plays a significant part in Matthew, and which in Luke?
(f) What journeys follow the birth of Jesus in Matthew and in Luke?
(g) Why did the family have to go to Nazareth in Matthew, and why in Luke?

8. Finally, find Luke 2: 41–52 – the only story of Jesus' childhood. Briefly give an account of what happened, in your own words.

Creative Writing

Either: Write a short play about the Nativity, using either St Matthew's or St Luke's version.
Or: Why was it highly significant that Jesus was born into a humble home and family, and not in a king's palace – as the wise men expected?

THE VIRGIN BIRTH

The Christian belief that Jesus was born of a virgin was never accepted by the Jews, and is one of the major difficulties encountered by thinking Christians today. A virgin is a girl or woman who has never had sexual experience, and it is unknown for any human to give birth to a child without sex being involved.

Many early Christians simply assumed that Jesus was the normal son of Mary and Joseph (see John 1:45). They believed that Jesus did not actually become the Messiah, or Christ, until the moment of his baptism – when the Holy Spirit came upon him. Some ancient manuscripts of Luke 3:22 actually report that the voice from Heaven at Christ's baptism stated: 'You are my beloved son, with whom I am well pleased. *This day* I have begotten you.' Jewish Christians, like the Jews themselves, believed that God was wholly spirit, and could not have a physical son. They were content to believe that Jesus was 'adopted' by God when he reached his manhood; he was the Anointed One, or Messiah, but not the literal son of God. These Jewish Christians included Jesus' own brothers, among them St James, who became the head of the Church at Jerusalem.

Other Christians, following St Paul's teachings, believed that God Himself had entered the world to live as a human being. This appearance of God in the flesh of a man was called the **Incarnation**, from the Latin word *carno*, which means 'flesh'. If God had done this, it was obvious that the idea of God as a single Almighty Person was insufficient – God was not only Father, but also Son and Holy Spirit. The idea that God is Three Persons in One is called the doctrine of the **Trinity**. The concept is a very difficult one to grasp, but it lies behind what Christians believe about the significance of Christ's life on Earth, and his death and resurrection.

If Jesus really was God Incarnate, then he could not just be the son of human parents. St Luke's Gospel tells us in 1:31–35 that the angel Gabriel was seen by Mary, and she was told that she would become pregnant. Mary could not understand this, as she was not married and had had no sexual experience. The angel explained that the Holy Spirit would come upon her and the power of God would overshadow her. The child to be born would be the son of herself and God, both human and divine. The fact that Jesus was sometimes called the son of Joseph does not prove that he was *not* virgin born, however, as Joseph was still his legal father, and this is all that the phrase may have implied. However, some people find this passage so difficult to accept that they think it could just be a legend or myth, and not the literal truth at all.

Matthew 1:23 is a quotation from Isaiah 7:14 in the Old Testament, where King Ahaz of Judah was to receive a special sign about the future safety of his kingdom. A virgin would conceive and bear a son, and before he was old enough to know the difference between good and evil, Ahaz's enemies would be overthrown. The Hebrew word for virgin simply means a young woman, and many scholars think that the young woman in question was actually Isaiah's own wife. The passage did not really imply anything to do with a supernatural virgin birth, or even a future Messiah.

There are several passages in the Old Testament where angels appeared to announce the birth of famous children (Genesis 18:1–15; Judges 13), but it was not claimed that these children were divine. Another passage gives the Song of Hannah (I Samuel 2:1–10). Luke's passage may have been based on the earlier one. The story of the slaughter of the children at Bethlehem can be compared to the story of Pharoah killing the babies at the time of Moses; just as the first Moses survived to found the Old Covenant, so did Jesus, who was like a second Moses, survive to found the New Covenant. This kind of reasoning was popular among the early Christians, and is known as **Typology**.

Other religions claimed that their gods or heroes were the result of gods visiting virgins, and this sort of legend was despised by the Jews as presenting a very inferior view of God. In the next century, the Christian writer Justin composed a famous dialogue with the Jew Trypho, in which Trypho derisively equated the Jesus myth with that of the birth of Perseus as the son of Zeus and the virgin Danae. He said, 'You should be ashamed to relate such things like the heathen. It would be better if you asserted of this Jesus that as a man he was born of human seed, and called to be Messiah on account of his faithful obedience to the Law.'

It is a fact that there are no other definite mentions of the virgin birth in the New Testament, which is perhaps surprising if it was so basic a belief of the Christian Church. St Paul's writings, which come before the gospels, and St Mark's Gospel, which was probably the earliest gospel in our New Testament, show no signs of the belief. Some scholars think that the first two chapters of St Luke's Gospel came from a different source from the rest of his book, and that therefore the original of this gospel had no reference to it either. Both the genealogies of Jesus (the family trees given in St Matthew's and St Luke's gospels) trace Jesus' line of descent through Joseph and not Mary – which is strange if they are trying to prove that Jesus was the son of Mary only, and not of Joseph.

However, there are no ancient manuscripts of St Luke's Gospel which do not contain those chapters, so we cannot prove that St Luke did not write them. Also, the birth stories given in St Matthew and St Luke are quite independent, which shows that there were at least two strands of tradition that accepted the virgin birth, and not just one.

Of two famous martyr-Christians, St Ignatius, the Bishop of Antioch, accepted the doctrine of the virgin birth, but Justin Martyr did not. Both of these Christians lived shortly after the New Testament was written, and there was certainly a difference of opinion even then.

The truth of the matter is still a mystery, and a matter of faith. It remains a very important question for those who believe that Jesus' death could not really save us from our sins unless Jesus truly was by his birth an incarnation of God and not just adopted by God at his baptism.

Questions

1. What does it say about the virgin birth in the following verses: Luke 1:34–35; 3:23; Matthew 1:16, 18, 20, 25?
2. What does it say about the parents of Jesus in John 1:45 and Luke 2:41–43?
3. What is a virgin?
4. What is meant by the word 'incarnation'?
5. What is meant by the word 'Trinity'?
6. What did Jewish Christians believe about the relationship of Jesus to Almighty God?
7. What was the prophecy in Isaiah 7:14 really about?
8. Describe briefly the appearance of angels in the Old Testament passages Genesis 18:1–15 and Judges 13.
9. Why do some scholars think the passages about the virgin birth may not be original to the gospels?

8

WHO WAS JOHN THE BAPTIST?

One of the things we now know is that the Jews were not just expecting the Messiah to arrive 'out of the blue'. Since he was coming to bring judgement, among other things, it was only fair that they should have a warning. God would not leave His people unprepared. Before the Messiah arrived, a messenger was going to come to 'prepare the way'. According to one of the prophecies, this messenger would be the prophet Elijah. Another prophecy connected with the messenger did not give his name, but said that there would be a 'voice crying in the wilderness' (Isaiah 40:3).

Elijah had been a famous prophet, and he had lived some eight hundred years before Jesus was born. He was a strange fellow who lived in the wilderness, and dressed in a rough garment of camel-hair. The reason why people thought that he might come back again was that there was *no record of Elijah ever having died* like normal people do.

According to tradition, on the east side of the Jordan was an area abounding in springs, near a cave in which Elijah was supposed to have lived. It was there that Elijah had been miraculously fed by ravens (identifying this wadi with the Brook Cherith of I Kings 17:5). A hill there is still called the Jebel mar Elias (Hill of Elijah), and marks the spot where he mysteriously disappeared from the earth. On one occasion, he had walked there from Jericho, passing Gilgal on the way, with his friend Elisha, when something very strange happened. Some people even interpreted what happened as the visit of some sort of flying saucer! Be that as it may, what is described in one place as a whirlwind, and in another place as a 'chariot of fire', suddenly descended on him and whisked him away, leaving his friend standing with his cloak, which had been left behind. Thinking that what went up must soon come down, fifty people searched for Elijah's body for three days, but it was never found. Instead, Elisha put on Elijah's cloak, and found that he had received all Elijah's prophetic powers.

So the rumour grew that Elijah had not died at all, but had been taken up alive to Heaven – and before the Messiah came, he would come down again to warn people to get ready for the Chosen One.

Now let us consider what happened at the start of St Mark's Gospel. Before Jesus had ever spoken one word that we know of in public, there was a disturbance, and a great deal of excitement in the country by the River Jordan. Hundreds of respectable Jewish people were making the journey there to see a strange, wild individual, hear him preach, and be submerged by him under the muddy Jordan waters. Ordinary people would never have agreed to do this had they not been completely convinced that this person was very special.

The person causing all the excitement was a young man, dressed in camel skins, the son of one of the priests. His name was John. He spent all day, every day, standing by the River Jordan preaching about the coming Messiah, and warning people that they must change their lives and show that they meant it by getting baptised, before it was too late. God would sort out any trees 'not bearing fruit' like a gardener – he would cut them down! So they had better make an effort to give up their sins quickly.

Because of the way he was dressed, and the fact that John was carrying out his mission in the area specifically connected with the work and disappearance of Elijah, the people naturally thought that John the Baptist must be Elijah the prophet, come back again as expected. Whatever the truth of the matter, he must have known that people would draw this conclusion, in view of how he was dressed and what he was doing, so presumably he intended to *represent* Elijah, if nothing more. Therefore we are bound to consider several possibilities about John. Either he was a deliberate fraud, a fake deluding the people and raising their hopes falsely for some obscure motive of his own; or he was stark-raving mad; or he was deluded into thinking he had been sent by God to do these things; or he *really had* received a genuine calling.

Questions

1. Who was the messenger who would come to prepare the way for the Messiah expected to be?
2. Where, according to tradition, had the prophet Elijah lived?
3. Why did the Jews connect John the Baptist with Elijah?
4. What alternatives must we consider about John?

Research

1. Find Malachi 4:5. Malachi was a prophet. Who did he state that the messenger, or 'forerunner' was going to be?

2. Find Isaiah 40:3. What did the voice cry in the wilderness?
3. Find II Kings 1:1–8. One of the Old Testament stories about Elijah. How was his appearance described there?
4. Find II Kings 2:1–3, 6–18. Describe in your own words how Elijah 'died', and what efforts were made to find his body.
5. Find Mark 1:1–8.
(a) Who was the person causing all the excitement?
(b) How was he dressed?
(c) What was he doing?
(d) What did he say in verses 7–8?

6. What conclusion did many of the people come to about who John the Baptist really was?
7. Find Matthew 11:7–15. What did Jesus say about John that connected him with Elijah?
8. Find Matthew 17:10–13. What did Jesus say about Elijah in verse 12, and who did the disciples think he was talking about?
9. Before we go any further with this mystery, we should perhaps have a look at the account of John's birth, and see if there are any clues to be found there. Find Luke 1:5–25.
(a) Who were Zechariah and Elizabeth?
(b) What was Zechariah's profession?
(c) Why was Elizabeth unhappy?
(d) Verse 11. What happened when Zechariah went into the Temple to burn incense?
(e) What did the angel say in verses 16–17?
(f) What was the angel's name?
(g) What happened to convince Zechariah that he really *had* seen an angel?
(h) What happened to Elizabeth?

10. Find Luke 1: 39–80.
(a) Who visited Elizabeth?
(b) What happened when she greeted Elizabeth?
(c) Copy out verse 44.
(d) How long did Mary stay (verse 56)?
(e) What was the baby called?
(f) When did Zechariah get his voice back?
(g) Copy out verses 68–69 and 76–77 of his speech.

As John's parents were old when he was born, it is possible that they died while he was still a child. Near the Dead Sea was a religious community whose members were called Essenes. These people often adopted orphans, and trained their most promising youths as missionaries. Some people think that since John appeared so near to their Dead Sea settlement, at the age of about thirty, with a similar message to theirs, that he himself was actually brought up as an Essene. They apparently did go round the country calling on people to repent, for the Kingdom of Heaven was at hand. Sometimes they baptised people to symbolise giving them a new life. John and the Essenes lived so close to each other that, at the very least, they must have been aware of each other's activities – but many modern scholars now think that the differences between the Essenes and John are far greater than their similarities.

Creative Writing

Either: Write a short play about the appearance of the angel Gabriel to Zechariah.

Or: Imagine that you are either Elizabeth or Mary, and write a poem or a diary passage about your meeting.

9
WHAT DID JOHN TEACH?

The teachings of John the Baptist are unfortunately only hinted at briefly in the gospels. With the arrival on the scene of Jesus himself, the work of the Baptist faded quickly into the background – rather like a best man at a wedding, who has been so important at the preparation stage, but who stands quietly aside on the arrival of the bridegroom. John knew that his role was one of vital importance, however. When the Messiah came, the new age of God would have begun, and it was John's duty to warn the people before it was too late for them.

He knew that by no means the whole of Israel would respond to his message, but those who heard his warning and accepted what he was saying would become a special community gathered out of the whole mass of the people, a kind of holy remainder when all the others had decided against changing their lives and been weeded out.

John shattered the self-assured belief that simply the fact that they were Jews – descendants of Abraham – would be quite enough to protect them from the wrath of God, which they all agreed would fall on those with whom God was not pleased. They had assumed that since they were already God's chosen people they would escape the terrible judgement reserved for everyone else. John fervently believed that this idea was simply not good enough – when God struck, the judgement would fall on *all* men, whoever they were. What was more, that time of judgement could happen at any moment. The very next hour might bring their salvation or damnation. The Messiah would arrive like a gardener ready to take a harvest. Were the people wheat or weeds? Were they fruitful trees, or fit only to be cut down and burnt?

John ignored totally the religion of the Temple and the state system of worship. What he called for was not offerings and sacrifices of the sort the priests insisted upon, but the surrender of each person's soul to God in an act of spiritual renewal. He required from every person who came to him a unique, decisive act – a public submission to baptism in the river.

Only those determined to produce fruits worthy of repentance were allowed this baptism, those who were prepared to fulfil God's moral law by acting justly and loving their neighbours. The decision lay with them, and God would know whether or not the decision they had taken in their hearts was genuine. Once they had made the decision, John was prepared to welcome not only the ordinary people, but also those who were commonly despised and hated: the tax-collectors and the soldiers. All these types of people were welcome to come forward and receive God's mercy and be baptised, whereas some of the so-called righteous Pharisees and Sadducees were bluntly called poisonous snakes and sent away. John had seen through their hypocrisy.

John's form of baptism was by total immersion under water. It represented the starting of a new life, a complete break with the past, by having all one's previous existence with its sins and failures completely washed away. No matter what they had done, how many mistakes they had made, how little effort they had put into being religious – they could forget all about it, throw off their sense of guilt, and start again. It gave the people fresh hope for themselves.

It was a symbolic action. By that we mean that the outward sign of the washing of the body simply indicated something that was taking place inwardly in their minds and hearts. This made the people ready for the arrival of the coming Messiah; and it was thought absolutely necessary, for when he *did* come, people would be too late to change their minds – they would then face their judgement for the things they had done. For the people who submitted their lives in this way to God, and put themselves completely into His hands, it was believed that by opening their hearts they would make it possible for God to fill and baptise them with His Holy Spirit, and change them into new and radiant beings.

St John's Gospel gives us another reason why John baptised people, this being on a very practical level. It suggests there that John did not actually know who the Messiah would be, only that he was about to appear. He stated that God revealed to him that when he baptised the right man, he would know him beyond any doubt, because he would see certain signs which would be quite unmistakable. What John saw when he baptised Jesus we will consider shortly.

Questions

1. Why was John the Baptist like a best man at a wedding?
2. In what way would the arrival of the Messiah bring judgement?
3. What did John the Baptist call for from each person?

4. What sort of people were allowed to be baptised?
5. What did the baptism represent?
6. What is meant by a symbolic action?
7. Why did baptism give people fresh hope?

Research

1. Find Matthew 3:1–12.
(a) What did John cry in verse 2?
(b) What did he call the Pharisees and Sadducees?
(c) What do you think verse 8 means?
(d) What did he say about the Coming One in verse 11?

2. Find Luke 3: 7–17.
(a) What advice did he give to the multitudes (the crowd of ordinary people)?
(b) What did he say to the tax-collectors?
(c) What did he say to the soldiers?

The robbing of people by violence referred to the unpleasant practice some soldiers had of 'framing' farmers and landowners with false accusations of treachery, and then confiscating their property. In the 'good old days' before the reforms of the Emperor Augustus, soldiers had not been paid wages and had been allowed to help themselves to whatever loot and plunder they could get their hands on. Strange though it seems to us, many of them bitterly resented being paid wages, which meant that they were no longer officially allowed to go looting.

3. Find John 1:29–34. What did John say was his reason for baptising people, as given in verse 31?

Creative Writing

Imagine that you have made the journey to the Jordan to see the Baptist. Why did you go there? Describe the scene and how you felt when it came to your turn to be baptised. How would you feel after this?

10
THE BAPTISM OF JESUS

We have already seen how Jesus and John were related to each other. Their mothers were probably cousins. If Luke's version is correct, then Mary visited Elizabeth during her pregnancy, and probably did so again many times during the period up to Elizabeth's death. Unfortunately, we have no details at all of the relationship between the two boys, although they must surely have known each other.

The important question is: did John *know* that Jesus was the expected Messiah? Linked to this is the other mystery: did Jesus himself know he was the Messiah? He must have found out something from his mother, but, so far as we know, did not begin his ministry until he was about thirty years of age. There are many stories of his childhood, and legends about his journeys to places like Egypt and India and even Britain, to study at the ancient centres of learning, but we have no proof for any of these legends. All we have in our gospels is the sudden appearance of John in the wilderness, baptising people, and the submission of Jesus to baptism before he started his mission.

Let us have a look now at the narratives, and see what we can learn from them.

Find Mark 1:4–13.
(a) What was John baptising people for?
(b) What message did he give in verse 7?
(c) What would be so special about the Coming One?
(d) What happened when Jesus was baptised?
(e) What was the Holy Spirit said to be like?
(f) What did the Voice say?
(g) What did the Spirit do?
(h) How long was Jesus in the wilderness?
(i) What was happening to Jesus in the wilderness?

That is all that St Mark has to tell us. It is a very brief description of Jesus' baptism, and there is no mention at all of the details of his temptations. However, one problem of doctrine – that is, a difficulty arising from the beliefs of the Church – has already occurred. The Son of God was supposed to be sinless, and to know everything. If he was without sin, why did he submit to a baptism which was to wash his sins away? It looks as if Jesus may *not* have known that he was without sin, and may not have known that he was the Messiah.

Let's see if St Matthew's Gospel can give us further information.

Find Matthew 3:11–17.
(a) What did John say to Jesus when he came to him for baptism?
(b) Did Jesus agree to baptise John?
(c) What answer did Jesus make?
(d) What happened immediately after Jesus was baptised?

Now find Luke 3:21–22. This is all that Luke has about the baptism of Jesus.
(a) Does Luke mention the conversation with John that is in Matthew's version?
(b) Verse 22. What words are different about the Holy Spirit?
(c) If you are using a Bible with footnotes, do you notice a small letter ('k' in the RSV) by the word 'pleased'? It means that there is a footnote at the bottom of the page. If you look at it you will see that some old versions of the gospel add some more words to the story – 'today I have begotten thee'. This implies to some people that Jesus only really became God's son at his baptism, when he received the Holy Spirit. Many people think that this is quite a reasonable belief, but it means that they cannot also believe what St Luke has to say about Jesus being the Son of God at his birth. It would mean that Jesus was really only God's 'adopted' son.

St John's Gospel tells us something about the reason for the signs that John saw when he baptised Jesus.

Find John 1:31–34.
(a) What had God told John when He sent him to baptise?
(b) Copy out verse 34.

So it seems that John's mission was really two-fold: first, to prepare the people for the coming of the Messiah by the baptism of repentance; secondly, to identify the Messiah by recognising certain signs when he came. If St John's Gospel is correct here, probably only John would see the signs of the Messiah, and even he did not know until he saw them which man was to be the Chosen One.

Now, all the gospels mention these signs: the heavens open, there was a mysterious voice (which may have been heard only by John and Jesus) and the Holy Spirit descended on and remained on Jesus 'like a dove'. Only Luke's Gospel mentions 'in bodily form'. It is unlikely that this meant that a bird actually did flutter down. Birds were regarded as omens in the ancient world; but it is more likely that the *symbol* of the dove was intended, not an actual bird. The dove represented peace, purity and compassion – and the reason why John described the Holy Spirit as being 'like a dove' was not because it was in any way a real bird complete with feathers (as many church windows confusingly portray it), but because, when John baptised Jesus, he was suddenly made aware of those very qualities radiating from Jesus in a way that was quite unlike any other man, and he recognised him us the one they had all been waiting for.

Further Questions

1. What was the two-fold purpose of John's mission?
2. Which gospel says the Holy Spirit descended in bodily form?
3. What symbol is used for the Holy Spirit?
4. What three things did this symbol represent?

Creative Writing

Jesus had to make a moment of decision, and that moment altered the rest of his life. It was like reading books all about swimming, and then one day deciding to get into the water. It was like being in love with someone, and then one day promising to live with them for the rest of your life. Once that kind of decision is made, it can never be gone back on. Life can never be the same again.

In what ways would life be different from now on for Jesus? What sort of things in his life do you think he would have to give up?

11
THE TEMPTATIONS

Now we must consider why Jesus went off into the wilderness for six weeks. St Mark's Gospel implies that Jesus was driven there by the action of the Spirit. Jesus felt that he was being compelled to go out into the lonely desert, and that there he would be able to concentrate his mind on what had just happened, and work out how he would commence his work of bringing the Kingdom of Heaven to earth.

In the desert, we are told, Jesus was disturbed by three temptations, three tests that he had to pass. Now, how does one interpret these temptations? The devil is mentioned, and so are mysterious trips to high mountains and temple pinnacles. Are we supposed to

The Wilderness near the Dead Sea   *After his baptism Jesus spent a long time in this region, and faced his temptations. It is very hot and barren, and lies below sea level.*

take all this literally, or is there some other interpretation? If Jesus was really the Son of God, is it possible that he would have been tempted at all into doing something *evil*? Were the temptations really evil in any case? Let's think about it.

Would there have been anything evil about turning stones into bread, or jumping off the Temple pinnacle? We are naturally supposed to assume that Jesus could have done these things if he had wanted to. If Jesus had launched himself from the Temple and landed in a broken and mangled heap below, that would have been the end of his ministry! In the gospels there are stories about Jesus performing similar miracles, and these were certainly not supposed to be thought of as evil. In Mark 6:34–42, he changed five loaves and two fishes into enough food to feed 5,000 people; in John 2:1–10, he turned water into wine; and in Mark 6:48–50, he walked on water.

If we are meant to accept that Jesus did do these three things, then surely he cannot have thought it evil to do so? Changing stones into bread and floating down from the Temple pinnacle were not really very different from these three examples. So what were the temptations all about?

Was it that they were temptations to use his powers selfishly – for his own benefit? That is quite possible, and may well be the reason why Jesus refused to do them. Was it because Jesus thought it would show a lack of faith on his part if he put God to the test? Again, there is probably a lot of truth in this, and certainly many of Jesus' miracles of healing seem to have relied on the strong faith either of Jesus or of the person seeking a cure. Yet if God is real and His powers are real, why should He object to being put to the test? He was willing enough to oblige for several of the Old Testament heroes (see Isaiah 7:14). It might be that our pious reluctance to test God really stems from our knowledge that our faith is *not* strong enough. We are frightened of making fools of ourselves, frightened that it will not work. If we put God to the test because we do not trust Him or His providence then it reveals that we do not really know Him or love Him, and have not understood His love for us.

Jesus probably had much deeper reasons for resisting those temptations. If it was true that Jesus had only just fully realised who he was, his next move might well have been to work out what he was going to do about it. Many people see the temptations as thoughts that were passing through his mind as he considered ways of starting his mission.

At the time of Jesus, the economic conditions of the majority of the people were terribly poor. They suffered from lack of food, from unemployment, lack of money and poor health. Their physical needs were very great. If Jesus really had the power to produce food, to see to the people's physical needs, how could he deny this to his nation's hungry children? Modern missionaries and Oxfam workers often start their missions in disaster areas in precisely this way – feeding programmes. It is quite possible that Jesus considered using his powers for some similar venture.

To be aware of the possibility that he could put right man's distressing physical conditions must have put a tremendous responsibility on Jesus. He was surrounded by poor, hungry people. What better way or starting his ministry than by turning stones into bread? Wouldn't that be a good thing? Now we should begin to see the knife turn in the depths of that temptation. With what agony of mind must Jesus have chosen *not* to feed them.

The answer he gave to Satan was quite simple: 'Man shall not live by bread alone, but by every word that proceeds from the mouth of God.' He must have realised that to give in to this impulse would have meant spending the whole of his time repeating and repeating the miracle, for well-fed people soon become hungry again – and the minute he stopped this activity the situation would become just as bad as it had been to start with. Oxfam's slogan once used to be 'Help us to *stop* feeding them'. The point of that was that the people needed helping to become self-sufficient, and the pouring in of mere food supplies could never be more than just a temporary help.

Jesus would never have been able to save people from their ultimate death. He must have realised that it was far more vital to give something more important than food – something that would make people happy *even though* they would die. He had come to give them hope, courage to face life, love and trust, the ability to have compassion and forgive, and to gain a glimpse of God's eternal world where all people would find their place.

Now let's think about the second temptation. This was to jump off the pinnacle of the Temple. One edge of the Temple overlooked the Kidron Valley, and for anyone to survive a leap down would certainly be impressive. It was not such a bad idea.

As it happened, the Jews were expecting the Messiah to appear with a demonstration of wonder in the Temple (see Malachi 3:1). If Jesus could walk on water, he perhaps could have achieved this miracle without hurting himself. Satan very cunningly quoted a Messianic prophecy at him – or, if you find the idea of a real Satan too hard to accept, perhaps the thought of this prophecy entered Christ's mind and he wondered if it would really be true. The thought was: 'For He will give His angels charge over you, to guard you in all your ways. On their hands they will bear you up, lest you dash your foot against a stone.'

Earlier verses in the same Psalm 91 are even more encouraging: 'You will not fear the terror of the night, nor the arrow that flies by day . . . a thousand may fall at your side and ten thousand at your right hand; but it will not come near you.'

Most of Christ's life he was pestered by people who wanted to see him do something extraordinary. Occasionally Jesus *did* do some strange things, but they were usually done in secret, or out of unavoidable circumstances, or out of deep compassion. He never showed off, and most people would not have respected him if he had. Also, one must realise that it is only too natural *not* to believe in people who say they have seen miracles. You have to see them with your own eyes. Like the feeding, Jesus would have been involved in continually satisfying people's curiosity.

So, if the temptation was really to do what the people demanded out of their curiosity, this he refused. It would not be his method – his mission was more important than that.

Another possible meaning involved in this temptation is more subtle. Jesus, who loved God with all his heart, probably knew that in the life ahead of him he would run into enormous dangers. We do not know at what stage Jesus knew that he would have to die, but the second temptation gives us a clue that, even at the beginning of his ministry, Jesus faced up to this possibility in his mind, and passed the test.

If he had flung himself off the Temple pinnacle, it would have been a direct challenge to God, to see if God would save him. It would have been called God's bluff, as it were, putting his life deliberately in danger to prove to himself that God would get him out of trouble and rescue him. The test here was really to see whether Jesus was prepared not only to serve God with his life but even go beyond that – did he love God enough to die for him, if need be? There was all the difference in the world between taking a course of action knowing that you would be protected and treated in a privileged manner, or taking it on even though it might mean your death.

What Jesus was really saying – as was proved by his words in Gethsemane – was, 'So be it, Lord. I will serve you and love you and do your will even though it means losing my life.' It implied a genuine belief and trust in God, that even though he might die, yet he was in God's hands and all would be well. The devil might pester him with the question, 'Are you sure?' The rest of Jesus' earthly life proved that he *was* sure.

At last came the final test: to gain ownership of the world by serving the devil. This really needs a little background explanation.

At the time of Christ, the world was ruled by Rome, and that great nation was not welcomed by every one of its subjects. Apart from the benefits the Roman civilisation brought, it also gave the nations terror and slavery, and ruthless brutal treatment. In Palestine, there were many zealous patriots who refused to acknowledge the Roman authority. These were the people known as Zealots. They were prepared to fight and die for their beliefs. They waited expectantly for a Messianic leader to come and lead their mission of ridding the country of the Roman occupation. Their battle-cry as we have already seen was 'No friend but the Zealot; no tax but the Temple tax; no king but God alone.'

Jesus must have been very tempted to have become their leader, and be just the sort of Messiah that everyone wanted him to be. After all, many of the Old Testament prophecies said that he would be a great king and would vanquish all his enemies. If Jesus had started a military campaign, and people had flocked to join him, maybe he could have driven out the Romans – or perhaps become the Emperor of the World himself. Then he would have had the authority to see to it that laws were put right, slaves were freed, orphans and widows taken care of, and so on.

What a temptation this must have been. As it happens, Jesus had to face this one more than once during his ministry. St John's version of the feeding of the 5,000 reveals how, after the miracle, the people tried to *force* Jesus to be their king, and he had to get away quickly to the hills to avoid their insistence. When Jesus revealed at Caesarea Philippi that he really was the Messiah, he also told his disciples that he knew his mission would end in his death in Jerusalem. St Peter immediately tried to tell him that this was nonsense – he would be successful and triumphant. Jesus then saw the third temptation all over again, and spoke defiantly to what he could see as Satan behind Peter's words. A third time that Jesus must have been sorely tried was during his last night, in the Garden of Gethsemane. He did not *have* to wait there for his betrayer to come and have him arrested. He could easily have escaped and avoided his death – and he certainly did not want to die. He begged God to let the cup pass from him, meaning that he did not want to go through with the dreadful suffering he knew he was about to face. Yet again he triumphed over his own fears and thoughts for himself – that agonised plea ended with the words, 'Not what I want, but what You want.'

Jesus could see beyond the setting up of an earthly kingdom. Where would it have ended? And how would it end? We can learn about Alexander the Great, or Julius Caesar, or Hannibal, or Napoleon – all great military leaders, but they are history. Their message, if they had one, does not live now. It does not affect our lives.

And again, Jesus could probably see even further depths in this temptation. At that time, the Pharisaic party believed that the world was in the grip of the devil, indeed, that he was the 'Prince of this World', and that only by becoming a spiritual person and rejecting the selfish and worldly impulse could one ever hope to reach God. There are still many who would accept this notion. Therefore it followed that ambition, self-seeking and pride would entangle a person more and more in the things of the Earth, and the influence of Self and Evil. Jesus himself said elsewhere, 'You cannot serve God and self-interest.'

Jesus was not so much being tempted to serve the devil as what the devil represented: self-interest and ambition. Scholars point out that all the answers Jesus gave came from the Old Testament passage of Deuteronomy, Chapters 6–8, where Moses and the people of Israel had been in the wilderness for forty years and were poised to enter the Promised Land at last. In Deuteronomy 6:5 Israel was told that if they were truly to be God's people, then they must worship no other God but Him, and love Him with all their heart, soul, mind and strength. As the Israelites wandered in the wilderness, their love and trust in God were severely put to the test – and found wanting! Their love was sorely challenged to see if it was complete and unconditional; but Israel craved after proofs of God's existence and proofs that He cared for them, which simply revealed their basic suspicion and unbelief, and lack of trust. Jesus faced the same tests, and passed them triumphant.

The first temptation, of not demanding anything for himself, but depending totally on the will of God, showed that Jesus loved God with his whole heart. The second, not to endanger himself deliberately and thereby challenge God to save his life, showed that he loved God with all his soul or life, and was prepared to accept whatever God sent. The third, to reject the appeal of ambition or personal success, showed that he loved God with all his mind, with all the personal wealth, resources, abilities and ambitions that he had.

In the world's eyes, Jesus was a failure. The outcome of his mission was his execution. He was beaten by his enemies, put to death, and that was that! But Christians believe that the death of Jesus was the very opposite of a defeat – it was his greatest victory, the culminating victory over self and the devil. At the cross, the principles of Jesus were put to the final and most demanding of all tests, and he did not give in.

Questions and Research

1. Find Matthew 4:1–11.
(a) What were the three temptations?
(b) Make a chart in three columns, stating:
  (i) What the temptation was.
  (ii) What answer Jesus gave.
  (iii) The place in the Old Testament where that answer came from. (You will find this by looking up the verse in the footnotes.)

2. Would there have been anything evil in turning stones to bread, or in jumping off the Temple pinnacle?
3. Give three examples of similar things that Jesus is said to have done during his ministry.
4. What were conditions like for the majority of people at the time of Jesus?
5. If you had the power to produce food, and you met a hungry child, what would you do?
6. If you were hungry and you heard of a wonder-worker who would feed you, what would be your natural reaction?
7. What things in life are more important than food?
8. Are these things possibly what God might will for us?
9. What Old Testament prophecy led Jesus to believe that he might be able to leap down and not be hurt?
10. Why was Jesus reluctant to perform this sort of miraculous trick?
11. Which group of people waited for a Messiah to lead them against the Romans?
12. What advantages would being a king have given Jesus?
13. Make a list of the three places where Jesus was tempted again to be ambitious and successful.
14. Who misunderstood Jesus' need to face death, and got called 'Satan'?
15. How did Jesus end his prayer in Gethsemane?
16. What did the Pharisees think that ambition did to a person?
17. What did the 'devil' really represent?
18. How was the death of Jesus really a great victory?
19. Look up and read these passages carefully, to see for yourself how Jesus faced his temptations all over again: John 6:11–16; Mark 8:27–33; Mark 14:32–36.

Creative Writing

Either: Find Mark 8:35. What do you think Jesus meant when he said that those prepared to lose their lives would find them, and those that clung to their lives would lose them?

Or: How can an ordinary person in an ordinary life keep the standard of loving God with all their heart, mind, soul and strength? Take the example of either a student at school, or a housewife, or a person at work, and indicate how they could attempt to live in such a way.

THE DEATH OF JOHN

John's mission came to a sudden end when he made a very dangerous enemy, Herodias, the granddaughter of Herod the Great. This energetic lady had been married to her uncle, Herod Philip Boethus, who lived in Rome, but after some twenty years of marriage she had left him for another of her uncles, Herod Antipas, the ruler of Galilee. John the Baptist was horrified by what he thought was disgraceful conduct.

Strangely enough, by Jewish Law, if Antipas' brother had died childless, it would have been Antipas' duty to marry his wife or wives, and produce a child which would be counted as his dead brother's. As it happened, Herodias had already had a child by her husband, and in any case, the husband was still very much alive. Therefore her 'wedding' to Antipas was not considered lawful by the Jews, and they were very shocked.

John criticised the couple openly, and for doing so was promptly arrested and flung into prison. The famous historian Josephus tells us that he was put inside the great fortress-prison of Machaerus, down near the Dead Sea. Here he was allowed to have visitors, and his disciples came to see him regularly. Even Herod Antipas used to go and have conversations with him, so he cannot have thought too badly of him.

John knew that Jesus, his cousin, had now begun his mission, so he may have thought that soon the Romans and the Herodians would be overthrown, and he would be released. As time passed, he grew worried, and wondered whether he had made a mistake. Jesus had made no effort to form an army or have him set free. He sent Jesus an important message. He asked him if he really was the Chosen One, or should the people start looking for someone else? Jesus' reply to him indicated that he certainly claimed to be the Messiah, but not quite the sort of person that John had been expecting.

Then, suddenly, John was put to death. According to St Mark's Gospel, John met his end at Herod Antipas' birthday party, when the daughter of Herodias by her former husband danced publicly

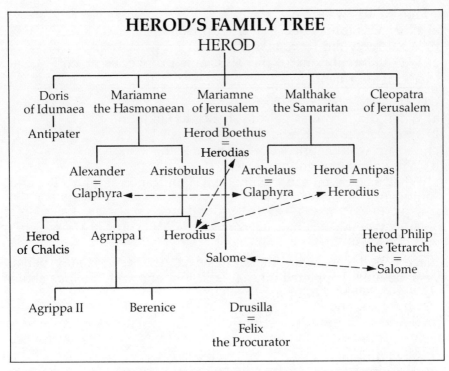

HEROD'S FAMILY TREE
HEROD

- Doris of Idumaea
  - Antipater
- Mariamne the Hasmonaean
  - Alexander = Glaphyra
  - Aristobulus
    - Herod of Chalcis
    - Agrippa I
    - Herodius
      - Agrippa II
      - Berenice
      - Drusilla = Felix the Procurator
- Mariamne of Jerusalem
  - Herod Boethus = Herodias
- Malthake the Samaritan
  - Archelaus = Glaphyra
  - Herod Antipas = Herodius
    - Salome
- Cleopatra of Jerusalem
  - Herod Philip the Tetrarch = Salome

for his guests, and was promised any reward, even up to half his kingdom. Herodias seized the chance to get rid of her enemy, and demanded John's head. The embarrassed Antipas had him executed immediately, and the Baptist's head was carried into the party on a plate. John's disciples went to the prison and took away what was left of his body and buried it, and then went and joined Jesus and his followers.

The most significant things about John's life and mission were, first, his work in calling the people to be ready for the Messiah when he came, and show their allegiance by being baptised and starting new lives; and secondly, his role in being the man chosen to identify the Messiah when he finally did come. Even Jesus himself may not have known for certain that it was himself – he certainly did not start his mission until he had been baptised by John.

Questions and Research

1. Find Mark 6:17–20.
(a) Why had Herod Antipas put John in prison?
(b) How do we know that Herod respected John?
(c) In what prison do we think John was locked away?

2. Find Matthew 11:2–6.

(a) What was John's question from prison?

(b) What reply did Jesus make?

(c) Was this reply one of the Messianic prophecies or not? (Look back at your list.)

3. Go back to Mark 6:21–30.

(a) When did Herodias get the chance to kill John?

(b) Who danced for Herod and his guests?

(c) Explain what happened as a result of this dance.

(d) What happened to John's body?

(e) What would you say was the real significance of John's life and mission?

Creative Writing

Imagine that you are a guest at Herod Antipas' birthday party. Describe what happened on that occasion, and your feelings about the tragic death of John the Baptist.

13
THE EARLY MINISTRY

Jesus' belief in himself as the Messiah may have started with his baptism, or it may have begun very much earlier, when he was a child – possibly Mary may have told him of her visions, and her hopes for him. No one can say at what specific moment Jesus knew that he was the Messiah. But we do know that he did not start his ministry until after his baptism, and his temptations in the wilderness. As a result of his temptations, we know what Jesus decided *not* to do about his ministry, and why. So how *did* Jesus go about his work, and what was his work going to be? How was he going to influence people to repent and change their lives? It seems that he chose three methods – teaching, healing and using the example of his own life.

But he couldn't do it alone. Let's start at the beginning of his ministry, and examine exactly how he went about it.

The call of the disciples

1. Find Mark 1:14–15. What was Jesus' first move?
2. Find John 1:35–62.
(a) Who was standing with John the Baptist?
(b) Why did they follow Jesus?
(c) Name one of those disciples.
(d) Who did he bring to Jesus?
(e) When Jesus met Simon, he 'looked at him', and gave him the nickname Cephas, or Peter – the Rock. Peter did not actually develop his rock-like qualities until after the death of Jesus. What does this suggest to us about the ability of Jesus to judge peoples' characters?

3. Find Mark 1.16–20. Here we have a different version of the call of the first disciples. This could mean that one version is correct and the other incorrect, but not necessarily so. The event mentioned in St John's Gospel could have taken place before the one

in St Mark's and would explain why they were so willing to leave everything and follow him.

(a) Where did Jesus see Simon and Andrew?
(b) What was their profession?
(c) Where did Jesus see James and John?
(d) Who was the father of James and John?
(e) What happened when Jesus called them?

4. Find Luke 5:1–11. Here we have yet another version of a meeting between Jesus and his first disciples. This could be another account of the meeting in Mark, or it could refer to a separate occasion.

(a) Who were the four disciples mentioned, and what was their relationship to each other?
(b) Why didn't Simon want to bother with fishing?
(c) What was Simon's nickname?
(d) What happened when Jesus told him to try fishing again?
(e) What did Simon say to Jesus?
(f) What did Jesus tell him?

Notice how the natural reaction was fear and astonishment.

5. We are not told of the call of all the disciples. Two others are mentioned in St John's Gospel. Find John 1:43–51.

(a) Who was the next disciple called?
(b) Whom did he fetch?
(c) What was his reaction on being told that Jesus was a Galilean?
(d) Why did Nathanael change his mind about Jesus?

The point is, I suppose, that Nathanael must have suddenly realised that Jesus knew something about his thoughts 'under the fig-tree' that nobody could possibly know. Perhaps he was wondering about the fate of the nation, and when the hoped-for Messiah would finally arrive – we don't know. But whatever it was, the idea that Jesus knew his thoughts was enough to convince Nathanael. Again, we have here an indication of Jesus' super-normal powers, his ability to read the mind and character of a person. Maybe Nathanael had been thinking about the way to heaven, for Jesus' speech in John 1:51 seems to be referring to Jacob's dream at Bethel (Genesis 28:12) – but this time the way to heaven is not a ladder, but Jesus himself.

6. Find John 2:1–11. Also in St John's Gospel we have the account of the first recorded miracle of our gospels. This one was not a healing, but something completely different – an act of kindness to save a friend from embarrassment.

(a) Where did the miracle take place?
(b) Briefly explain in your own words what happened.

The Sea of Galilee *Quiet beaches like this one were typical of the places Jesus knew, and where he taught. The large tree is a modern eucalyptus.*

(c) What does this tell us about Jesus' attitude to fun and parties?

This miracle is one of those referred to in St John's Gospel as a **sign**. The fourth gospel includes very few of the stories from the Synoptic Gospels, and it seems that those it does give were all carefully chosen to illustrate something specific about the significance of who Jesus really was.

The sign meant that what happened revealed something deep and important about Jesus and his kingdom. The external event was a pointer to an invisible truth that not everyone would see and understand.

With the coming of Christ, something had occurred which overshadowed all the works of God in the past. What Jesus really gave was himself. Jesus himself was the good wine that was better than anything else that preceded – and God did not give His blessings through Christ in limited measure. The wonderful new wine was not just a couple of bottles, but 120 gallons!

The rejection at Nazareth

Sadly, at the start of his mission Jesus did not meet with absolute success. When he went to preach in his own synagogue at Nazareth, the people were so alarmed by the claims that he was making for himself that they very nearly killed him. They had known him as a child and a young man – they could not accept his new role, and his claim to be fulfilling the prophecies of the Old Testament.

7. Find Luke 4:16–30.
(a) Where had Jesus been brought up?
(b) What reaction would you expect his neighbours to have to him?
(c) Copy out the quotation from Isaiah that Jesus read out.
(d) What did Jesus say about this passage?
(e) In verses 24–27, Jesus mentioned two Old Testament prophets who had more satisfaction from foreigners than from their own kindred. Who were they, and to whom did they go?
(f) What was the reaction of Jesus' neighbours to his speech?
(g) How was Jesus very nearly put to death?

In Mark's Gospel, the order of events is different, and the occasion when Jesus was rejected at Nazareth occurs much later than it does in St Luke's version. We do not know which of the two versions is correct. Here, Luke's version is preferred because it is a fuller account with more details, and biblical scholars have noticed how it does sometimes look as if Mark's order of events is faulty. Luke, on the contrary, took great care to write down his stories in order, a claim he made in the opening verses of his gospel. It is much more likely that the Nazarenes would have been reluctant to believe in Jesus at the start of his ministry, rather than later – when he had become famous for his miracles.

8. Find Mark 6:1–6.
(a) What do we find out about Jesus' previous profession?
(b) What do we find out about his family?
(c) What important parts of the account as given in St Luke's Gospel are left out of St Mark's?

Work in Capernaum

9. Find Luke 4:31–37.
(a) Where did Jesus go?
(b) What was the reaction to his teaching there?
(c) What happened in the synagogue?

10. Find Luke 4:38–39.
(a) How do we know that Peter was married?
(b) What happened at his home?

11. Find Luke 4:40–44.
(a) What was the result of these miracles of healing?

The Synagogue Ruins at Capernaum *These ruins are of a large and wealthy synagogue, probably built directly over the one paid for by the centurion of Capernaum whose slave Jesus healed. That centurion may have used a room in his own villa as the synagogue. At this site Jesus taught regularly.*

(b) What did Jesus do at dawn?

(c) Why did he seem reluctant to go on healing?

12. Find Mark 2:13–14.

(a) Whom did Jesus call next? What was his profession?

(b) What was the reaction of the Pharisees to Jesus mixing with this sort of person?

(c) What reply did Jesus make?

(d) Verses 18–20. What was another reason why the Pharisees disapproved of Jesus?

(e) Find Matthew 9:9–13. Here is another version of the call of the tax-collector, but what is he called this time?

(f) Find Mark 2:21–22. Jesus compared himself to two things, and the Pharisees didn't like it. Why not?

(g) Find Mark 2:23–28. Give another reason why Jesus upset the Pharisees.

13. Find Mark 3:1–6. The mounting opposition of the Pharisees came to a head when Jesus again entered a synagogue to teach.

(a) A certain man was waiting for him. We don't know his name, but what was wrong with him?

(b) Why do we suspect he had been 'planted' there?

(c) How were the Pharisees trying to catch Jesus out?

(d) How do we know that Jesus could read their minds?
(e) What question did he ask, and what answer did they give him?
(f) What happened to the man?
(g) What did the Pharisees decide to do?
(h) Who were the Herodians?

14. Find Mark 3:7–12.
(a) What was Jesus' reaction to the mounting opposition in the towns?
(b) What was the reaction of the crowds to him?
(c) Why did Jesus make use of a boat?

The Twelve Apostles

Jesus' early mission came to a head with his choice of twelve of his many disciples actually to help him with his work. They became known as **Apostles** – which means no longer 'learners' or disciples, but men 'sent out'. The Apostles are named in the following passages: Matthew 10:2–4; Mark 3:16–19; Luke 6:14–16; and Acts 1:13. Funnily enough, the gospels do not agree exactly even over names as important as theirs. The only Apostles named in St John's Gospel are Simon, Andrew, James, the Beloved One, Philip, Nathanael, Thomas and Judas Iscariot. Many scholars think that the Nathanael mentioned in John's list is the same person as Bartholomew, since Bartholomew is really a surname; and that the extra Judas in Luke's list is the Thaddaeus of Matthew.

15.
(a) Copy out the list as given in St Matthew's version.
(b) These would be his closest friends and helpers. We know, however, that many other people counted themselves as his disciples. Open your gospels anywhere, and see if you can find some names of people who would have counted themselves among his disciples. Don't forget the ladies.

Jesus goes home

Having chosen the Twelve, Jesus drew his initial campaign to a close. He went home, intending to rest. Unfortunately for him, the crowd he had attracted had no intention of letting their new master get away.

16. Find Mark 3:19–35.
(a) Did the crowd leave him to rest?
(b) How do we know that Jesus was probably very tired and overworked?

(c) What did the scribes accuse him of?
(d) How did Jesus answer that accusation?
(e) What did he say was the one sin that couldn't be forgiven? (There is a note about this in the section on forgiveness.)
(f) Who came to Jesus, probably to take him away to rest?
(g) What did Jesus do?
(h) Some people have thought that Jesus did not get on too well with his family. What do you think?
(i) Copy out verse 35.

Creative Writing

Choose any of the gospel incidents considered in this chapter. Imagine that you are one of the people who met Jesus. Describe your meeting, what happened (or what you saw) and how you felt about it.

14
THE SYNAGOGUE

A synagogue was a meeting place used by the Jews for their acts of worship, scripture reading and discussion. The name comes from the Greek words meaning to come together or to meet. Nobody is quite sure when the first synagogues were formed, but it was probably during the Old Testament period when the Jews were in exile in Babylon and could not get to the Temple to worship. They began to gather together on the sabbath days for prayer, reading of their scrolls, and generally to encourage each other to remain faithful to God in the difficult circumstances in which they found themselves.

Any group of twelve men gathered for these religious purposes had the right to call themselves a synagogue. When the Jews returned from their Exile, the Temple – which had been burnt down – was rebuilt and its services began again. However, by that time they had got used to their practice of meeting together, and continued to do so. Later, special buildings were provided in which to hold these meetings, and these became known as 'synagogues'. In the same way, the word 'church' now implies a building to most people, though originally it meant the people who were in it, not the place where they met. By the time of Jesus there were synagogues in every town and village.

These buildings were usually very simple, with seats for the men placed all around a raised platform from which the speaker read from the Law or addressed those gathered there. The women and children were not allowed to sit with the men, but were given space at the back or at the side, or if there was a gallery, they could go up there and watch. Any man – a person over the age of thirteen – could speak in the synagogue, or be invited to read the scriptures, but women were never allowed to speak. The men were obliged to have their heads covered, usually by a shawl called a tallith – and in modern times by hats or little round caps.

Synagogues were not run by the priests, who carried out the sacrifices at Jerusalem, but by a locally respected man who was elected their ruler or president, and a group of elders or respected

THE SYNAGOGUE

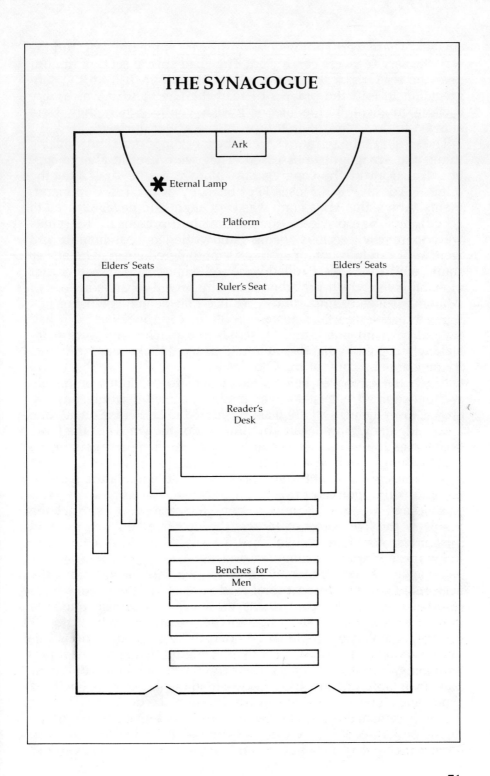

Ark

Eternal Lamp

Platform

Elders' Seats

Ruler's Seat

Elders' Seats

Reader's
Desk

Benches for
Men

citizens. These were responsible for the care of the building and the way the services were conducted. They had special seats of honour near the reader's desk. They could invite any man from the congregation to lead the prayers or read the Law, and it was a very exciting moment in the life of Jewish youths when they were allowed to do so for the first time, at the age of thirteen.

The scrolls of the scriptures were the most important and valuable things the synagogues possessed. They were kept in a large cupboard in front of the congregation, known as the Ark, after the original Ark in which Moses kept his copy of the Ten Commandments. Above the Ark a lamp was kept alight and never allowed to go out, as a sign of God's eternal, watchful presence. The scrolls were extremely precious, being handwritten on parchment, and were kept carefully wrapped in an embroidered cover. The staves round which they were rolled were sometimes topped by a cluster of small bells, which probably originally served to drive away evil demons. It is very important to realise that people could not just go to the shelf and take down a book to read. Books as such had not yet been invented, and all scrolls and parchments were painstakingly copied by hand – a chore that would take many months, if one wanted a copy of the Old Testament!

When the Law was being read, it had to be done completely without fault. If a mistake was made, the reader would have to start all over again, as there was considered to be a curse on anyone who added anything or left anything out of the words of the Law. Sometimes the words were pointed out with a special pointer, so that nothing could be missed. Nowadays, the pointers of many synagogues are made of silver, and have a little miniature hand at the end with a pointed finger.

The Law was divided into sections for each week, so that the whole of the five books of Moses (the first five books in the Old Testament) could be recited once a year. Adult Jews commonly knew these scriptures from memory.

Synagogues were not only used for worship. Apart from the services of prayer and scriptural readings held in them, they were also used as schools, courtrooms for specifically Jewish offences, and for weddings and discussions. The Jewish courts had the authority to sentence people to be fined or flogged for various offences, and even possibly to condemn certain offenders to death by strangling, burning or stoning. One could be stoned for adultery or blasphemy. Stoning involved being hurled forcibly down from three times one's own height, and if not found to be dead, one's chest would be crushed by a heavy stone that it took two men to lift.

On the kinder side, the rulers of the synagogues also dealt with the sharing out of benefits to the poor, and organising help and relief where necessary for people who had been struck down by various misfortunes.

The synagogue as an institution played a vital part in the preservation of Judaism through its various periods of oppression, and served as a force to unify all the members of the Jewish nation – whether they were in Israel, or away in some distant country. By the time of Jesus, many devout Jews were highly contemptuous of the Temple hierarchy, where the office of High Priest went to the highest bidder. They turned away from the sacrificial system to the more personal religious life they found in the synagogues. The early Christians seem to have based their organisation and meetings round the idea of the synagogue, even after the majority of them were no longer Jews.

Questions

1. What does the word 'synagogue' mean?
2. Why did the Jews start having synagogues?
3. How many men formed a synagogue?
4. Describe the layout of a typical synagogue, and copy the diagram.
5. What was a tallith?
6. Who ran the synagogues?
7. At what age was a Jewish youth counted as a man?
8. What were the most valuable possessions of a synagogue?
9. How often was the whole Law read through?
10. What else was the synagogue used for besides services?

Research

1. Find and write out Matthew 4:23.
2. Find Mark 1:21–28.
(a) What did Jesus do on the Sabbath?
(b) Why were the people 'astonished' at Jesus?
(c) Who interrupted the service?
(d) What did Jesus do?

3. Find the following references. State, in each case, what event took place at the synagogue: Mark 3:1–6; Mark 6:1–6, Luke 13:10–17.

4. Find Mark 5:21–24, 35–43.
(a) Which synagogue ruler came to Jesus for help?
(b) What help did he need?
(c) Describe, very briefly, what happened.

5. Find Luke 7:1–5.
(a) Who had a sick slave?
(b) Who did he send to Jesus?
(c) Why was this Roman popular with the Jews?
(d) State, very briefly, what happened.

Creative Writing

Imagine that you are at a synagogue service, and that Jesus is there. Describe what happened, and what the reaction was when Jesus interrupted the service to do a healing. (Choose one of the events you have studied in this chapter.)

15

THE MINISTRY OF HEALING

Although Jesus rejected the idea of becoming known as a wonder-worker, and realised that only by the example of his own life and his words as a teacher would he have a lasting effect on mankind, nevertheless he did become extremely famous and popular as a healer. It seems natural that someone of Jesus' great compassion *should* have healed the physical ailments of those who sought him – and sometimes even of those who had *not* asked him for help.

During his three-year ministry, Jesus was followed by large crowds of invalids wherever he went. Sometimes, we are told, he did not even enter a town, with its narrow back-streets, but stayed out in the countryside. Sometimes he worked all day, not even taking the time off to eat (Mark 6:30). When he cured the paralysed man, the crush of people round the house in which Jesus was teaching was so great that the friends of the invalid were obliged to let him down through the roof, after removing some tiles. (Incidentally, the mention of tiles in Luke 5:19 suggests that the house was in the typical Greek style not uncommon in Galilee. It also suggests an eyewitness detail, for the average Jewish house was not tiled.)

However, Jesus could not possibly heal everybody. Many people must have heard of him and not got to him. Many people must have touched him in the same crowd as the woman with the haemorrhage, and yet we are not told that they were all healed – just as many people have longed for healing from places connected with Jesus or the Holy Spirit (such as Lourdes, for example), and have come away in the same sad physical condition.

Even as 'Man shall not live by bread alone', so it was important to Jesus that Man should not simply go to him for bodily health. Jesus had a lot more to offer, a far richer reward then simply a longer life here. (One might say here that many folk who have been to Lourdes for healing and who have not been healed, have nevertheless had their lives changed at Lourdes when they felt themselves to be in the caring presence of Jesus, and have later died without fear or disappointment.)

What of the people that Jesus *did* heal? Only a handful are mentioned in St John's Gospel, but hundreds in the first three gospels. Some are mentioned at length and in moving detail, many are simply referred to in general paragraphs where we find out that the whole village assembled with their invalids, and he healed them all (for example, Mark 6:55–56).

Jesus healed by several different methods, which fall into two main categories – healing **by personal contact**, and healing **from a distance**. In areas where Christ was little known, or with people who did not appear to have sufficient trust in him, Jesus used methods already family to them – such as anointing with saliva, a substance believed by the ancients with some justification to have curative properties. Sometimes he increased his ability to draw faith from them by touching them, or taking their hands. When a person was suffering from a mental disorder, or spirit-possession, and was not perhaps in control of his own mind, Jesus used command – exerting his divine will over theirs.

When the invalid's malady was caused in some way through sin – perhaps paralysis caused by a guilt complex over some remembered misdeed – Christ removed the blockage first by forgiving the sin and putting the tormented mind at rest, and then the healing followed. It has been suggested that many of the healing miracles worked by Jesus were of psychosomatic ailments (which are caused or made worse by worry) and that by curing the mind, the body would then naturally right itself. One can certainly imagine that healing of this sort would be very effective.

When the invalid himself or herself had enough faith in Jesus, or when a friend had sufficient faith for the sick one, the healings could take place without any form of contact at all.

Therefore, to summarise, we could say that Jesus healed:

1. By mechanical means (e.g. saliva) – a technical term for using something as an aid.
2. By touch –
   (a) on the affected part;
   (b) on the hand; and
   (c) on the head, or any other part, when the person was affected all over.
3. By being touched.
4. By command.
5. By forgiveness of sins.
6. By the faith of the invalid.
7. By the faith of someone else on the invalid's behalf.

From a survey of the few healings described in detail in the gospels, we can draw several conclusions which repay study. First, however, we must go through the gospels and catalogue the instances.

1. Healing by mechanical means

1. Find Mark 7:31–37. Write the story in your own words. How was the man healed? Did Jesus say anything special to him? Was the healing done publicly or secretly? Did Jesus give the man any instructions?
2. Find Mark 8:22–26. Again, write out the story of what happened. How do we know this healing did not work properly the first time. (This is a very important point, for it is the only example we have of some kind of a limit to Jesus' powers – perhaps when he was very tired. That makes the work of Jesus all the more poignant, for if it cost him an effort to heal we can imagine the depth of his love and compassion when dealing with all those crowds.)
3. Find John 9. This is one more example of Jesus using saliva to heal. Read the chapter through. What was wrong with this invalid? What did Jesus do? What did he tell the man to do, and with what result?

It seems that it was not unknown at the time of Christ for doctors to use saliva in their medicine, and it was firmly believed right up to this century that to rub one's eyes with fasting spittle – the mouthful there before swallowing first thing in the morning – made them stronger. There *are* curative properties in saliva, and all animals lick their wounds, but Jesus was probably here simply using a popular method to bolster up faith where there was not much in evidence.

2. Healing by laying on of hands

This was Jesus' most usual method of healing. Sometimes Jesus would touch the part that was poorly or deformed, or very often he would touch the person on the head, or hold their hand.

4. Find Mark 1:29–31. This healing presumably took place on a sabbath day, after Jesus had taught in the synagogue at Capernaum. Who was Jesus staying with? Why was there no meal ready for him? What did Jesus do about it?
5. Find Luke 13:10–17. On what day of the week did this healing

take place? What was wrong with the woman Jesus saw? Why was the synagogue ruler indignant when Jesus healed her?

Oxen and asses worked hard for a living, but even they were allowed to rest on sabbath days, and were released from their burdens. What was the reaction of the people who had criticised Jesus when he pointed this out?

6. Find Luke 14:1–6. This is another sabbath-day healing. Where was Jesus being entertained to dinner? One of the people there had dropsy, a disease that causes water to be retained in the limbs, especially the legs, so that they swell up. Why were the Pharisees watching Jesus? Did Jesus know what they were thinking?

Jesus again spoke of sabbath-day regulations. A person was not allowed to lift a burden or carry things about; yet, if an animal fell down a well on a sabbath day, the law would swiftly be broken to pull it out. God's laws were intended to be kind and compassionate. It was a relief for slaves and animals to be able to have a rest. Yet obviously God did not intend to cause suffering by His sabbath laws. Acts of kindness, and healing, were quite in keeping with God's intentions for the sabbath day. Indeed, God never stopped His work of healing just because it was the sabbath, did He?

7. Find Mark 1:40–45. If a leper came near a person, he was obliged to shout, 'Unclean! Unclean!' so that healthy folk would keep well away. What did this particular leper do that put Jesus in danger of catching the disease? How did Jesus feel about this man? What did he do? Jesus did not want the leper to tell anyone, but he was far too excited. What did Jesus command the leper? Were his instructions obeyed? What was the result of that?

Lepers were not allowed to live in towns where they might pass their disease on to other people. Leprosy was one of the most serious diseases of the ancient and medieval world, and there were no known cures for it. There seem to have been several different diseases called leprosy in the Bible, some of which apparently did get better; but equally the person who caught leprosy had to go away from his people and live with other lepers until he died.

Enough people recovered from one form of the disease for there to be a set ritual that the priest had to carry out before a leper could go home. Find Leviticus 14:3–9. Give a brief outline of what cured lepers had to do.

8. Find Luke 22:47–51. This was actually Jesus' last healing before his execution. What was wrong with the man Jesus healed?

Find John 18:10–11. Who cut the man's ear off? What was the man's name?

Find John 18:26. How did one of this man's relatives nearly cause the arrest of Peter?

9. Find Mark 5:21–43. This moving incident involved a little girl who died. Fevers and sickness were very common among children who lived near the Sea of Galilee. Many disease-bearing mosquitoes plagued the area, and it was extremely hot and uncomfortable through the summer months. Who was the father of this little girl? Why did Jesus not get to her in time to save her from dying? What happened while Jesus was still speaking to the woman and the crowd? Who witnessed what actually happened when Jesus got to the little girl? Why did the mourners laugh at Jesus at first? Describe what happened when Jesus went into the child's room. 'Talitha' was Aramaic for a little lamb, and a term of affection. What were Jesus' final instructions?

10. Find Mark 9:14–29. This is another healing involving a child. This boy was described as having a 'dumb spirit', but his symptoms seem to indicate that he was an epileptic. What symptoms did the father describe for the boy? How long had he had the disease? Why did the boy's father think a spirit was trying to destroy his child? What did the father say when Jesus told him that all things were possible if only he would believe? Describe what happened when Jesus ordered the spirit to leave the boy. At what stage did Jesus take the boy's hand and pray?

In this modern world many people no longer believe in evil spirits at all, and they think that when people of the time of Jesus believed that sickness was caused by spirits, it was simply because they lived before the time of medical advances. Medicine, however, has not completely explained away certain cases that really do seem to be caused by 'possession'. It may be that a sick person has been possessed by a part of his own subconscious mind; some doctors who work with mentally sick people feel that there is a noticeable difference between those who seem to be possessed by something other than their normal selves, and those who are simply suffering from a disease of the brain.

It is worth noticing that Jesus certainly believed in the reality of evil spirits, and made a distinction between his ministry of healing and that of exorcism.

3. Healing by being touched

On one occasion, Jesus healed someone without consciously willing it. A woman in the crowd had been in a wretched condition for many years, and despite all her efforts, nothing had cured her. Instead, she was gradually getting worse. In her despair she reached out and touched Jesus as he passed, firmly believing that just to do this would cure her.

11. Find Mark 5:24–34. What was wrong with the woman? What did she do? What did Jesus say? What was the reaction of the disciples to this? How did Jesus know that someone had been healed?

This incident is very important, for it is the only one we have that actually mentioned power leaving Jesus to cure a person. It is interesting to notice that, after Jesus' death, when St Peter was involved with his own ministry of healing, the sick were carried into the streets on their beds so that his shadow might fall on them and heal them (Acts 5:18). St Paul, who also had a healing ministry, used to bless handkerchiefs and aprons and send them to invalids and possessed people, and they were cured (Acts 19:11–12).

4. Healing from a distance

All the people we have studied so far actually experienced physical contact with Jesus, and were cured. But there were many who were cured without actual physical contact. These were cured in several ways – by a direct command from Jesus, by their own faith, by the faith of someone who loved them, by experiencing forgiveness of sins, or by Christ's prayers.

One very exciting healing occurred when Jesus had been rowed across the Sea of Galilee one night, had climbed the cliffs on the far side, and was passing through a graveyard inhabited not only by the dead but also by a man possessed by evil spirits.

12. Find Mark 5:1–20. Why was the madman not chained up? What did he do at night? What were Jesus' first words to him? Why did the man say his name was Legion? How did this healing have an unfortunate effect upon some pigs? What was Jesus' command to the healed man? How was this different from his usual instructions?

This healing gives us an interesting example of a mistake in St Mark's geography. The text should read Gerasa (modern Kersa), and not Gadara, since Gadara was several miles away from the cliff edge. Gerasa was not far away from the big Roman garrison at Hippos. The Romans were very fond of sausages, and were probably the customers of the men who kept the pigs. It is rather interesting that the emblem on the standards of the legion stationed here was a wild boar.

Notice how, in this miracle, the first conversation took place between Jesus and the entity possessing the madman, and not the madman himself. The possessing demons knew that Jesus was the Son of the Most High God, and were frightened. The asking of the name was a common way of gaining control over such a spirit.

It is a well-known fact that many animals are far more sensitive to atmosphere than people. Possibly the unfortunate pigs panicked when the demons, or atmosphere of evil, left the man, and so fell to their deaths in the sea.

Another example of healing by command occurred at the start of Jesus' ministry when the Pharisees were annoyed with him for healing on the sabbath.

13. Find Mark 3:1–6. What was wrong with this invalid? Why does it look as if he had been placed in front of Jesus deliberately? What did Jesus ask the people who were watching? Why was Jesus angry with them? How did he cure the man?

Yet another healing by command took place in a synagogue. This time it was a man possessed by a demon.

14. Find Mark 1:21–28. What did the possessed man shout out? Who was supposed to be speaking? What did Jesus do about it? What was the result?

Notice again how it was the demon within the man who spoke and who recognised that Jesus was the Holy One of God.

5. Healing by forgiveness of sins

One healing was concerned with the forgiveness of sins. It was a case of paralysis. It does sometimes happen that when a person's mind is suffering great distress because of guilt and shame or fear, particularly if this is repressed, the physical body suffers as a result. It was not impossible that the feeling of guilt or remorse over something he had done had paralysed this man. We do not know – we can only guess that possibly this was the reason why Jesus spoke to him as he did. Jesus did not usually mention forgiveness of sins to the invalids he healed.

15. Find Mark 2:1–13. Briefly describe what happened. Why were the Pharisees so annoyed with Jesus? If they believed (and they did!) that man's sickness was God's will, what would that imply about the power of Jesus?

It is interesting to note that in the only other recorded case of Jesus dealing with paralysis, in John 5:1–14, the method was once more by the forgiveness of sins.

6. Healings by faith

Other healings were a result of the faith of the invalid.

16. Find Luke 17:11–19. Why did the lepers stand at a distance? How many of them were there? What did Jesus tell them to do?

The fact that the lepers left Jesus and started to look for a priest indicates that they did have faith in him – for, as they left Jesus, their leprosy had not yet been cured. It might have seemed a waste of time to them, and yet they went. One wonders whether they would still have been cured if they'd stood there arguing. St Luke's Gospel has a particular interest in any incidents connected with Gentiles, women, outcasts, sinners and Samaritans. Into which category of interest does this incident fall?

17. Find Mark 10:46–52. What was wrong with this invalid? What was his name? What did he cry out to Jesus?

Jesus was not literally the Son of David. David was the best-loved Old Testament king, and many Jews believed that when the Messiah came he would be a descendant of David. We know that both the Virgin Mary and Joseph the Carpenter were of David's line, and so Jesus did fulfil this requirement. To call somebody 'Son of David' was therefore highly dangerous, for the Romans would arrest anybody claiming to be a Messiah. They thought the Messiah would be a military leader, perhaps a ringleader in the Zealot resistance movement.

Why did many people tell Bartimaeus to be silent? Did Jesus accept the title? What would this tell the people who saw the miracle?

7. Healing by the faith of another

This final category is the one that is probably of the most interest to us – for we ourselves will at some time or another pray for our loved ones when they are sick. When someone else has faith enough to ask Jesus for healing for someone else – perhaps because the sick person is a baby, or unconscious, or mentally deranged, or is dying – this is called absent healing, or distant healing, as happened in the case of the centurion's servant.

A centurion was a Roman officer in charge of a hundred men. Centurions were usually tough, hard characters who had proved themselves to be excellent soldiers. They were rarely wealthy, and although they might have been loved (or hated) by their troops in the same way as our modern sergeant-majors, they were seldom loved by the people of the land their army was occupying. This centurion seems to have been an exception in two ways: he was quite wealthy and he had impressed the local people.

18. Find Luke 7:1–10. Why did the local people think this centurion was worth helping? What did he want Jesus to do? Did he approach Jesus himself?

As it happened, Jesus did not actually enter the centurion's house. The centurion was a man who was used to being obeyed. When he gave orders, he expected them to be carried out.

What did he expect Jesus to do? What was Jesus' reaction to this man's faith?

Gentiles, especially Romans, were one of St Luke's characteristic interests. He presented this Roman officer in a very good light. St Matthew's version gives somewhat different details.

19. Find Matthew 8:5–13. What was wrong with the servant? What does this version leave out of the narrative?

It is interesting to compare this healing with a similar one in St John's Gospel (John 2:46–54). Instead of a centurion at Capernaum, it mentions an official; and instead of a slave being sick, it is the man's son. Some scholars have wondered if this is another version of the same healing. Other details are not so similar, however, as you will see if you read the narrative. Notice how the official checked the time of the healing with his servants, and found out that the boy was cured at the very hour when the official had his conversation with Jesus.

The healing of the epileptic boy and Jairus' daughter are also healings that did not have anything to do with the faith of the invalid. The gospels tell us of two others, both involving youngsters.

20. Find Matthew 15:21–28. Who came to Jesus for help? What was

wrong with the child? What was the reaction of the disciples to this woman? What did Jesus say?

This is a very surprising incident, for we find it hard to imagine that Jesus would refuse to heal anyone, let alone a little girl. Yet it seems that Jesus had not at this stage considered extending his healing ministry to those who were not Jews. (The centurion's slave was probably a Jewish man.) But the woman surprised Jesus by her faith and her persistence. She had no intention of giving in.

What did Jesus say about children and dogs? What do you think he meant by this?

If the children meant the Jews, and the dogs meant the Gentiles, then it seems that Jesus had no intention of extending his ministry beyond helping the Jews. That seems so unlikely; the story is embarrassing to those who see Jesus as universal saviour. Yet the very awkwardness of the story suggests that such a tale would never have been invented if it did not really happen. Perhaps it shows the real human nature of Jesus – that the persuasiveness of the woman was able to change his mind, and make Jesus think again about helping her?
What did the woman say to Jesus? What was the result?

Find Mark 7:24–30. Notice how Mark's version leaves out the sentence about only being sent to the House of Israel. The entire story is left out of St Luke's Gospel, even though he had a special interest in Jesus' dealings with women and non-Jews.

The healing at the gate of the city of Nain involved another dead person. Jairus' daughter had only just died when Jesus healed her, but this boy had presumably been dead for some hours. In Galilee, people were usually buried the same day that they died. They would not be placed in the ground, but in a cave with a stone rolled over the entrance to stop animals getting in to eat the meat of the corpse. Relatives often inspected the dead person during the first few days, just in case they were not really dead after all.

21. Find Luke 7:11–17. Where did Jesus see this dead youth? What do we know about him? Give a brief description of this very dramatic healing, and the effect it had on the crowd watching.

The significance of Jesus' ministry of healing

An examination of Jesus' healing ministry leads us to several very important conclusions. If the narratives are true, and Jesus really did heal sickness, and if he was indeed the Son of God, then the sickness cannot have been inflicted by God in the first place. In other words, despite what some well-meaning people sometimes say, sickness is not, and never can be, God's will. How can anyone seriously imagine that God would deliberately inflict dreadful suffering on people? Could we accept a God who was more cruel than we are ourselves?

A second important conclusion must be that sickness is not a punishment sent by God for our sins (see John 9:2), except in so far as we punish ourselves for our own wrongdoing by such things as repressing guilt, or damaging our bodies by indulgence in harmful practices like breathing in nicotine and tar and poisoning ourselves with alcohol and drugs.

Jesus could cure the complete personality, physical, mental and spiritual. Healings are recorded of physical disorders such as poorly arms, legs, eyes and skin, and virus and bone infections; mental disorders such as epilepsy and paralysis; and spiritual disorders caused by demon possession. He usually only cured those who had faith in him. Many people must have touched him in the crowd as he went to heal the daughter of Jairus, for example, and yet, so far as we know, only the woman with the haemorrhage was cured. When that woman touched him, Jesus apparently felt power go out of him, so this implies that Jesus did use some sort of power to cure people and work his miracles. Possibly excess use of this power made him tired. The only cure we are told about that did not seem to work at first was that of the blind man at Bethsaida, which may have followed the feeding of the 4,000.

Although Jesus often ended the day exhausted, having had no time even to eat, he used prayer and contact with God to renew his strength rather than sleep (see Mark 1:35; Luke 5:16, 6:12, 9:18). After working hard, he often stayed up all night instead of going to bed, and seemed refreshed the next day.

It seems that Jesus had absolute command over life and death, but only attempted to bring back those who had recently died, especially if they were young persons. We have no record of Jesus being called to the death-bed of elderly persons, but presumably, in his acceptance of life beyond the death of this present body of ours, Jesus would have taken the view that bodily death was inevitable and acceptable in due course. One imagines that he would have helped those at the end of their lifetime to die in peace. (Modern medicine, that keeps many people alive beyond the time when they would naturally have passed on, has to face the particular dilemma of whether it is better using medicine to help a person to die more easily, or to keep on attempting to prolong life at all costs – even when it drastically increases the suffering of the person concerned.)

The ministry of Jesus reveals his great love, compassion and self-denial, for he had not come primarily as a healer, and the work with invalids must often have exhausted him and impeded his progress as a teacher. Yet he never turned them away. Even a visit from his own family had to take second place to his great work. Nothing distracted him from it. Even in the excitement of his arrest, after his agony of mind in Gethsemane, he paused to heal the stricken ear of Malchus.

Of course, the mission of healing did not stop at Jesus himself. He considered it important enough to pass on his power to his disciples, and they were even sent out on practice missions during his lifetime. It is important to notice that Jesus' works of healing were not used as proofs that he was the Son of God. If that had been so, what would it have proved about all the others who were also given the power to heal? However, it was intended to demonstrate the action of God, and was a sign that the Kingdom of Heaven had already come among them.

Most of the references to Jesus' work as signs come in St John's Gospel, where it stresses that many people came to believe in Jesus as the Son of God because of the signs that he did. Indeed, a concluding verse of that gospel states quite bluntly that Jesus did a great number of signs, and that those included in the gospel were deliberately chosen so that the reader would come to believe that Jesus was the Christ (John 20:30).

The signs were not just the healings, however, but the whole of Jesus' activity and his teachings; his death and resurrection was the greatest sign of all.

After Jesus' departure and the coming of the Holy Spirit, the ability of the disciples to heal was one of the chief marks of their calling, and the gift spread to many of the early Christians. For example, Ananias of Damascus cured St Paul's blindness. The ability to heal was seen as the direct action of the Spirit of God, and all possessors of the Holy Spirit were healers in one sense or another. The important ingredients were prayer – a bringing of oneself into the presence of God, and a becoming open to His power: right-living and self-control.

Questions and Research

1. John 9:16. Why did some people think Jesus could not have been a sinner?
2. John 7:31. Why did some people think Jesus must have been the Christ, or Messiah?

3. John 2:23. Why did many people believe in Jesus?
4. John 6:14. What was the reaction of the crowds after Jesus had fed the five thousand?
5. John 6:2. Why did multitudes (crowds) follow Jesus?
6. John 12:37. Did people always believe in the signs?
7. John 4:48. What did Jesus say that sounded rather indignant?
8. John 29:29. What words did Jesus say to encourage Christians who had not had the opportunity to see the signs that took place during his lifetime?

General Questions on the Healings

1. What were the two main methods of healing used by Jesus?
2. What is meant by 'mechanical means'? Give two examples of where Jesus used this method.
3. Which invalids recognised Jesus as 'Son of God'? Who was speaking on those occasions?
4. Which four healings were done on a sabbath day?
5. Which invalids were asked to keep their cures secret?
6. Which invalid was asked to publicise his cure?
7. Which invalids were Gentiles (non-Jews)?
8. Which healings were done by the faith of another?
9. Which healing was by forgiveness of sins?
10. Why did this healing offend the Pharisees?
11. Which invalids were raised from the dead?
12. Which healing didn't work properly the first time?
13. Which invalid 'drew power' from Jesus?
14. Which invalid called Jesus 'Son of David'? Can you remember why this title was significant?
15. Which invalids were female?
16. Which invalids showed the greatest faith in Jesus?
17. Who was 'Legion'?
18. Who was Jairus?
19. Which healing had a disastrous effect on some animals?
20. Which healings were only in St Luke's Gospel?

16
THE MASTER'S VOICE, SIDE TWO

Most of Jesus' preaching was intended to show people the way to find God, to enter into a state that he called **eternal life** or the **Kingdom of Heaven**.

We are at a great disadvantage in that we cannot actually go to hear Jesus teach, or find out what he was really like from the people who knew him. We can study the gospels, and even though we may feel him speaking through them, it is hardly the same thing.

Each gospel, in any case, presents a slightly different picture of Jesus. St Mark reveals a man of action and drama and power; St Matthew presents a Messianic figure who fulfilled all the Old Testament prophecies – the Jewish Expected One, descendant of David and so on; and St Luke shows us a man of great love and compassion whose arms reached out to embrace the whole of humanity, including the unworthy, the lost, the despised.

If we only study the Synoptic Gospels – the first three – we miss a lot by not getting to know the Jesus of the fourth gospel, the Jesus who brings the revelation of the spirit and nature of God.

Let us consider some of his words as given in that gospel. We might get a glimpse of what Jesus was like, and the authority, confidence and compassion that struck the people who actually *did* listen to him with amazement and wonder. It is in pondering words like these that all of us are challenged with the problem of belief. Who was this person Jesus? Was he a madman, or a deliberate liar? A money-making fraud and imposter? A well-meaning but deluded idiot? A con-man with delusions of grandeur? Or was he really the 'Son of God'?

Project

Find these verses in St John's Gospel. Either read them round the class, or write them out. They could be produced as a little booklet with a special cover:

John 1:1–5, 10–13; 3:3–6; 4:23–24; 5:24; 6:35; 6:51; 10:11, 16, 18; 14:1–3, 8–9, 12; 14:18–19, 27–29; 15:13; 11:25–26.

17
THE TEACHINGS OF JESUS: HIS METHODS

Although Jesus undoubtedly became very famous as a healer, the healing part of his ministry was not his main concern – because he knew that any effects of physical healing could only be temporary. Sooner or later all men's earthly lives would be ended by death. What was of vital importance to Jesus was to give people in all places and all times something much more important than physical well-being – he had come to bring life of a completely different order to all who accepted him; a view of life and an insight into existence that far transcended earthly life. He had come to bring eternal life, or the Kingdom of Heaven.

Jesus used many methods of teaching. His most direct teachings were probably **in the synagogues** on sabbath days. It was quite in order for visiting rabbis to address the congregation, especially if they had a reputation for wisdom and learning. We have no evidence that Jesus was a properly trained rabbi, a training that required years of study in the Law and its interpretations, but he was often called rabbi, and had impressed many synagogues with his message. The usual procedure for speakers in the synagogue was to take a passage from the scriptures, read it, and explain its meaning. We have an example of Jesus doing this in Luke 4:16–30. We can also see there how the congregation was rather shaken by what Jesus said, and so offended that they tried to kill him!

His second important method was to use **parables**, and there are many examples of these in the gospels. Luke 15 has three well-known ones.

Thirdly, Jesus would teach by **giving an example**, such as the pattern prayer given in Matthew 5:7–15. Then, he would teach by giving **answers to direct questions**, for example on marriage and divorce (Mark 10), on inheriting eternal life (Mark 10), or on paying taxes (Mark 12).

Occasionally Jesus would **correct their faults**, as in Luke 5:29–32; 6:6–11, 32–36; or **develop discussions into instruction**, as in Luke 6:37–42; 7:18–35, 36–50. Sometimes Jesus would **test his disciples**, as when he challenged Peter to walk on water (Matthew 14) or when he sent out the disciples on practice missions (Luke 9). Finally, sometimes his teachings came in a moment of **revelation**, as when Peter, James and John saw Jesus in his glory as the Messiah when he was transfigured on the mountain (Mark 9).

Project

Make a chart showing all the methods Jesus used to teach his disciples. Put the methods (given in capitals) on the left-hand side, and briefly give an example for each on the right-hand side. Do not write out the full story or all the verses given – just a line or two to say what each incident was will be enough.

18

THE PARABLES

All Jewish teachers used the method of speaking in parables to put across their lessons. A parable is a saying with a message, a meaning for those who want to know – those who have 'ears to hear'. The actual word parable comes from putting together two Greek words – *para*, meaning 'alongside', and *ballo* meaning 'I put'. They are comparisons, one thing being put alongside another, in order to make a particular point.

Jesus was attempting to teach his hearers something about the Kingdom of God, or the kind of conduct expected from those who wished to be in it, and in many cases he taught in parables for exactly the same reasons the other rabbis did: to make his point in a striking and imaginative way that would enable the student to understand the lesson and remember it. For this reason, Jesus often used background material familiar to his audience – illustrations from farming, fishing and family life.

It has often been said that parables are 'earthly stories with heavenly meanings', but this is not strictly true, as not all parables are stories as such. Certainly the best-known ones are **stories** – for example, the good Samaritan, the prodigal son, the ten bridesmaids, the rich man and Lazarus – but most of the others are very much shorter.

Sometimes it is said that parables are **allegories**. An allegory is an elaborate story in which each part is supposed to represent something else. It is true that three of Jesus' stories *may* have been allegories, or they may have been given allegorical interpretations which were not the original teaching of Jesus but were added later by the leaders of the Church – for example, the sower, and the wheat and the tares (Matthew 13:1–23, 24–30, 36–43). However, one parable which *does* seem to be an allegory is that of the vineyard in Mark 12:1–11, and we have no reason to believe that this is not a genuine parable of Jesus.

Sometimes it is said that the parables are **fables** – imaginary tales with morals to them. Again, some of them might be, but certainly not many are. Some of Jesus' parables are very short, and simply state that the Kingdom of Heaven is like something. We call these similes.

There remains another category of parable which is certainly striking, but is terse and cryptic, and to which the meanings were not given. The disciples were left to puzzle these out for themselves. Such parables might be called **riddles**, and examples are the mustardseed, the leaven, the seed growing secretly, the pearl. It seems that Jesus taught in riddles so often that it baffled his disciples, who got quite agitated and demanded to know *why* he spoke to people in parables, and not openly.

In Mark 4 we have a clue as to why Jesus did so. A quotation is given from Isaiah in which it is suggested that Jesus taught in riddles deliberately so that certain people *would not be able to understand him*. St Matthew obviously found this idea hard to accept, so the wording in his version is altered to suggest that it was not Jesus' fault that they couldn't understand him, but the fault of the people. Certain people just did not wish to understand.

Nevertheless, despite St Matthew's opinion, there are reasons why Jesus could have desired a certain measure of secrecy and ambiguity. If Jesus had stated openly that he was the Messiah, he would have been arrested immediately. All Messianic claims were regarded as revolutionary. Jesus was not the only person who had claimed to be the Messiah – there had been others, whose missions had ended with the Roman army capturing them and putting them and their followers to death. In A.D. 6, for example, when Jesus was presumably twelve years old, Judas of Gamala had been crucified with some 6,000 of his followers, for claiming to be the Messiah. A religious leader, if harmless, might simply have been ignored, but the Romans always kept a very close watch on crowds, and they would not have ignored someone with the influence and following that Jesus enjoyed. Once they discovered that he was making Messianic claims they would have dealt with him immediately.

Also at this stage, Jesus could have wished to gather round himself only those followers who had the interest or stamina to work out his teachings for themselves, or at least find out from those who had. Although he never made open claims to be the Messiah, certain people may have come to that conclusion – rather like a ploughman suddenly finding buried treasure (one of his riddles). It was a 'secret' known only to those who had 'eyes to see'. To many people, Jesus probably appeared to be giving homely advice, or tips on good farming! Not everyone would get the message.

Therefore it seems that, although Jesus did often teach in parables to make his lessons clear and memorable to the disciples, there were also times when the teaching was a 'Messianic secret' known only to those few who could understand the riddles.

Questions

1. What is a rabbi?
2. What is an allegory?
3. Which three parables of Jesus are given an allegorical interpretation?
4. What do some scholars think about the interpretations of these?
5. What does the word 'parable' mean?
6. What is a simile?
7. Give three examples of parables that are stories.
8. Give three examples of parables that are riddles.
9. Why did rabbis teach in parables?
10. Can you suggest any reasons why Jesus might have deliberately taught in riddles?
11. What was the Roman attitude to Messiahs?
12. Name the unfortunate 'Messiah' who was executed.
13. What was the 'secret' known only to those who understood?

A few riddles

One riddle Jesus gave them to puzzle over concerned his own particular trade, that of carpentry.

1. Find Matthew 7:2–5.
(a) Write out verse 5.
(b) What does this particular parable try to stop us doing?
(c) A modern rephrasing of this parable might be that 'the pot shouldn't call the kettle black'; or even that 'people in glass houses shouldn't throw stones'. Explain in your own words what the riddle really means.

Another riddle was about an animal particularly shunned by Jews – the pig.

2. Find Matthew 7:6.
(a) Copy out the verse.
(b) Why would it be foolish to throw down pearls for pigs?
(c) What do you think Jesus meant by the pearls and the pigs?

According to the Law, pigs were unclean animals, and to call someone a pig was, and still is, a term of abuse and contempt. These pigs were interested in food, not pearls. Jesus obviously knew that certain people would not be the least bit interested in his teachings; they were only after a good time and plenty of comfort and easy living. They would just trample on the pearls. One must make it very clear that Jesus was not referring to people who were poor or not very intelligent – no one had *more* time for these than Jesus – he meant those wilful persons who simply had no time for, and who scorned, the good and deeper motives of life. He said elsewhere that the one sin that could not be forgiven was the inability to recognise the working for good of the Holy Spirit.

The next two examples would be easily understood by a thrifty housewife and a home-brewer.

3. Find Mark 2:21–22.
(a) What did Jesus say about patching clothes?
(b) What did Jesus say about brewing new wine?
(c) Was Jesus comparing his teaching to the new wine or the old wineskins?

If a piece of unshrunk cloth is used as a patch, the first time the garment is washed it shrinks and the tear gets worse. If fermenting wine is placed in a skin bag that has already been stretched by use, the bag would burst and all the wine spill out. There was going to be a lot of tension bringing Jesus' teachings together with the old understanding of religion, and Jesus knew it.

The stories

St Luke was a gifted and fluent writer, and it is a characteristic of his gospel to present Jesus' teaching in stories. All the parables in the list below are in his gospel. Write out this list. (The parables are dealt with more fully later in the course.)

1. The Good Samaritan (Luke 10:25–37).
2. The Prodigal Son (Luke 15:1–2, 11–32).
3. The Two Debtors (Luke 7:36–39, 40–44).
4. The Rich Fool (Luke 12:13–21).
5. The Unjust Judge (Luke 18:1–8).

The story of the good Samaritan is one of the best known, and probably one of the most important, of all Jesus' teachings. Jesus was asked by one of the Jewish teachers what it was that a person had to do in order to gain eternal life. Jesus replied that what was necessary was to keep the Law as revealed by God. The rabbi gave the summary made familiar to devout Jews by one of their leading Pharisees, Rabbi Hillel. It stated that a person should love God with his whole heart, soul, mind and strength. The whole of his life, energy, reason and deepest feelings were to be devoted to living in kindness and forgiveness, peace-making and righting of wrongs. Therefore, equally important, a person should also love his neighbour as much as he loved himself.

Another New Testament passage later pointed out that, if a man says that he loves God but behaves badly or meanly to a fellow being, he must be a liar. For if he does not love his neighbour, whom he can see, how can he claim to love God, whom he cannot see (I John 4:20)?

4. Find Luke 10:25–37.
(a) What did the lawyer (scribe) ask Jesus?
(b) What summary of the Law did he give in verse 27?
(c) What was the question the scribe asked in verse 29?
(d) Write out the story of the Good Samaritan (verses 30–35) in your own words.
(e) Which of the three passers-by was really the good neighbour?
(f) What final words did Jesus say to the scribe?

It was most significant that the person the Jewish scribe had to agree was his neighbour was a hated Samaritan. The Jews recoiled

The Road to Jericho *This dangerous and barren road ran all the way from Jerusalem to Jericho near the Dead Sea. It was infamous for its bandits, and Jesus mentioned it in his story of the Good Samaritan. It was up this road that Jesus travelled to Jerusalem for the last week of his earthly life.*

with horror from having anything to do with Samaritans – as a modern person might recoil from a teenager in offensive or menacing dress, or from a dirty, smelly person. What Jesus was trying to teach was that a Christian should find love in his heart for every person. No matter what he was or what he had done, he was a brother – and a brother in need should never be turned away.

Nowadays people are called Good Samaritans if they help others. An organisation called simply the Samaritans exists to talk depressed people out of committing suicide. Everyone appreciates kindness and compassion, but we should be careful how we even think of others. Sometimes we are called upon to be helpful and merciful to people we, or society, do not like. Sometimes we are given help from people we would never expect would help us. When misfortune strikes, that is when we find out who our friends really are! No one who refused help to a person in need could be considered a real Christian.

5. Find James 1:27. What did St James say was pure religion?
6. Find James 2:14–17. What did St James say about the sort of person who was supposed to believe in God but did not help his neighbour?
7. Copy out James 2:26.
8. Find I John 4:20. What sort of man did St John say was a liar?
9. Find I John 3:17. Copy out this verse.

19

THE KINGDOM OF HEAVEN

Perhaps the main theme of the teaching of Jesus was that at last the Kingdom of Heaven had come within the reach of ordinary people. It was not something far distant and way beyond their understanding or hope of ever gaining it; it was within their grasp, waiting to be discovered. It meant the acceptance of the rule of God in men's hearts and lives.

The Jews believed that God was the creator of the world, and therefore the true ruler of every part of it. He was especially *their* king, for he had entered into a covenant relationship with them and had guided their history through the centuries. At certain times, the Jews had been ruled by earthly kings like David and Solomon, but nevertheless they regarded those kings as only ruling on behalf of God – they were His vice-regents. Prophets could, and did, rebuke them and warn them when they felt that they were not carrying out God's wishes properly.

Since the Jews as a nation had been defeated by foreign powers, they had developed a longing for a Day of the Lord, a day when God would send His Messiah to challenge their enemies and restore the rule of God on earth.

So, when Jesus spoke of the Kingdom of God, or the Kingdom of Heaven, he cannot have ignored this background of ideas that he had inherited by being born a Jew. However, it seems that when he taught, he was thinking of a kingdom in several different senses.

The Pharisees believed that the world was in the clutches of evil powers and spirits and that the work of God was to fend them off and destroy them. The more people that joined in the work of God, the quicker His kingdom would come 'on earth as it is in Heaven'. When a person began to realise that this life was not the sum total of everything, but that there was an eternal order of things and an aim for human endeavour, it changed the whole aspect of his existence. What had been ordinary and commonplace suddenly became charged with excitement and a sense of fulfilment. Purpose and dedication took over what had previously been aimless and random. Anxiety and fear about the problems of life and the fact of death lost their sting of agony. There was confidence and hope.

In the sense that people could suddenly discover this deeper awareness of the meaning of life, Jesus was teaching that the Kingdom of Heaven *had already come*. It was obviously not an earthly, political kingdom, but a brotherhood of people with a certain kind of insight – people who accepted the sovereignty of God in their hearts and spirits. People could find within themselves the quality of 'eternal life' after a moment of revelation, and this would colour and alter their whole view of life thereafter. It meant the realisation of personal happiness and fulfilment.

This is probably why Jesus thought of the Kingdom as a secret which only certain people would understand and know. Not everyone would have arrived at a state where they were concerned about the ultimate problems of life. But when they *began* to be concerned, and started to look seriously for answers, the chances were that they might stumble on them and discover, to their surprise, that the clues had been there all the time, waiting to be found.

And once the clues are picked up, the trail towards discovery becomes an all-consuming interest, like yeast gradually spreading and working its way through dough. What had seemed like hard work becomes a joy and a delight. Before one is really aware of it, the sense of ever-growing love and serenity floods through every part of one's activities, pervading every moment and experience of life. To find this, said Jesus, was worth more than anything else on earth.

It meant that a person had passed from ordinary life into eternal life long before the end of his own particular time-span here on earth.

One of the most damning features of much of our church worship today is that it bores rather than fascinates. All too often visitors turn away feeling that the Kingdom of God is not to be found there. What is experienced by individuals may not always be obvious – but enthusiasm is generally catching. Where the congregation *is* aware of God's presence with them, it usually shows in their sincerity and humility, their peace of mind, and their general attitude to life.

However, at the same time Jesus also taught the idea that the Kingdom of Heaven was an actual state of being that would come about in the future, and bring a just judgement on us for our lives and actions. What had been started among us would reach a final stage of fulfilment when we faced our own judgement. If we had done good things, even if they appeared to go past unnoticed, God had seen them and we would be credited accordingly. Likewise, if we thought we had 'got away' with doing bad or mean things unnoticed, God had seen, and we would have to pay the price.

Jesus chose not to speak about the Kingdom in plain, straightforward terms – he chose parables, and sometimes riddles. Not everyone could see what he was talking about. In a sense, the Kingdom he spoke of was secret; but when people *did* see, when 'the penny dropped', they understood exactly what Jesus meant.

Our task now is to analyse the parables, and see if *we* can see what Jesus meant.

Questions and Research

(A) The sowing of the Kingdom

1. Find Mark 4:1–20. The Sower.
In this parable, we have a description of a farmer sowing his seed with hope in his heart that he will eventually be able to reap a harvest, despite all the difficulties and dangers the seed will have to face before it ripens to bear fruit. Those of you who have ever tried your luck with a packet of seeds probably know already that so much depends on the weather – the right temperature, the right time for sowing, the right rainfall. Very often we plant seeds that never come up at all!

The farmer in Israel used to throw his seed out of a basket or container, a method called 'broadcast' sowing, and then plough the land up afterwards – so, very often, the seed did fall on a piece of land choked with weeds, or the bit that would be left as a pathway. Some seeds would soon be pecked up by birds, or shrivel away in the heat if there was no depth of soil for them to put roots down into. Anyone who has been to Israel will assure you that it is a very rocky, thorny and stony land.

In fact, it was almost a miracle that any seed managed to survive at all, and that was certainly how the primitive farmer saw it. The seed was a common symbol for the mystery of resurrection, or for life arising out of death. God guided the whole process from the 'dead' dry seed to the waving cornfield, through His mighty creative power.

To human eyes, a great deal of the farmer's labours seemed futile and fruitless, and time and time again there seemed to be failure and disappointment – yet, thanks to God's divine love and compassion, the harvest does not fail. There comes a time when the land is rich with waving corn.

In the parable of the sower, it is this confidence that, in spite of every failure, the Kingdom of God will come at last which is the climax of the story. God made a beginning with the seed, and there will be a harvest of great reward to come. Jesus even exaggerated the outcome to make his point – some grain will bear fruit even a hundredfold, highly unlikely in real life!

(a) What did sowing 'broadcast' mean?

(b) What was the seed a common symbol for?

(c) Write out the parable as given in verses 3–8.

(d) Make a note that the farmer is God, and that He is sowing His message into the hearts of different kinds of people.

(e) What happens to the seed that falls on the path?

(f) Why does the seed sown on rocky soil die so quickly?

(g) What happens to the seed sown among thorns?

(h) Despite all these setbacks, does any of the seed manage to bear fruit?

(i) Verses 10–13. Did the people understand what Jesus was talking about?

(j) Note that, in the explanation given, the people become the seed sown, and not the types of ground receiving the seed. As the explanation does not fit the parable exactly, some scholars think that it may not be original, but was perhaps added later by someone in the early Church. Make a list of the different things mentioned, and say what they are supposed to represent.

(k) Of the people listening to Jesus, have a guess at how many per cent would fall into each group!

(l) What does this parable teach about the Kingdom of Heaven?

2. Find Mark 4:26–29. The Seed Growing Secretly.

This parable also concerns the life-cycle of grain from seedtime to harvest. Once again, it is the confidence in God's guidance towards the coming of the Kingdom that is stressed. Out of nothing, in spite of apparent neglect, and not put off by failure, the growth towards harvest takes place. After he has ploughed, the farmer apparently does nothing; but his crop is growing steadily from shoot to ear, and then to ripening corn. Suddenly, the moment of harvest arrives and the Kingdom has come. The farmer then gathers in his successful crop.

Some scholars think that this parable is another version of the parable of the sower. If you leave out the allegorical interpretation of the sower, which may not have been original, it is certainly very close in meaning.

(a) Briefly write out the parable.

(b) What happens to the seed, once it is planted?

(c) In what sense was the growth of this seed hidden?

(d) How does Jesus describe the moment when the person suddenly realises the truth of what has gradually been dawning on him?

(e) Explain how this parable could be another version of the parable of the sower.

Another version was preserved in the teachings of St Clement at the turn of the first century. It read: 'The sower went forth and cast the seeds into the ground; they fall on the ground, parched and bare, and suffer decay; then from their decay the greatness of the providence of the Master raises them up, and from the grain more grow and bring forth fruit.'

3. Find Matthew 13:24–30, 36–43.
This parable is only to be found in St Matthew's Gospel. As in the other seed parables, the seed is sown and the harvest awaited, but this time a sorting-out is required before it can be gathered in. Like the parable of the sower, it is presented as an allegory – but again, many scholars think that this allegorical interpretation was put forward by the early Church and not by Jesus himself, although there are not definite proofs that this is so. The allegorical interpretation raises the question of the origin of evil and the reasons why God does not immediately remove it.
(a) Briefly write out the parable.
(b) If God was the farmer, responsible for the 'good seed' in the world, what was suggested about the origin of the 'bad seed'?
(c) Could the farmer tell the difference between the wheat and the weeds?
(d) Why didn't the farmer want to have the weeds pulled up too soon?
(e) What does this tell us about God allowing evil to exist in the world?

People often wonder why God lets the suffering and evil go on. One possible reason is that some people love the bad ones very much, and would like to see them given every chance to mend their ways. God gives them this chance, although He knows the harm they might do. Bad people are often frightened, or unhappy – things seem to happen to them. They seem to be worse than they really are. Others are so lucky to have love and security – they should try hard to be like God, extra loving and ready to help those who are struggling without much success.

(B) The Kingdom grows out of all expected proportion

The power of the Kingdom spreads out and transforms. It passes rapidly from person to person, altering lives as it goes. It grows rapidly, too. 'As small as a grain of mustard-seed' was a Jewish

102

proverb. Mustard seed is as tiny as dust, yet in a very short time the mustard shrub grows up into a large bush, from six to ten feet tall, big enough to shelter birds among its branches. Who would have expected such a tiny little seed to produce a plant big enough to give haven and shelter? The Kingdom takes over one's whole life, and changes and shapes it. One moment life is ordinary, humdrum, rather pointless. Then, suddenly, something brings home to the individual the realisation that God is real, that there is life after death, that our actions and thoughts *do* matter – and life is never the same again.

Who would have thought that a small piece of yeast or leaven would rise through and alter the shape of a whole mass of dough? Again, Jesus was exaggerating for effect – the three measures of meal mentioned in Matthew 13:33 would have been enough to have provided for over 150 people, an enormous quantity.

Like this, the influence of Christ spreads out through those who know him, like ripples on water, to others of distant lands and times. So it goes on throughout history and space.

4. Find Matthew 13:31–32.
(a) Write out the parable of the mustard seed.
(b) Why was this particular plant chosen by Jesus for his parable?
(c) What was the result of the mustard seed growing into a shrub?
(d) How would one describe the growth of this plant?

5. Find Matthew 13:33.
(a) Write out the parable of the yeast.
(b) What happens when you put yeast, or leaven, into dough?
(c) How is this like the Kingdom entering and affecting human lives?

(C) The Kingdom is of enormous value

Finding the Kingdom is like a merchant suddenly discovering a rare pearl, the most extraordinary and valuable he has ever seen. He sells all his possessions so that he can buy it – for it is worth much more than anything on earth to him. Or it is like a ploughman stumbling across a hoard of buried treasure. He realises its value, covers it up, rushes off and sells everything in order to raise enough money to buy the field from his employer and make the treasure his. He's a dishonest fellow, but no fool. Discoverers of the Kingdom give up everything they own to possess it – but they do not lose by it. It is worth so much more. It is more valuable than riches or power – it is worth more than life itself.

6. Find Matthew 13:45–46.
(a) Write out the parable of the pearl.
(b) What did the merchant give up in order to have the pearl?
(c) Was he gaining or losing by this deal?

7. Find Matthew 13:44.
(a) Write out the parable of the hidden treasure.
(b) Was the ploughman being honest or dishonest?
(c) Was he gaining or losing by his action?
(d) What is the point of both these parables?

(D) The Kingdom demands our growth and progress

We have already seen that although, in some people, the Kingdom spreads and pervades their lives, and they become a refuge and an influence for good on others, this is not always the case. Some of the seeds planted fell by the wayside, or got choked by thorns! In the parables of the talents and the pounds, Jesus taught that if we do not make progress and grow towards goodness, then what we have found will be taken away. We will have lost our chance. The Victorian preachers used to terrify their congregation with threats of hellfire and damnation, and modern society has swung away to the other extreme – one of toleration of almost anything. Anything goes!

To study the words of Jesus is to bring us up sharp. God is not prepared to reward selfishness and laziness, and sloppy standards of living. He loves and He forgives, but He does not just wave a magic wand to take away all the inevitable results of our uncaring lives. It is vitally important that we do care and we do try.

We cannot be forced to use our talents, but we can certainly be blamed if we don't use them. God expects back more than He gives out. Nothing can stand still, in life or in nature, or in our talents or experiences. If we are top of the class at the age of 12, and decide that we need learn no more, we will be bottom of the class by the time we reach 14. Nothing can stay the same. The person who has a talent and does not develop it and use it, will lose it. There must be progress, or there will be regression. There can never be a standstill.

8. Find Matthew 25:14–30.
(a) What did the master give to each of his servants?
(b) What did the first two servants do with their money?
(c) What did the third servant do?
(d) When the servants gave back their talents, had the third servant cheated the master out of anything he owed him?

(e) What did he say about his master in verse 24?
(f) If the master is supposed to be God, what does this tell us about His expectations for us?
(g) What happened to the talent of the third servant?
(h) Copy out verse 29.

9. Find Luke 19:11–28.
(a) How many servants were there this time?
(b) How much did they each receive?
(c) Only three servants have the return of their money reported. How much did each of these three return?
(d) What is the point of both of these parables?

(E) The Kingdom demands our acceptance of its gifts

These parables take up the point made in the previous parables. It is thought that they were aimed specifically at the Jewish race, who had had the chance of being God's special people, but instead of accepting the Messiah, they had not recognised him and had rejected him. The banquet was a well-known symbol for the coming of the Messianic Kingdom. God's new Chosen Race would be those who did believe in Jesus as the Messiah, whether or not they were Jews. In the first parable, the people who had been invited to the banquet at first made excuses and did not go. In the second, a guest insulted his host by not being properly prepared. Was this guest an uninvited gatecrasher, or deliberately insulting his host? The real point was probably that the man without the garment was a fool – the summons to the feast had caught him unprepared.

The rabbis, who had a similar parable, taught that the garment was repentance – being sorry for one's shortcomings and trying to put them right. They said that a man should be repentant and prepared every day of his life, since he knew not when his end would come. Likewise Jesus stressed that a Christian should always be prepared for the coming of God's Kingdom, and not be caught out. The rabbis' parable was that a man had given out invitations to a party, but had not specified the time of the feast. The sensible people got ready in clean garments anyway, while the foolish just carried on working. Like good Boy Scouts, the sensible were prepared and not caught napping.

10. Find Matthew 22:1–10.
(a) Write out the parable of the marriage feast.
(b) What happened to the people who had been invited to the feast?
(c) Who finally went to the feast?

11. Find Matthew 22:11–14.

(a) Which guest was thrown out of the feast?

(b) Why was the giver of the feast so offended?

(c) What type of person do you think is represented by the man who had not bothered to put on his special garment?

12. Find Luke 14:16–24.

(a) What excuses were offered by the unwilling guests in this version?

(b) See if you can spot what details about this version are different from that in Matthew 22:1–10.

13. Find Luke 16:1–13.

(a) Write out the parable of the unjust steward.

(b) Was the steward honest or dishonest?

(c) Why did Jesus commend his action?

(d) Verse 9 probably means (i) use your worldly wealth in order to do good, and so make friends who will stand by you when it fails; (ii) make friends that are not simply influenced by your money or influence, for these are the sort that will stand by you when you have nothing; or (iii) use your wealth in order to do good, and you will receive your true reward in heaven. Write out these three possibilities.

(F) The Kingdom will come suddenly – we must be ready and awake

The following parables all contain a warning. We must not waste any of our opportunities or we may be caught out. We must live every moment as if it were out last, or as if it were a test. Treat every person as if he were Christ in disguise, for we do not know when our time of judgement will come. There may not be a later opportunity to put things right, or do the things we have put off until later.

14. Find Luke 12:35–38. Write out the parable of the master returning.

15. Find Luke 12:39–40. Write out the parable of the thief in the night.

16. If we knew that the thief was about to break in, or the master about to return and catch us lazing about, we would do something about it. How should we live every day of our lives?

17. Find Matthew 25:1–13.

(a) Why were five of the bridesmaids rather foolish?

(b) What happened while they were away finding oil?

(c) What happened to these bridesmaids?
(d) Copy out verse 13.

(G) The coming of the Kingdom brings our judgement

These parables all tell us that there will be a time or judgement.
We will all be drawn up, like fish in a net that gathers up all sorts.
Good fish are kept, but bad fish are thrown away as being useless.
The parable of the wheat and the tares shows how God leaves the
longest possible opportunity for the evil to sort itself out, but there
will one day be the harvest, and the judgement. The ten bridesmaids show us how, if we are not ready when this judgement
comes, it will be too bad! We will have had our chance. It is up to
us to be prepared.
   The parable of the sheep and the goats tells us on what our entry
into the Kingdom of Heaven is based. How will we know whether
we are sheep or goats? Thankfully, it will not be based on how
intelligent we are, or even on what we believe – for we are not all
of one mind about belief in God. It will be based on what we have
done – the record of our lives. No amount of excuses will help us.
Our actions will show us for what we are.

18. Find Matthew 13:47–50.
(a) Write out the parable of the dragnet.
(b) Will the good and the bad 'fish' all get the same fate?

19. Find Matthew 25:31–46.
(a) How would the farmer know which of his flock were 'sheep'?
(b) Did the 'sheep' know that they had done all those things to
    Jesus?
(c) Copy out verse 40.
(d) Why did all the goats protest?
(e) What did Jesus say to them in verse 45?

20. Find Matthew 7:21–29. We are judged on the quality of our
    lives. The foundation we need to build on is to hear the words
    of Jesus *and do them.* Pious belief is not sufficient, if our actions
    do not back up our words. Doubtless many people go to church
    who are *not* really Christians, just as many people do not go to
    church who are just the kind of people God wants and will
    welcome. Copy out verses 21–23.

(H) God is generous to late-comers

Just as in the parable of the prodigal son the behaviour of the good
brother disappointed his father, so many Christians disappoint God

by being ungenerous to late converts to the way. We seem to have a natural suspicion of outsiders, an unwillingness to welcome them – especially when they are people whose past is known, and not noted for its saintliness! In the parable of the labourers in the vineyard, the farmer pays the same wages to people he hires very late in the day as to those who have worked hard all day (like that elder brother). Those who came first see this as being unfair.

This is where *you* are put to the test, to see if you have understood what the Kingdom is all about.

As Jesus said, it is not the fairness of God that is under question, but His generous love. Think about it. Try to imagine yourself as the parent of two children, one of whom never fails you, and one who goes wrong. When the wrong one comes back, you don't stop loving the loyal one, do you? Of course not. But how pleased and relieved you are to see the lost one come back. When you are a farmer hiring unemployed men in a time of depression, those who are given work and pay for the day are the lucky ones. If the farmer goes out again late in the day, to see if he can help anyone else out by bringing them wages, is it right or wrong for the first labourers to complain that he is being unfair?

21. Find Matthew 20:1–10.
(a) Write out the parable of the labourers in the vineyard.
(b) Why did the farmer give those whom he hired last the same wage as those who came first?
(c) Was he being unfair, or exceedingly generous?

Lists showing two ways of looking at the Kingdom

It is here now	*It will come in the future*
The sower	The dragnet
The seed growing secretly	The wheat and the tares
The mustard seed	The ten bridesmaids
The leaven	The marriage feast
The pearl	The wedding garment
The treasure	The talents and the pounds
The talents	The sheep and the goats
The pounds	The master returning
The labourers in the vineyard	The thief in the night
The firm foundation	The dishonest steward

Finally, find Luke 17:20–21, and Luke 9:27. What did Jesus say in these passages about the Kingdom of Heaven?

20
THE SERMON ON THE MOUNT

Chapters 5–7 in St Matthew's Gospel are traditionally known as the Sermon on the Mount. It is a collection of teachings gathered together by the author of the gospel, and was probably not actually all said as one sermon on one occasion. Bits and pieces of it occur in various *different* places in St Luke's Gospel; and it seems more likely that Matthew deliberately gathered it all together in the same way as he deliberately collected parables together in chapters 13 and 25, than that Luke split it all up.

Both Matthew and Luke place the sermon after the occasion when Jesus called his twelve special disciples, but Luke places some of the teachings in what he saw as the correct place in his narrative. For example, Matthew 6:6–15 comes in Luke 1:1–4, after Jesus at prayer; Matthew 6:25–33 comes in Luke 12:22–31, after the parable of the rich fool; and Matthew 7:7–11 comes in Luke 11:9–13, after the story of the friend at midnight. Luke probably did this deliberately as he had information about the original settings of these teachings of Jesus. One of his main concerns was to give the life of Jesus 'in order', which many scholars think means 'in the correct chronological order'.

In the sermon, Jesus set out the characteristics of the real inhabitants of the Kingdom of Heaven – what a person must be like, or do, in order to gain entry. In later work, we will consider the main Christian qualities of love, forgiveness, humility and courage, faithfulness and truth. Here, in Matthew 5:1–16, we will consider in depth a section of Jesus' teaching known as the **beatitudes**.

The word *beatus* means blessed or happy; and Jesus was pointing out that the key feature of the citizen of the Kingdom of Heaven was his happiness, his sense of fulfilment and rightness. The beatitudes are a series of two-lined verses in which Jesus outlined the necessary qualities for a person to develop if they were ever to find true happiness. You will probably find some of the things listed rather surprising, as they are not at all what one might expect to be the ingredients of a happy person – until one really starts to consider what the phrases mean. For example, Jesus thought that people who were mourning were happy, and also those who were being cruelly treated because of their beliefs.

Questions and Research

1. What is the difference between the ways that St Matthew and St Luke give the teachings in the Sermon on the Mount?
2. What does the word *beatus* mean?
3. Find Matthew 5:1. Why is this sermon known as the Sermon on the Mount? Now find Luke 6:17. Why is his version known as the Sermon on the Plain?
4. You need one finger in Matthew 5:1–16, and one in Luke 6:17–24.
(a) How many beatitudes are there in Luke?
(b) How many are there in Matthew?
(c) How many 'woes' are there in Luke?
(d) How many are there in Matthew?
(e) Which beatitudes are on the same subject in both versions?
(f) Which ones does Luke leave out?
(g) What is the difference between Matthew 5:3 and Luke 6:20, and Matthew 5:6 and Luke 6:21?
(h) Is there any difference in the type of beatitudes that occur in these gospels?

5. From the verses in Matthew, write out a list of the types of people that Jesus said would be blessed, or happy.

Those who find happiness

The first sort of person that Jesus thought would find happiness was the **person who was poor in spirit**. In St Luke's version, it simply says the person who was 'poor'. It should be obvious to everyone that there is all the difference in the world between being poor, and being poor in spirit. Sadly, we can never know for certain which version represents the actual words of Jesus. Luke seems to be dealing with physical characteristics, whereas Matthew seems to have a more spiritual level. But what is spiritual about being poor-spirited? That really doesn't sound a very attractive quality – and, indeed, modern translations of the Bible wrestle with the problems of finding the words that mean the right thing. The New English Bible has the words 'blessed are those who know that they are poor'.

It is difficult to know exactly what Jesus meant, but he most likely had in mind the sort of person whose spirit was not cluttered up with greed, ambition, pride, hate and self-seeking. One of the

110

sayings of Jesus not in the Bible but known from other sources states that, 'Life is a bridge – pass over it, but build no house upon it.' It suggests an attitude rather like the Buddhist principle of detachment. Nothing should be so valuable to a person that it could not be given up. To cling to one's possessions and ambitions does not always bring happiness; quite the contrary – it can court disaster. A good phrase to remember is that 'a man's true possessions are those that would survive shipwreck'. All those old platitudes about the best things in life being free and you can't take it with you really do mean something. People obsessed with getting and gaining always want more; they never reach satisfaction. They are always worried and fretting. Too much attachment to things can be a trap, and so can too much attachment to people sometimes. Those who work in hospitals know how quickly and easily a life can be snuffed out, hopes shattered, plans dashed. If we are grateful that we have two legs, aware that we may not have them tomorrow, and able to cope mentally with the consequences of that – then we will have found happiness beyond the comprehension of those whose lives are dedicated to ambitions and possessions. Being poor 'in spirit' no doubt means a great deal more than just a willingness to give up earthly goods if need be – it means giving up self-seeking and greed as well. St Peter stated in Mark 10:28 that he had left everything to follow Jesus. Jesus replied that those prepared to let go would find rewards a hundredfold.

The second category or person who would find happiness was the **person who was mourning**. Mourning means grieving over the loss of a loved one. These people were capable of knowing true happiness, because they were also capable of deep feeling and compassion. Because they had known hurt, they could share sympathy in a way that people who have never suffered cannot. Some people are afraid of being hurt – they draw back and become hard, and build a shell around themselves. If they become so hard that they are incapable of sharing sorrow, then they will never know real joy. Without trust in another there is no real love. The person who cannot entrust himself to another but remains enclosed within himself is like the man who built a very high wall around his garden to keep out all intruders. Sadly, his beautiful flowers and trees withered and died, through lack of light. To restore their loveliness, he had to break down the barrier he had created. People's feelings are like that, and how cruel we can be when we thoughtlessly trample over the deeply felt emotions of others. However, it is probably true that one never really appreciates the beauties and benefits that life offers until one has had to experience losing them and living without them. How sad it is that one only really realises fully what life means when one is faced with the sad fact of death.

Jesus may also have meant here the type of person who is conscious of the shortcomings and sorrows of the world, and longs in his soul to put them right. That sort of person, the one not encased in his own hardness, will know true happiness.

Thirdly, Jesus placed the **person who is meek**. What a wretched word that is – it now means almost the opposite of its original meaning. To most of us nowadays someone who is meek is timid, even cowardly. Really it means someone who is self-controlled, who has the strength not to hit back, to lash out or to take revenge. It is so automatic for us to hit back, with our minds if not with our fists, and to dislike those who dislike us. But, says Jesus, a Christian is to turn the other cheek and not hit back. The way it was put in the Old Testament (for the idea was not new), was that God stated categorically, 'Vengeance is Mine'. In other words, we are to leave the dealing with our enemies to Him. We need not worry ourselves about the wicked getting away with it – people reap what they sow. Those who are malicious and spiteful and jealous and burnt up with hate usually land themselves in a terrible mess. There is no need for *us* to want revenge or think spitefully – people who deliberately act badly usually pay the price for it sooner or later. We should rather try to understand what it was that made them this way, and be sorry for them. We should try to see men as God sees them, like that father grieving for his lost son.

The next category was those who **hunger and thirst for righteousness**. St Luke's version again adopts a different interpretation, and merely commends those who are actually hungry. He may have been influenced by a group of early Christians who thought that poverty in itself was a good and holy thing, and who despised the rich. Hungering for righteousness is completely different.

The concept of righteousness implies a longing to see justice and mercy prevail, both in our own lives and in society in general. A truly righteous society begins with individuals caring about their own standards and actions, and not just leaving the responsibility to others. Before anyone can alter the state of the world they live in for the better, they must first see to it that they themselves are as far beyond reproach as possible, otherwise they will simply be accused of being hypocrites. A person who is consciously doing his best is not a burden on others, but the strength of the community rests in him and those like him.

Next come **the merciful**. These are people who are actually in a position to hurt others, but who do not take advantage of their opportunity to do so. It is all too easy to hurt people with our quick and thoughtless words, as well as our unkind actions – but the Christian should try to control his desire for revenge, and stop the chain of repercussions that inevitably gets set in motion when people do wrong things. If you have been victimised, or attacked, or cheated, instead or rounding on the enemy you should try to understand what it was that made him act in that way, and put it right, if possible. As St Paul said, don't repay evil for evil, but try to overcome evil with good. At best, it will stop your enemies from being your enemies, and turn them into friends; at worst, if they will not change towards you, at least you will have done your best not to sink to the same level.

The sixth group of happy people are **the pure in heart** – those without mixed loyalties or motives. One cannot really compromise as far as God is concerned. The nearer one tries to get to the Kingdom of Heaven, the more important it is to have the right motives and actions even over the very little things, and not give way to the temptation to take it easy, or ignore just that little instance. No doubt we ordinary folk can afford a little satisfaction if we just manage to keep the Ten Commandments; but the nearer one gets to God, the more one realises that it is not enough not to hit back at enemies – one must not *think* back either. The secrets in our heart of hearts must be as pure as possible, or God will see through us.

The final two categories of happy people are involved with those who fling themselves into the world of conflict and try to deal with it. **The peacemakers** are those who are not only at peace in themselves because their consciences are clear, but they actually manage to radiate peace to others. They have the type of character to which people in trouble will turn for refuge and strength. One cannot but admire great Christians like the missionary to China, Gladys Aylward, who once had to walk inside the locked gates of a prison full of rioting murderers and maniacs. She walked straight in, took the axe from one desperate prisoner, and sat down quietly. Miraculously, the riot stopped and she was unharmed. Her sense of peace, and her courage, calmed the men, and they too sat down around her.

Persecution is just about inevitable, so those who were putting up with it were also blessed people. All those who attempt to put right injustice and selfishness are bound to run into opposition, sometimes even physical torment. Yet who suffers most – the person who dies for his faith because he will not be untrue to what he firmly believes is right and good; or the person who bows to his enemy and gives in? That person will never be happy. **The persecuted** martyr may suffer, but in himself, he will know peace of mind.

This Christian standard set by Jesus has often been criticised as being too high, too demanding, too difficult for the average person to keep. Jesus knew this perfectly well, but he thought the Christian *should* be conspicuous, *should* be a contrast to the non-Christian. He should be like salt, which was of no use if it didn't flavour or preserve; or like light, which was of no use if it was covered up. Hollow religion was meaningless – lukewarm Christians-in-name-only were of no use. A religion that simply expects its members to wear a badge or a uniform, and perhaps give up certain things and observe a few ceremonies, was not really what Jesus had in mind. His rules were hard, for they meant real effort to change the character of a person.

One might well think it was impossible – but folk who *have* been changed know that, with God's help, it *is* possible.

Questions

1. What translation does the New English Bible have for 'poor in spirit'?
2. What is meant by detachment?
3. Why are people obsessed by material things never truly happy?
4. How is it that people capable of grief can be called happy?
5. What does the word 'meek' mean?
6. Why is it so difficult for us to be meek?
7. What did Jesus say we should do when someone hit us?
8. What does righteousness mean?
9. What are merciful people?
10. What did St Paul say about taking revenge?
11. What is meant by the 'pure in heart'?
12. Why are peacemakers so important?
13. Why is persecution inevitable when you are trying to do the right thing?
14. In what way has this standard set by Jesus been criticised?

Research

1. Find Matthew 5:1–12.
(a) Write out the rewards of the happy people – the second halves of the beatitudes. This list represents what membership of the Kingdom of Heaven is all about. It shows the results of joining it.
(b) Sum up by bracketing off the list of rewards for being citizens of the Kingdom, and stating that they add up to: **consolation, freedom, fearlessness** and **satisfaction**

2. Find Matthew 5:13–16.
(a) How did Jesus compare Christians to salt, and light?
(b) What use is tasteless salt and a light covered up?

114

(c) Copy out verse 16.

3. Find Matthew 6:25–34.
(a) What did Jesus say about worrying over silly things like clothing and what you looked like?
(b) What do you think Jesus had in mind when he said that we should 'take no thought for the morrow'?
(c) Copy out verse 34.

4. What does it say in Matthew 6:19–21 about real treasure?
5. Mammon means worldly wealth and ambition. In verse 24 Jesus said that we could not serve both God and ambition at the same time. Why not?
6. What is said in Matthew 7:1–5 about judging others?
7. What does it say in Matthew 7:7–12 about our efforts to find God and our ultimate happiness? Copy out verse 12. This is often called the Golden Law.
8. Find Matthew 7:15–23.
(a) What did Jesus call the people who *looked* good but were really hypocrites?
(b) How would you know a truly good person?
(c) What would Jesus say to those who claimed to believe in him, but who had not really carried out his wishes?
(d) Copy out verse 21.

9. Write out the parable of the houses build on the different foundations. What was the true, solid foundation that Jesus referred to in verse 24?

Creative Writing

How far do you think it is true to state that a person cannot be a Christian unless he goes to church? What sort of qualities do you think one should find in every Christian?

21
THE LAW AND THE TRADITION

As far as the Jews were concerned, the chief way in which God had revealed Himself and His will to mankind was by the Law, the Torah. This Law consisted of the first five books of the Old Testament, known in Greek as the Pentateuch (from *penta* meaning 'five', and *teuchos* meaning 'book'). As this Law had been given to Moses under the direct inspiration of God, it was sacred, never to be broken. The contents of the books were actually quite varied, containing historical stories and legends; codes and taboos about marriage, food, clothing and property; religious and civil laws; priestly rituals; and rules about observing sabbaths and sacrifices. To get the flavour of it, have a look at Leviticus (see especially Chapters 14, 15, 19).

The Torah, or Pentateuch, was considered to be the complete revelation of God's will. The answers to all man's questions were to be found in it. It gave full guidance as to how man was to conduct his life and worship. Prophets and holy men came and went, and often gave fresh insights into the books of God, but none would ever dream of questioning its sacredness. The wishes and commands of God were written there for man to read and understand.

As a devout Jew, Jesus knew and loved the Law. He stated (Matthew 5:17–18) that not the tiniest part of it was to be ignored or broken. Whoever relaxed the least of the commandments and taught others that it was all right to do so, would be called least in the Kingdom of Heaven. Jesus claimed that he had certainly not come to oppose God's will! He accepted that the Torah was the will of God, and stated that he certainly had no intention of going against it. He had not come to abolish the Law and the prophets, but to fulfil them (Matthew 5:17). In his love for the Law, he shared the opinion of both Sadducees and Pharisees.

However, there was something about the attitude of both to the Law which disturbed Jesus, and because Jesus challenged both parties to reform the way they thought about the Law, he inevitably offended some and disagreed openly with others – although one

Reading the Scrolls *Modern Jews still treat their hand-written scrolls with enormous respect. The men cover their heads and wear prayer-shawls. The boy has become a 'Son of the Law', and is reading aloud from the Law, using a special pointer so that he does not miss a single word. Jesus would have done this at the age of twelve.*

must remember that there were also many devout people who would have agreed with him wholeheartedly. (No doubt the Pharisaic school of the Rabbi Hillel would have done – see below, p. 95.)

Many Sadducees were no longer as devout as they should have been. The chief priests were sometimes even hated and despised by their people – they had become too sympathetic to the Romans, and too fond of their enormous wealth. They refused to agree with the Pharisees, who were trying to interpret the Law in fresh ways, so that ordinary folk would better understand it and be able to keep it. Jesus would certainly have favoured what the Pharisees were trying to do. Pharisees believed in keeping the Law in every detailed particular, but they had begun to worry about whether man's ability to interpret the Law was fully adequate. Had they left anything out? Were they in any way falling short? It was as if they were seriously afraid that God, their loving Father, would punish them in some way if a trifling regulation was carelessly overlooked. They argued that it was not for Man to decide which of God's Laws were important or trifling – only God knew that. All were to be kept equally. So, to make certain that absolutely nothing would be overlooked because they had not done enough, they worked out a series of extra commandments which they regarded as a hedge or barrier, to prevent them from doing wrong.

The changing circumstances of life meant that new suggestions were constantly being made out of their eagerness not to offend God in any way. It was all rather like a twentieth-century person trying to sort out the laws of a medieval society. What would we do with a law that stated that we were not allowed to sharpen our pikes on a Sunday? Or polish our armour? What would be the equivalent in modern terms? Bayonets? Could it include tools and gardening equipment? For armour, should we read metal, and therefore forbid ourselves polishing our cars? This sort of argument was precisely what the rabbis practised on the old Law.

In fact, rabbinical scholarship was one of painstaking 'exegesis', that is to say, a careful accumulation of all possible interpretations of the scriptures. No attempt was made to decide once for all which was the true one, the object was just to preserve as many as possible. The pupil would ask his teacher for his opinion, and remember it along with the rabbi's name – in his very words, if possible. A good pupil tried to memorise the views of *all* the authorities.

It was a fact that the laws tended to be 'Thou shalt not' rather than 'Thou shalt', and tended to be concerned with controlling a person's outward conduct rather than his heart and his motives. God was seen rather as a Judge, awarding prizes and merits to those who could manage to keep all the laws, and punishments to those who did not. Therefore it became a matter of great concern not to leave out any of the little laws (if a person was *really* pious) in case they might offend God. When God said He wanted a tenth of their crops given to His service, they took this quite literally and even offered up a tenth of the herbs growing in their yards – mint, anise and cummin.

However, there were by the time of Jesus three main ways of approaching the Law. One was to keep it exactly as it was stated, with no changes or allowances at all. This was the way favoured by the priests and Sadducees. They considered that the Tradition of the Elders was simply the opinions of men and had nothing to do with God's wishes, and therefore they did not think that they were obliged to study it or keep it.

The second way was the one we have been looking at, the way developed by the rabbis and handed down from teacher to pupil. The explanations of the laws that they taught were called **Midrashim**. The main difficulty with them was that not everyone would see eye to eye over the meaning of any given passage of scripture, so arguments would arise and people would not know which version was supposed to be binding. However, the Pharisees were trying to make sense of sometimes very difficult and obscure passages, and regarded these interpretations as their duty in helping mankind to do the right thing.

These traditions were eventually fixed in writing. The oldest known collection is the **Mishnah**, a re-edition of earlier collections undertaken in the second century. A parallel collection was called the **Tosephta**. The **Talmud** is a continuation of and commentary on the Mishnah, and still exists in two versions – a fourth-century Jewish one, and a fifth-century Babylonian one. By the third century there were said to be 613 regulations, 365 of them negative, and 248 of them positive. Presumably there were not quite so many in the time of Jesus, but there were certainly enough of them for Jesus to see them as being a burden to the people.

Living according to the principles of compassion was the third way of dealing with the Law. This was the way favoured by Jesus, as it had also been by the prophets of the Old Testament. Jeremiah 31:31–34 speaks of the Covenant of the Heart. The point was that if men earnestly desired to please God and to live a good life, they would have God's laws in their hearts, and not in any book or on a tablet of stone. In any situation it would become unnecessary to look up and follow the exact letter of the Law – it would mean simply having God's principles in one's heart and living to the best of one's ability.

Jesus knew that, in their zeal to please God, the Pharisees had created a way of life that might suit them, but had become a burden instead of a blessing for ordinary people. This burden had never been intended by God, who wished His people to love and serve Him gladly.

The tradition of the Pharisees had grown very complicated. One example concerned the sabbath laws. The written Law said: 'Keep the sabbath day holy.' On that day there was to be a rest from labour for man and beast, housewife and slave. It was to be a day of gladness, joy and thanksgiving. The Pharisees went on to define very carefully what the limits of work were. Work included such things as reaping, threshing, ploughing, bearing heavy burdens and so on. What was a burden? Anything more than the weight of one dried fig – therefore no objects of more than this weight could be carried on the sabbath. Chairs could not be dragged across a sandy floor, as that was ploughing. A few ears of corn could not be plucked or rubbed, as this was reaping and threshing. They could even debate seriously whether or not one should 'carry' a false tooth on the sabbath, or eat an egg laid on the sabbath. Journeys of more than 1,000 cubits were not allowed (a cubit was between 23 and 28 centimetres) and no cooking was allowed on the sabbath.

It was obvious in many cases that the Pharisees' zeal for the Law had led them too far. The Tradition laid tremendous restrictions on the people, and heavy burdens of guilt on the common folk who found its strictures impossible to keep, although they adhered firmly to the Law of Moses. Jesus himself argued against the weight limit – if an animal fell down a well on the sabbath, they would certainly haul it out and become guilty of a 'sin'. Yet surely God would consider this the right thing to do, rather than let the animal drown and pollute the community's water supply?

The rabbis by no means agreed with each other in any case. At the time of Jesus, the most influential leaders of opinion were Shammai (the Severe) and Hillel (the Gentle). Hillel's leading pupil was Gamaliel, the teacher of St Paul, and one of St Paul's leading statements was that he found the burden of sin caused by people not being able to keep the laws completely unreasonable.

One example of their differences was over divorce. The Mosaic Law stated that to divorce his wife a man had to have a written and legal document, and it was quite all right for him to cast her aside if he had reasonable grounds. The rabbis went carefully into the question of what were reasonable grounds for divorce. In this instance, Hillel thought the ancient law was fair enough, but Shammai taught that the only grounds for divorce should be the wife's unchastity. He thought that the old law was very one-sided and unkind to the woman, since the woman would have no rights of appeal and would simply be thrown out to fend for herself. This would mean that unless she could find some other man to support her, she would become an outcast who must either starve or become a beggar or prostitute. It was a serious matter. Jesus went even further than Shammai in his attempts to protect women, and said that there should be no grounds for divorce at all. St Matthew's Gospel adds one clause – 'except for premarital unchastity'. The reason for this exception was presumably because, in God's eyes, a woman's committing of herself in the act of love *was* a marriage, and that if she married someone else after giving herself to a man, that so-called marriage was really adultery, and not valid. People in the twentieth century have found this teaching difficult to accept now that women can fend for themselves quite adequately. Possibly Jesus would give a different ruling if he were to return now. His principles seem to have been those of kindness and humanity, not of creating prisons for unhappy women.

Jesus had not come to throw over the Old Law, even though they sometimes thought this of him. Far from it. He had come to supersede it, to take it further, to its logical conclusions. The Law, which had been given for the guidance of ignorant and primitive men, was being fulfilled in the Christian life. Those hearing Jesus teach would either see his words as marvellous prophetic inspiration, or dreadful arrogant blasphemy. They would see Jesus as either a great new rabbi and prophet, or a rogue deserving to be put to death.

Questions and Research

1. What were the first five books of the Old Testament called?
2. What was this whole section called?
3. Find Leviticus 19 and pick any five laws as examples. Try and choose five different sorts of things.
4. What did the Pharisees consider needed to be done to the Law?
5. What did a rabbi's pupil try to do?
6. In what sense did God become a kind of judge?
7. What way of keeping the Law did the Sadducees favour?
8. What were the Midrashim?
9. How many regulations were there said to be by the third century?
10. Give three examples of the sabbath traditions.
11. Did Jesus agree or disagree with these?
12. Who were the two leading rabbis?
13. Which of these was the kindest?
14. What was the third way of keeping the Laws?
15. Find Jeremiah 31:31–34, and copy out that passage.
16. Would Jesus agree or disagree with this?
17. Find Matthew 5:17–20. What did Jesus say here about the Law and a person's righteousness?
18. Find Matthew 5. Here is a list of five examples from the Old Law that Jesus examined in his teachings:
    (a) Murder (5:21–22)
    (b) Adultery (5:27–28)
    (c) Oaths (5:33–37)
    (d) Revenge (5:38–39)
    (e) Love (5:43–44)
    In each case, explain what Jesus said the Old Law was, and in what way *his* law went further and took the meaning of the Law to its logical conclusion. Notice how these examples fully justify Christ's statement that he had not come to destroy but to fulfil the Law of God.
19. Find Matthew 7:28–29. What was the reaction of the crowds to all this?
20. How did Jesus' teaching differ from that of other rabbis (Matthew 7:28–29 again)?

Creative Writing

Every society has to have laws, otherwise selfish and violent people can act in a way that damages and frightens others. God's laws are of the sort that govern our innermost thoughts – they are intended to make us kind and generous and forgiving. Imagine two situations: (a) the laws governing the organisation of a church service, and (b) the laws governing a club for difficult and deprived children. Which of these two kinds of Christian and caring work do you think the more important, and why?

22
PRAYER, CHARITY AND SELF-DISCIPLINE

Prayer, for many people, consists of asking God for things wanted, or for help in difficulties, or reciting various poems and praises to Him. All too often there is no real feeling that the prayers mean anything at all. Is there really anyone listening? Very often no attempt is made to see if there is an answer – and if answers come along, they are seldom recognised as such. Very few of us actually hear voices from heaven, but many people seem to think there ought to be, just in answer to their requests. What a noise there would be if God obliged.

True prayer is really bringing oneself into a state of communion with God. It is a two-way channel. It brings a Christian the feeling that God is not just an abstract power or dymano, but has a personality that cares about each individual. It brings the awareness that out of life's loneliness or moments of despair, Someone is listening and directing the overall pattern of events. It brings the confidence that although things may seem bleak and hopeless, if one tries to do the right thing, the kind thing and the honest thing, and goes forward trusting in God, then everything will work itself out according to His plan, and all will be well.

One fault in us is that our prayers are so often just asking for things, and that when we ask for something, we always want the answer to be 'yes'. The answer could equally well be 'no', or even 'not yet'. How often, when we get *those* replies, do we try to fool ourselves that there has been no answer at all.

In the Sermon on the Mount, the question of one's *motives* for praying is carefully examined. Motives are of vital importance. If the Christian is genuinely trying to belong to the Kingdom of God, then his motives must be correct. If he is merely doing acts of kindness and holiness simply in order to get human praise, to be well thought of – then he will get the appropriate reward. No doubt he *will* be well thought of, by those who don't really know him. But this person must be completely unaware of the presence of God, who can read his heart and his innermost thoughts!

Those who are aware that God knows their motives do not bother

123

with self-seeking, or desire praise from others. On the contrary, they make every effort to keep their good works and devotions a private matter between themselves and God. It is enough that He knows. In fact, it even becomes an embarrassment if anyone else knows. Jesus said, 'Let not your left hand know what your right hand is doing.' As soon as a good deed becomes public property, the special relationship between the doer and the receiver, and the doer and God, is in danger of being lost.

Rabbinical almsgiving was occasionally accompanied by loud trumpet blasts, so that those being given the charity would know where to come. Needless to say, this sometimes resulted in a degrading scramble among those unfortunates who needed the help. They were allowed no pride at all. Often, no doubt, those who were most in need would get shoved to the back by the strongest. In these cases, the so-called charity of the rabbi was really simply a display of his generosity, and not a genuine effort to alleviate suffering at all. If his motive was really to do good and not just to show off – why was there a need for the trumpet announcement? The person whose giving is the most generous is probably the one who does it anonymously, so that no one knows the source of the gift but the giver and God.

Fasting was a regular act for pious Jews. Fasting means going without food, and the object of the exercise was to discipline and purify the body, and improve the concentration for acts of worship. Inevitably, the holy man who fasted a lot tended to look pale and drawn. So those who wanted to give the impression that they had gone without more than they really had, used to make their faces grey with dirt and ash. Jesus despised this play-acting and hypocrisy. No doubt the general public was taken in and paid great respect to the fasters, but Jesus knew that God could see through the charade. To want people to notice how good you were was a sign of weakness and insecurity in your character, not a reason for merit. Jesus suggested that even if you *were* fasting, you should rub oil into your face to give it a healthy glow, and not go round looking miserable and hungry. You should act in such a way that nobody would ever guess the extent of your severe religious practices. It was a matter between yourself and God only.

Again, prayer was often performed in public, and often in a pompous and long-winded manner – to impress the passers-by. Jews raised their arms to heaven to pray, and covered their heads with a shawl (called a tallith) so what they were doing was always conspicuous. Jesus didn't think there was anything wrong in praying in a public place, so long as the prayer itself was not made public just to show others how devout you were. He said that we should not pray like hypocrites on street corners in order to be seen, but we should do it in secret. We shouldn't be trying to make an impression on our neighbours, but be doing it out of our love for God. And there was no need to pile on long, repetitive prayers. It was not the length or pomposity that counted, but the intensity and honesty.

God is not subject to flattery like an oriental potentate. God is probably not particularly impressed with the average church evensong or school assembly – unless special and genuine efforts have gone into them. Listen honestly to what is said: notice the attitude of the supposed worshippers. No wonder so many people think there is no one listening, and turn away from religion. Talking to God shouldn't be like making a speech in a public meeting.

We shouldn't just reel off a list of 'I wants' either. God knows what we need before we ask Him. So why, then, should we pray? What is this attempt at communication for?

First, in this age of rushing about and not having the time to do all sorts of important things, it is of value in itself to develop an ability to switch off the noise and the world and enter into a state of peace – rather like walking into a beautiful private garden in the middle of a crammed housing estate. In a time of quiet, one has time to think about the incredible wonder of the universe in its shattering immensity and its incredible microscopic details, and to ponder on its origin and its continued orderly existence. One can try to conceive of a Being permeating all this, and caring intensely for every part of it – seeing the sparrow fall, being aware of life in all its forms in a way that we could never be aware of it except in brief flashes of understanding.

Secondly, in prayer, one has time to consider whether or not our world is completely aimless in its existence, or whether it is struggling gradually towards being a better place; and whether or not we humans have a responsible part to play in improving our earth. It is so easy to destroy and devastate, both in the realm of nature and of human relationships. We should be trying to work out what is God's will, to see it done on earth 'as it is in heaven'.

However, unless our minds are in harmony with God's mind, we will never be able to 'see' what is God's will at all. So there must be no barriers between us, caused by guilt or selfishness or unwillingness to serve in whatever situation we may find ourselves. The resignation of our wills to God's must be complete – there should be no holding back. We know that we must not harbour any malice or ill-feelings in our hearts for those who have wronged us, and this is possibly the hardest of our feelings to deal with. Jesus thought that it was absolutely vital that we should be able to forgive others. If we still bear malice, then we are still in need of help ourselves, and are not really ready to be giving help in furthering God's kingdom. We would still be nursing a barrier between ourselves and God. We will be forgiven to the extent that we can forgive others.

Then, we can ask for our daily needs to be taken care of – as they surely will be if we are busy doing our duty to the best of our abilities; we can ask for the strength and help to be led out of temptation successfully when we are faced with it; and for guidance not to get ourselves trapped into evil in any shape or form. Once we have achieved for ourselves the ability to pray and feel ourselves draw close to God, then we shall have no need to keep on saying, 'Oh please God do this, oh please God do that.' We shall do our best to *help* God act by working out how we can help practically, or by pitching in all our energy to bolster up someone who is 'low', all our love to rescue someone who is being swept away.

Questions and Research

1. Find Luke 11:1–4.
(a) What was Jesus doing?
(b) What were the disciples doing at this time?
(c) What did they ask Jesus?
(d) Copy out Matthew's version, given in Matthew 6:9–13.

2. What is true prayer?
3. What did Jesus think about the person who only did good in order to show off?
4. Find Matthew 6:1–4.
(a) Why did some people sound trumpets before they gave help to the needy?
(b) What did Jesus say about it in verse 3?

5. Find Matthew 6:5–15.
(a) How did the hypocrites say their prayers?
(b) Where did Jesus suggest one should go to pray?
(c) Can you think of other places that would be ideal for saying one's prayers?
(d) What do you think Jesus meant by 'heaping up empty phrases'?
(e) In what sense is God like a 'father' to us?
(f) What is the most important part of Jesus' prayer, as given in verse 10?
(g) What did Jesus say about forgiveness in verses 14–15?
(h) Why is forgiveness so vital?

6. Find Matthew 6:16–23.
(a) What is meant by fasting?

126

(b) How did some people try to make others think they had been fasting more than they really had?

(c) What did Jesus think you should do?

(d) Verses 19–21 are one of Jesus' riddles. People in those days kept their clothes and precious belongings in big wooden chests, which were often attacked by moth and maggot (see the footnote to find the maggots!). What do you think Jesus meant by your 'treasure'? This is a hard question, and needs quite a lot of thinking about.

(e) Rewrite verses 22–23 using the word 'motive' instead of 'eye'.

Creative Writing

Prayer can be a great help to people. It can help you to sort things out in your mind, to see a situation realistically. It is a good thing, in any case, to think about other people and how you could help them, if they were in difficulties.

(a) Make a list of things that you might pray for.

(b) See of you can work out how praying for people can help them, and also help you to be a better person.

WHAT DID JESUS TEACH ABOUT PRAYER?

Apart from his teachings in the Sermon on the Mount, the events of Jesus' life reveal that prayer was of fundamental importance for him. He used to start his days by rising before dawn, which could be as early as 3 a.m., and going off by himself into the countryside to pray. There he could be alone for a while with God, before the hectic round of his day's activities started. When his busy day was over – and sometimes he did not get the chance to eat (Mark 3:20) – he would pray again in the quiet of the evening. Sometimes he spent the entire night in prayer; one example of this was the night before he called twelve of his many followers to be his special helpers.

Several short prayers of Jesus are recorded in the gospels, and although it cannot be proved for certain that these are his exact words, the prayers are consistent with his character of love and compassion and absolute trust in God. Even as he was nailed to the cross, he prayed that God would forgive the men responsible for his execution, and, according to St. Luke's Gospel, Jesus' last words before he died were the touching prayer that was often said by a devout Jewish child before falling asleep, 'Father, into Thy hands I commit my spirit.'

Jesus taught three parables about prayer: the Pharisee and the publican, the friend at midnight, and the unjust judge. All three are to be found in St Luke's Gospel, the gospel that above all others showed Jesus to be a person of great love and compassion, who cared deeply about ordinary people struggling to do the right thing as best they could.

In the first of these parables the scene is at the Temple where two men have come to pray. These two men are completely different. One is an extremely holy and devout person, a Pharisee, who has made enormous efforts to carry out the will of God in his personal life. He feels that he was been successful, and is heartily grateful that he has never to his knowledge fallen into sin. He fasts often, he pays his tithes on everything he possesses, he has never been dishonest in any of his personal dealings; and he thanks God that he has managed to be better than other people.

The other man is the complete opposite. He is one of the despised tax-collectors – very likely an informer against his countrymen for the Romans, and quite capable of taking advantage of his privileged position to squeeze money from his hard-pressed neighbours and put it in his own pocket. The lowest of the low.

Yet he knows that he has done wrong, and he is ashamed. He does not know how to face God – he cannot find the words that he would really like to say. He knows that he has no right even to stand next to the righteous Pharisee, so he mutters his plea for God to forgive him, and then sadly goes away – leaving the Pharisee to stare after him with dislike and contempt on his smug self-satisfied face.

Jesus said that the prayer of the tax-collector was more valuable to God than that of the Pharisee, although the Pharisee was a good man and the tax-collector was a sinner. The reason was that the sinner was *actually praying*. He was making a real contact with God because he was aware of his faults and his need to be forgiven. His heart was crying out in its despair and shame – he knew his shortcomings and he wanted to be made better. Out of his despair came real awareness of God and communion with God. The Pharisee, on the other hand, was not praying at all – he was simply reciting to himself a list of his merits. If he had really been aware of God's presence, he would have felt the fierce need to protect and help his brother who stood there in such a wretched state.

The other two parables Jesus told about prayer gave people confidence to try, and to keep on trying even when there seemed to be no obvious result. They are about persistence, which means not giving up too easily. If one has prayed for the solution to some problem, one may not be aware of the answer the first time – but God is very much greater than an unjust judge or a lazy friend. He certainly listens, and we should not lose heart.

In the parable of the friend at midnight, the scene is that of a family man in his one-room house, in the communal bed with all his family around him. He hears a knocking at the door, but he does not want to get up because it will disturb everybody, so he tells the person knocking to go away. However, the knocking goes on, so eventually the man does get up to see what he wants – because it looks as if the family is going to be disturbed anyway. The man in need would probably not have dreamt of bothering a stranger in the middle of the night, but he was confident that his friend would get up and help him. If the lazy friend gave in and came to him, how much more will our Father in Heaven? We can approach Him with confidence and trust, and He will not turn us away or ignore us.

The story of the unjust judge is also told with a twinkle in Jesus' eye. This judge was corrupt, and not the least bit interested in hearing the case of a poor widow, because he knew she was not going to be able to pay him very much. He had rich, influential clients to see to. But he gave in eventually because she kept on coming back – she made herself a nuisance – and he wanted to get rid of her. How much more will God help us in our times of difficulty than this crooked official?

Jesus assured us that we ought to put our requests before God. 'Ask, and it will be given to you; seek, and you will find.' Very few people manage to find anything if they never look. It is really up to us to ask and to seek – and then who knows what we might find?

One point about making requests in prayer should be a reminder that sometimes the answer is going to have to be 'no'. Sometimes we pray for very unsuitable things, or dangerous things, or impossible things, or things that would be very bad for us if we were given them, or things that would make life unbearable for others if we got our own way. We must not forget that God sees a far wider view of things than we do.

We can be so blind and unreasonable if we have not fully thought out what the will of God must be in any situation. What about the case of two conflicting armies, where both sides are praying devoutly to win the battle? If we all prayed, 'Please God, don't let me miss that bus,' the bus would be travelling backwards instead of forwards!

God is not likely to tamper with the laws of nature on our behalf – the effects on the rest of the world would be disastrous! So, fire will always burn, things will always fall from heights, bullets will always hit targets. *We* are God's hands and feet. The only way a child can be saved from a napalm bomb that will burn it up is when men are convinced that it is wrong to fire them, and stop doing so. That is one reason why the Christian who keeps quiet about the injustices of this world is 'a light under a bushel' – a useless object when it could be doing so much good.

Questions and Research

1. Find Luke 18:7–14.
(a) Which two men stood praying in the Temple?
(b) What did the Pharisee say in his prayer?
(c) What did the publican do?

(d) Why was God more pleased with the prayer of the publican than that of the Pharisee?

2. Find Luke 11:5–13.
(a) Why didn't the man want to help his friend?
(b) Why did he decide that he would, in the end?
(c) Was God more or less likely to help those who prayed to Him?
(d) Copy out verses 9–10.

3. Find Luke 18:1–8.
(a) What sort of person was the judge in this parable?
(b) Why did he finally give in and deal with the widow's case?
(c) Was God more or less likely to help than this judge?

4. Find the following references, and note what is revealed about Christ's own practice of saying prayers: Mark 1:35–39; Luke 5:16; 6:12.
5. Find Luke 9:28–36. On one occasion when Jesus was praying, he was watched by his three closest disciples, and they saw some extraordinary things happen. Describe briefly what they saw.
6. Find Luke 22:39–46. What happened when Jesus prayed in Gethsemane? How did this prayer help Jesus?
7. Find Luke 23:33–34. What did Jesus pray when he was nailed to the cross?
8. Find Luke 23:46. What were the last words of Jesus before he died?

Creative Writing

For some people, prayer is a time of quiet communion with God, perhaps with no words at all. It is a feeling that, just for a few moments, one can sit and let peace and love and happiness radiate through. Sometimes prayer is an urgent cry for help – again, words may not be necessary. The need is obvious.

Many times, however, prayer is trying to get into contact with God – to find out what His will is in any given situation so that you can do the right thing to help matters along. Putting thoughts into words is not easy, but sometimes it does help.

See if you can write a short prayer that might sum up the thoughts, and give help, in these situations:

(a) A person who is frightened to go to sleep in the dark.
(b) A person who has trouble with someone who dislikes them and is spiteful.
(c) A person whose close relative is dying.

WHAT DID JESUS TEACH ABOUT FORGIVENESS?

One of the most important aspects of the teaching of Jesus was his awareness of the fact that so many people were depressed, and discouraged from trying to be religious because they knew that they were failures in one way or another. Perhaps they had not been able to live up to the high standards demanded by the Pharisees. There may have been lots of times when the ordinary people were simply unable to keep all the traditions imposed upon them, and therefore felt that it wasn't really worth the effort to try.

Some people had obviously been real sinners – they had cheated and lied and bullied and threatened, and so on. They had committed tax offences, sexual offences, slandered innocent people, borne malice and hatred. All this nonsense about God and right-living was simply not for them – the holy ones could keep it.

The Pharisees and the sinners had a healthy contempt for each other, and avoided each other like the plague. It would have been impossible for any of these folk to have become Pharisees anyway; they simply would not have been accepted. The Essenes – probably the strictest of all the religious groups at the time of Jesus – expected a person to complete several years of training before he could join them, and looked down on all the outsiders. Jesus was the very opposite.

To him, the Pharisees were certainly holy men, but some had forgotten the most important thing – how to love and to forgive. They would not bend their rigid standards to help the weak. And Jesus was concerned with those who were weak, those who could never make the grade without a little help. His whole ministry was one of putting things right, of reconciliation.

He knew that this would sometimes require a great deal of patience and effort. Peter once asked him how many times he ought to forgive his brother when he offended him. If he kept on doing the wrong thing, would seven times be enough before one lost patience? Jesus said that this would be nowhere near enough, one should forgive 'seventy times seven' – in other words, since you would no longer be counting, simply to go on and on forgiving without limit.

This would be no easy matter, but it was vital. If we cannot forgive others, it means we have hardened our hearts. How then can God's forgiveness and love to *us* get through? We ourselves would then be cut off from God's mercy.

Jesus pointed out that those who have been forgiven the most are perhaps those who can love God more than those who have never felt the need for forgiveness. Maybe to know heaven, we must first know hell. In the same way, it is often said that only people who have known the pain and fear of real sickness truly appreciate their good health.

God rejoices over the lost sheep, or lost coin, or lost son, that finally gets found. It is not His will that any should perish or go astray. Jesus said that there was more joy in heaven over the sinner who finds God than over ninety-nine just persons who have never left Him. This is not because God doesn't love the ninety-nine just as much – they are already part of him, and should be rejoicing with him.

God was like the farmer who knew that one of his sheep was lost. The farmer did not *have* to go out in the dark, giving up his sleep, running the risk of danger and making himself tired and uncomfortable for that wretched animal. He could have shrugged his shoulders and stayed in bed, and written off the sheep – after all, he had plenty of others. But no – the good shepherd cannot bear the thought of what might be happening to that lost sheep. Is it in danger, trapped, dying? He will not rest until he has found out, and brought the sheep home if he can.

The story of the woman who had lost a coin was probably another that Jesus told with a twinkle in his eye; perhaps he had seen this very thing happen to someone he knew. Houses in Capernaum were built of black basalt slabs, and coins could easily get lost in crevices in the floor, needing the light of a lamp to find them. The coins referred to were possibly the bridal coins, the price paid for a woman who married, that indicated her worth. Some valuable brides had head-dresses made up of hundreds of coins; this lady only had ten. How horrified she would be to lose one of them. Just as the missing coin meant so much to her, so we mean a great deal to God, especially when we go missing.

In the parable of the prodigal son, the reaction of the elder brother, although understandable, was so disappointing. He had always been his father's right hand, yet instead of sharing his joy at the return of the foolish youth, he became jealous. The Pharisees felt like that over Jesus caring for prostitutes and tax-collectors; sometimes respectable church people feel like that over drop-outs and teenage vandals, when they turn up for help. Instead of opening their arms to them, they are frightened that they will do something dirty or dangerous, and they think it is not right that they should get such a large share of attention when they certainly have not deserved it. God is surely disappointed then, for those who needed help will slip away once more, unhelped. The true Christian should be the lifeline, the arm to lean on, and not just a self-righteous critic.

Jesus was so concerned to express God's love and forgiveness that he told one parable that is rather hard for us to understand. There was a farmer who needed workmen to labour in his vineyard (the place where grapes were grown). Unemployed people were to be found in the market-place just standing about, possibly begging. At dawn the householder went and hired some men, and agreed to pay them a certain wage. Several times he went again to the market and hired more people, and, of course, those he took on later did not do nearly so much work as those who had been at it all day. When evening came, the steward had the job of handing out all the wages. To everyone's surprise, the householder decided to give every man the same pay, no matter how much work he had done. Those employed just an hour or so were delighted, but those who had done a full day were very annoyed and began to grumble about it not being fair. One wonders what modern trades union shop stewards would make of such a decision!

The point of the parable was that the householder had made a decision to be generous to the late-comers. He had given all of them work, and all should have been grateful – but the first labourers sought to improve on the bargain originally struck, because they did not see why those who had come late to the job should get a full day's pay. You may, indeed, wonder why he didn't give the first men a bit more. Perhaps if they had not been so cheeky and resentful, but had been impressed with his generosity and kindly nature, he might have rewarded them more. Who knows?

Those full-day workers were like the elder brother in the parable of the prodigal son. Some people love and serve God all their lives, and certainly they will be loved by God and taken into His kingdom. Others only find God late in life, perhaps after suffering or making mistakes – but when they do find Him they are welcomed in also. If the full-time workers have really loved and appreciated God, they will share his delight in forgiving and extending his generosity to late-comers, and not be resentful or jealous.

Jesus saw just one sin as being beyond the reach of forgiveness. Those of us who consider that surely nothing would be impossible for God to forgive may well find this a difficult saying to understand. The one unforgivable sin, according to Jesus, was blasphemy against the Holy Spirit. But what exactly does that phrase mean? Presumably, if one simply cannot recognise the healing, loving, cleansing power of God when it comes – if one turns one's back on it – then an impenetrable barrier is erected between oneself and God. It is not so much that God *will* not forgive, but rather that He *cannot*. His only alternative would be to force the issue, to over-power the unbeliever, and this would be to take away his free will and render his reactions automatic, to dehumanise him.

There is a very famous picture by the artist Holman Hunt of Jesus standing out in the cold, knocking at a closed door. It is called 'The Light of the World', and Jesus is bringing his light with him. But if we do not open that door, Jesus does not force it open – he must go on waiting, outside.

Questions and Research

1. Find Matthew 5.
(a) What did Jesus teach about forgiveness in verses 7–9?
(b) What did Jesus say would happen to a person who bore malice to his brother (5:22–25)?
(c) How did Jesus think we should react towards our enemies (5:44–45)?
(d) What did Jesus teach about forgiveness in the Lord's Prayer (6:12, 14–15)?

2. Find Mark 2:1–12. How was forgiveness connected with the healing of the paralysed man?
3. Find Mark 2:15–17. Christ's whole mission was concerned with forgiveness. What did he say when the scribes asked why he was eating with tax-collectors and sinners?
4. Find Matthew 18:23–35. If we cannot forgive others, how then can we receive God's mercy? Give a brief outline of the parable of the unmerciful servant.
5. Find Luke 7:40–50. Those who have been forgiven the most find they can love God more than those who never needed forgive-ness. Write out the parable of the two debtors.
6. Find Matthew 18:15–22. What instructions did Jesus give there concerning forgiveness? What did Peter ask, and what was the reply?
7. Find Luke 15.
(a) What three parables of forgiveness did Jesus tell in this chapter?
(b) Which things represented the people like the Pharisees, who had never been lost?
(c) What was the reaction of the elder brother to the young wastrel when he came home?

(d) Why was the father so disappointed by this?
(e) Copy out verses 7, 31–32.

8. Find Mark 3:28–29. What was the one sin that could not be forgiven?
9. How could one explain the fact that God cannot forgive this sin?
10. Find Luke 18:9–14. Which of the two prayers was preferred by God, and why?
11. Find Luke 19:1–10.
(a) What did Zacchaeus do for a living?
(b) Why did the crowd 'murmur' about Jesus?
(c) What was the result of Zacchaeus' feeling forgiven?
(d) Copy out verse 10.
12. Find Matthew 20: 1–16.
(a) In what way was the householder obviously a kind man?
(b) What wages did he agree to pay the labourers?
(c) Did he pay the people he hired last any less than the first?
(d) What was the reaction of those who had worked all day?
(e) If the 'wages' are really 'entry into the Kingdom of Heaven', was the householder being mean to the first-comers, or generous to the late-comers?

13. Find Luke 23:33–43. Jesus died with forgiveness.
(a) What did Jesus pray about the men who nailed him to the cross?
(b) What did Jesus say to the thief who turned to him?

Creative Writing

Either: How can a Christian act as a lifeline to people in trouble? See if you can give some examples of how a Christian could help to repair the ruins of a bad person's life.
Or: Imagine you are one of the hired servants in the parable of the labourers in the vineyard. How did you and the other servants react to the householder's paying a full day's wage to the late-comers? You could write this parable as a playscript, if you wish.

25
WHAT DID JESUS TEACH ABOUT HUMILITY?

The word humility can have such awful overtones. One of Charles Dickens's most unpleasant characters was that dreadful fellow Uriah Heep, who was always being so terribly 'umble. When one meets people like that, it really takes an immense effort of will to think well of them and not despise the way they go crawling around. Can Jesus have really wanted people to be like that – sickeningly self-abasing? Can he really have admired it? Surely not.

In the section of the Sermon on the Mount known as the beatitudes, Jesus even stated 'blessed are the meek'. Now, to most of us, the word meek means timid, even cowardly. Can Jesus have really admired such people? It doesn't seem to make much sense. Certainly Jesus wasn't cowardly or always apologising for himself. What did he mean?

It is difficult to find a modern word that is the right equivalent, but presumably by meekness and humility Jesus meant the sort of character that was unpretentious, not arrogant. It certainly did not imply any sort of weakness – the very opposite. People on the whole have a tendency to hit back, to assert their rights. Jesus thought that this tendency should be under our control, and that this requires great strength of character. Again, it didn't mean that people were required to be submissive and ignore wrongdoing, or pass by on the other side. On the contrary, although they were to check their own tempers and passions, they would have been quite wrong not to have stepped in to help someone being abused. I think that Jesus would probably have made this difference between war in general and a just war. Surely one cannot believe that Jesus would condemn efforts to save Jews from the gas-chambers, or individuals fighting back desperately to save their families?

Yet, when it was his own self that was under attack, Jesus was prepared to be tortured and to die without hitting back. In his humility he was prepared to carry out God's will, and in his meekness he was not prepared to strike down even the soldiers nailing him to the wood.

Jesus taught that true greatness lay in being big enough to put others before yourself. At feasts and parties it was considered quite normal for the guests of honour to have certain seats that marked them out as important people. Even today in the East, this custom still survives. If guests are shown into an empty room, they are shown to the best seats, which are usually in the middle of one side or one end. If important persons come in after them, visitors go through the motions of leaving the best seats and going lower down. When entering a room in which a number of the seats are already occupied, it is polite for the visitor to try to sit on a seat at the bottom end of the room. The host will then urge him to take a better seat.

Jesus taught one parable about such a party. When the guests arrived, certain of them with high opinions of themselves looked around for the best places and sat there. Imagine their embarrassment when the host of the meal – who had a different opinion of who the important people were – asked them to move to a lower place. Other guests, who were not so conceited or pushing, had quietly taken humbler seats, and they were invited to move up. It is not wise to have too inflated a view of our own importance. God, who knows all our motives, may see things in quite a different light.

Nobody was more important to the disciples than Jesus himself, and yet, according to St John's Gospel, when he entertained them to a meal shortly before his death, he amazed them all by taking a towel and water, and washing their feet. This was one of the most disliked of household jobs, for it was usually done by the lowest servant, and nobody liked admitting that they *were* the lowest servant! Jesus pointed out that even if he was their lord and master, he had come among them as one who served. This was his example, and they were to follow it in their own lives.

He did not hesitate about washing their feet, or worry about what people would think of him, or feel small because he had performed this task. He did it deliberately, because he loved them. He was trying to teach them that real love does not mind the most humble of tasks, the dirty jobs, the humiliating chores. That is one of the marks of a Christian. When someone is sick in the wrong place, or the family pet does what it ought not, how does a Christian react? Leave the mess for someone else? Recoil from it? Or quietly and cheerfully deal with the problem, because one loves the sick person or pet? One of the most moving stories about the great Indian saint and politician, Mahatma Gandhi, involved such an example. He was trying to teach his backward people about hygiene, but some were lazy and thoughtless, and messed in the streets, leaving it for others to clear up. Gandhi went into the streets and buried their dung with his own hands.

God did not judge a person by what he showed of himself to the world. He looked to a person's heart. Many people gave rich and splendid gifts to the Temple in Jerusalem, but when Jesus saw a poor woman place a couple of copper coins in the box, he said that her offering was worth more to God than all the rich presents of the wealthy. Why? Because, although the gift was small, it was given with all her heart, although she had so little.

The greatest apostle is the servant of all – and not the sort of servant that constantly needs praising for what he does! All his acts of devotion should be done in secret, for trying to gain human praise merely discredits him in God's eyes. The truly great man does not think of himself at all – he only thinks of the work he is able to do, and the joy it brings him by drawing him closer to God. He may be a great person in the eyes of the world, but he himself will know how small and insignificant in the universe he really is – for he will see the universe with very different eyes from the world.

Once Jesus found his disciples arguing over which of them was the greatest. Jesus took a child and stood him in the middle of the room, and announced that if anyone wanted to be the first, then he must be the last and servant of all. He meant that a truly great person would not be proud or ambitious or worried about his position in life. He would be modest and eager to please and help others, but without drawing attention to himself. These qualities were often to be found in children who had not yet been spoilt by life's ambitions and desires. He who was closest to the child in his heart would probably also be closest to God.

The brilliant scientist and thinker, Sir Isaac Newton, thought like this. Just before he died, he said that he had been like a boy playing with pebbles on the beach, while all before him lay the vast ocean. That is an example of true humility. He was not pretending, or acting small. He was simply aware of the immense vastness of what he did not know.

Unless one can find this awareness, humility is a very difficult virtue to acquire. St Thomas Becket was apparently very bothered by it, as he had a hunch that he was a saint, but wondered if he really could be if he knew that he was. We all have this tendency to be very pleased with ourselves when things are going well. We need the awareness of God and the examples of great saints to help us keep things in proportion.

Perhaps Jesus himself, in submitting to the baptism of John the Baptist, which was supposed to be for the forgiveness of sins, revealed to us all just how sinless he was. For a man without sins would never for a moment be so conceited and self-confident as to believe that he had no sins!

Questions and Research

1. What did Jesus say about the meek in Matthew 5:5?
2. Find Matthew 5:38–39. What did Jesus teach there about self-control?
3. Find Matthew 18:1–6 and Luke 9:46–48 and 18:17. What did he say to those who were bothered about the greatest in the Kingdom of Heaven?
4. Find Luke 14:7–11. What did Jesus say might happen to a person who always assumed they would be given the most important seat? Write out a brief outline of this parable.
5. Find Luke 14:15–24, and write the outline of the parable of the feast. This could refer to the Jews rejecting Jesus and his turning to other folk to be the 'chosen race' and enter his kingdom.
6. Find Luke 18:9–14. Why was the humility of the tax-collector preferable to the prayer of the pious Pharisee?
7. Find Luke 21:1–4. Why was the widow's tiny offering more valuable to God than the other riches put in the treasury box?
8. Find Luke 9:23–27. Would any follower of Jesus have an easy time? Copy out verses 24 and 25.
9. Find Mark 9:33–37.
(a) Why were the disciples embarrassed?
(b) What did Jesus say to them in verse 35?
(c) Why do you think that someone who is prepared to be 'servant of all' is really a 'great' person?
(d) Find Mark 10:15. Copy out this verse.

26

WHAT DID JESUS TEACH ABOUT LIFE AFTER DEATH?

On several occasions it was reported that Jesus brought certain people back from the dead. The twelve-year-old daughter of Jairus, a synagogue elder, died while Jesus was on his way to heal her. Jesus took her hand and prayed, and the child came back to life. Jesus stopped a funeral procession to raise a widow's son at Nain. In the East, funerals often take place on the same day as a person's death, but it is safe to assume that the boy had been presumed dead for several hours. In St John's Gospel, an incident is recorded where Jesus restored to life a man who had been dead for four days, and was therefore considered to be totally beyond recall.

Pharisees, who believed in immortality and that people were living souls, thought it might be possible in certain circumstances to bring a soul back into the body of a person who had been dead for less than three days – but after that, it should have been out of the question.

The significance of this miracle was clear to the author of the gospel; it was a sign of God's power in Christ. Jesus himself was the resurrection and the life. Those who believed in him, though they might die, yet they should live.

Jesus taught tantalisingly little on the subject of life after death. Yet if the accounts of the raising from the dead were of events that really did happen, then obviously Jairus' daughter and the young man of Nain and Lazarus of Bethany had not ceased to exist when their bodies died. Neither, for that matter, did Jesus himself.

In this materialistic day and age there is an enormous hunger for proof of the supernatural, and of continued personal existence after the death of the material body. Such proofs as are given never really seem to be conclusive, or available to scientific checking procedures. Therefore they are treated with a great deal of suspicion, probably rightly. However, many people dismiss the evidence collected by the seekers into the realms of the soul as being just so much nonsense – an attitude which does not do justice at all to the literally thousands of perfectly respectable and intelligent persons who have had experiences which are difficult to explain in any way other than the existence of life after death.

Modern medical methods of reviving the newly dead have opened another interesting field of study: the recollections and experiences of those dead people who have been brought back to life. These recollections seem to add up to a sensible and complete picture of what happens at death and immediately after it, and presumably the same experiences would have been shared by the son of the widow at Nain, and Jairus' daughter, who were revived by Jesus. However, even here there is a catch in it; for those who simply refuse to accept the possibility of life after death, the assumption still remains that these revived persons had never been truly dead, and were simply undergoing a near-to-death hallucination, perhaps caused by a very high temperature.

There is always the possibility that by eternal life Jesus may not have meant a life that goes on for ever and ever after death at all. He was possibly referring to a different dimension to life, a deeper and more enriched awareness of living. Nevertheless, one of the main reasons why Jesus did not argue out the case for life after death openly was probably that he, and all his friends, and all the Pharisees, were all believers in it!

The Old Testament had frowned on necromancy, or attempts to contact the dead, and it was believed officially that the dead descended into the 'Pit' or 'Sheol', a shadowy place under the earth. Eternal life consisted only in passing on one's personality through one's children, and consequently it was considered to be a dreadful punishment for sin if God denied children to a couple. So serious was it, that if a couple were childless, a man could produce children for himself by promoting maidservants to the rank of a secondary wife; and if a woman's husband died childless, she was duty bound to marry his next of kin and have a child, which would be counted as her dead husband's.

As far as rewards and punishments were concerned, the good and the bad were supposed to receive their desserts in *this* life, in the forms of wealth, good health, large families and so on. The Pharisees, following perhaps the Persian influence, evolved the idea of punishment or reward in an after-life because it was becoming increasingly obvious that the good were the very ones who were dying young, and unrewarded, while the bad were absolutely thriving.

This meant that either God was being unfair, or that He did not care for His people, or that He had no power to save them, or that He did not exist at all. The Pharisees could not accept any of these options, so they reasoned that God must be rewarding or punishing His people in another life. Their heaven was the paradisa or garden.

The Jews had seen paradisas in Persian-occupied territories, and were impressed by them. Those who had suffered from arid, hard conditions longed for a place of green grass, lush fruit and water in abundance. The place of punishment was Gehenna, a burning rubbish-tip on which the dross of humanity was destroyed. This idea was based on the Valley of Hinnom in which the evil king Manasseh had made human sacrifice to the fire-god Moloch. After the king's death the valley had been desecrated and used as a rubbish dump, and was often fired to kill off the germs and smells.

From Paradise, spirits could return to earth as messengers (Greek = *angelois*) to give warnings or impart God's will. These angels, who to all intents and purposes looked like human beings, occasionally shining with brilliant light, were not to be confused with the wierd winged cherubim (which were rather like the Sphinx) or the seraphim (described as 'flames of fire'), who were the guardian spirits of the Old Testament; and they were certainly not the medieval idea of a cherub as a little naked winged boy, which was a depiction of the infant Roman god Cupid. There is no mention in the biblical literature of wings or harps for angels.

Sadducees ignored all these ideas as being innovations, new theories, and would have nothing to do with them. They stuck by the Old Testament refusal to encourage communion with the dead, and ignored the fact that, even in those times, one could find plenty of material to suggest that although the people were not *supposed* to believe in a personal survival after death, many of them did. I Samuel 28:8–25, for example, gives the famous story of King Saul communing with the ghost of Samuel, through the mediumship of the witch of Endor.

There are three notable places in the Synoptic Gospels where Jesus' belief in life after death was vouched for. The first was the occasion on which Jesus climbed a mountain with Peter, James and John, and was transfigured before them. The disciples saw his clothes shine with light, and two ghostly figures appear and speak with him. These persons were identified as Moses and Elijah. Now, if Moses had been dead for some 1,300 years, and Elijah some 800 years, this appearance surely suggests that they were still recognisable as persons, and were not just puffs of smoke; that they were still people, with no wings or other appendages, and were certainly not evil or frightening ghouls; that they must have been outside time; and that they could communicate with the living. People have puzzled over what this appearance of the two Old Testament personalities represented, but have often ignored the implications of what it suggested about their continued existence in an after-life.

Another important passage was the parable of the rich man and Lazarus the beggar, given in Luke 16:19–31. This parable was probably not intended to be taken as a literal description of what would happen after death, but it does hint at certain things which Jesus presumably believed to be true. It suggested that the good and the bad would be separated, and that those who had suffered on earth would be compensated while those who had been responsible for the suffering would be punished. It suggested that there was a great gulf between the two states which could not be crossed. And finally, it suggested that people on earth would not be impressed by the appearance and warnings of a ghost unless they happened to believe in them already. Jesus may even have been referring to his own rising from the dead, and we know for a fact that not everyone believes in him.

People who see ghosts are not necessarily convinced by what they have seen. The cause of the vision could have been indigestion, or a hallucination, or a hundred other things. Even if they were very impressed at the time, the memory would soon begin to fade and the person start to have doubts and find explanations. Psychic phenomena do not lend themselves readily to scientific proofs, as all psychical researchers know, to their annoyance.

During the last week of Christ's life, he was questioned on one occasion by the Sadducees, who – no doubt thinking that Jesus was a Pharisee – were trying to make fun of his beliefs. They asked him who a woman would be married to in heaven, if she had had seven husbands here on earth. They were trying to make Jesus look silly. It was a typical Saducean question. Jesus rounded on them in no uncertain terms, and told them that they were quite wrong in their beliefs. They knew nothing about the scriptures, or the power of God. Then Jesus said directly that when people rise from the dead they are not involved in marriage at all, but are 'like angels'. He also pointed out that when God stated that He was the God of Abraham, Isaac and Jacob, this implied that those persons were still living and recognisable entities (as Moses and Elijah at the transfiguration).

What does being 'like an angel' mean? Presumably, in this context, it means not having a physical body as we know it. No marriage. This might also imply no eating, digestion, physical ailments or physical anything. Taking this line of thought to its logical conclusion makes us wonder whatever we would actually *be* if we rid ourselves of our mouths, arms and legs, brains and so forth. This is a topic that obviously needs a great deal more thought than we can give it here.

Let us stop at the point where it seemed that we would still be recognisable as ourselves. No doubt we will know all the answers when we get there.

Questions and Research

1. What is meant by life after death?
2. How do modern medical methods of reviving dead people add to our knowledge?
3. Why is there 'a catch in it'?
4. What was meant by Paradise and Gehenna?
5. Which religious party did *not* believe in life after death?
6. Find Mark 9:1–8.
(a) Who did the disciples see up the mountain?
(b) Roughly how long had each of these been dead?
(c) Roughly how long was there in between the death of these two people?
(d) What does this imply about their relationship with time?
(e) Had they become in any way evil or frightening?
(f) Had they developed wings, or an interest in the harp?
(g) Did Jesus believe the 'dead' could communicate with the living?

7. Find Luke 16:19–31.
(a) Write out the parable of the Rich Man and Lazarus.
(b) Did the good and the bad live under the same conditions after death?
(c) Why was the rich man being punished?
(d) Why wouldn't God send back a ghost to warn his brothers?
(e) Copy out verse 31.

8. Find Mark 12:18–27.
(a) What was the Sadducees' question?
(b) Why were they trying to make fun of Jesus?
(c) What did Jesus say 'dead' people were like?
(d) What do you think this implies?

9. What are we told about life after death in these verses: John 11:23–26; I Corinthians 15:13, 17, 18, 19, 42, 44?

Creative Writing

Think of what St Paul said in I Corinthians 15:35–44 about the changes that occur during the life-cycle of a grain of wheat; or think of an acorn that becomes a towering oak tree. In some way, the waving corn or the mighty tree is contained in the seed. To look at the seed, you would never be able to predict what it was going to become; and in becoming a plant or a tree, the seed dies and is no more; it is cast off.

Either: Write a poem in which you are a potential oak tree locked in a tiny acorn, waiting to come into being.

Or: Imagine that you have just 'died' and discovered that you still exist but have entered a different dimension. Describe how you think you might feel, and what you think you might see.

27

WHAT DID JESUS TEACH ABOUT MONEY?

When the wise men travelled to Israel to find the man 'born to be King of the Jews', they naturally called at the palace of Herod the Great. But the infant saviour was not to be found there – the very place of his birth was in itself a clue as to the type of person Jesus was going to be. His parents had travelled from their home to Bethlehem, the city of David, in order to be enrolled among the tribe of David in a taxation census. No special provision had been made for Mary, who was heavy with child. They would probably have slept in one of the crowded *khans,* or inns, crammed in with about thirty other travellers, had it not been for the fact that Mary went into labour, and a place with some privacy had to be found for her to give birth. The couple sheltered in a stable, possibly in a cave, and there Mary's baby was safely born.

The wise men with their precious gifts were not the first visitors to pay homage to the child either. By the time they arrived the family were more comfortably in a house, and Jesus was possibly over a year old. The night of Christ's birth saw visions of angels appearing to some humble shepherds out on night-watch, and they were the ones who first bowed down in wonder before the baby in the manger.

When Jesus arrived at manhood, he took a firm stand against the evil and corruption brought about by money. Many Jews regarded good health and good fortune as being the direct blessing and reward of God – a proof that He was pleased with a person's life and behaviour. Jesus never stated that wealth in itself was wrong, but he realised that a person with great possessions was wide open to the temptations to be greedy and selfish and self-indulgent – far more so than the ordinary chap in the street. Incidentally, Jesus never said the famous phrase, 'Money is the root of all evil.' It was St Paul who said that, and the correct sentence is, *'Love of money* is the root of all evil' (I Timothy 6:10).

St Luke's version of the beatitudes made this opinion quite plain, as did several of the parables he recorded. In Luke 16:19–31, a rich man was made to suffer dire penalities after he died because he had ignored the poor man begging at his gate and refused to help him when he could easily have done so. In the next world he was punished for this; the poor man was consoled.

In Luke 12:13–21, Jesus scorned the sort of man who spent all his life building up a great stock-pile of material wealth. He did not realise that he was about to die, and that he could not take it with him. He entered the world with nothing, and he would leave it that way. All his worldly goods would simply pass to another. He had gained nothing of real benefit to himself.

In Luke 14:12–14, Jesus suggested that to earn real merit when entertaining guests at lavish parties, it would be better to invite the poor, the disfigured and the handicapped – people who would not be able to repay you. That would earn you treasure in heaven, where 'neither moth nor rust corrupt, and no thieves can break in to steal'.

One's good deeds and right-living build up the only form of treasure that really counts, the sort of possession that you *can* take with you.

A typical example of God's appreciation of real treasure was given when Jesus saw a poor widow give a couple of tiny coins to the Temple collecting-box. The amount was hardly worth anything, and rich people often gave enormous sums, yet Jesus said that *her* offering was worth more than theirs, for she gave out of her poverty all that she possessed. God knew, and He valued that gift very highly indeed.

Jesus was impatient of people who worried all the time about what they were going to eat or drink, or what they were going to wear. They were missing the important business of life. He didn't mean that people should not bother any more to look after themselves, or should make themselves a nuisance and a burden to others, but that their aim in life should not be only these time-wasting trivial things. They should be concerned with living kindly and considerate lives, looking after those dependent on them and seeking to make the world a better place than when they found it.

It seems that Jesus definitely thought that love of money *was* the root of evil. Once a rich young ruler who had lived an excellent life so far as the Law was concerned came to Jesus and asked him what more he had to do in order to gain eternal life. Jesus told him to sell all his possessions, and give his money away to the poor, and follow him. The young man went away sorrowful, because he couldn't do it. Jesus knew that anyone who couldn't see that the kingdom was really worth much more than anything else, was not yet ready to enter it. The kingdom was there, but a person still clinging to his possessions and ambitions would never see it.

Questions and Research

1. Luke 2:1–7. In what surroundings was Jesus born?
2. Luke 2:8–20. Who were Jesus' first visitors?
3. Luke 6:20–21, 24–25. What did Jesus teach about money in these verses?
4. Matthew 6:25–34. What is our attitude to clothing and luxuries supposed to be?
5. Matthew 6:19–24.
(a) What happened to earthly treasures?
(b) Where should our real 'treasure' be?
(c) Mammon was the Roman god of wealth and self-interest. What does verse 24 mean?

6. Luke 12:13–21.
(a) What was the parable of the rich fool?
(b) Copy out verse 15.

7. Luke 16:19–31.
(a) Why did the rich man suffer in the next world?
(b) What happened to the poor man?

8. Luke 14:12–14. Why was it better to ask those who could not repay you?
9. A well-known saying of Jesus that is not in the gospels is: 'It is better to give than to receive' (Acts 20:35). Why do you think this is so?
10. A saying of St Paul's was: 'Love of money is the root of all evil' (I Timothy 6:10). Do you think this saying is correct, and why?
11. Find Mark 10:17–31.
(a) Who approached Jesus?
(b) What did he want to know?
(c) What instructions did Jesus give him?
(d) What was the one thing the young man could not bring himself to do?
(e) Copy out verses 23 and 25. (A needle-eye was probably a narrow gate in the wall of Jerusalem. Any heavy-laden camels coming in from the desert with their merchandise would have to unload before they could go through. Those prepared to 'unload' their selfishness and ambition and pride could 'go through into the city', but for those who refused, the doorway was too narrow. They would have to go away again.)
(f) What would happen to those who *were* prepared to give up everything, like the disciples?

12. You might like to have these supposed sayings of Jesus from an Arab source known as Asin's collection:

Jesus said: My seasoning is hunger, my undergarment is fear, my
outergarment is wool; my fire in winter is the rays of the sun,
my lamp is the moon, my riding-beast is my feet, and my food
and fruit are what the earth brings forth. At night I have
nothing and in the morning I have nothing, and yet there is
no one on earth richer than I.

Jesus said: Eating barley and sleeping on dunghills with dogs is
a small matter when one seeks Paradise.

Jesus said: Do not look at the wealth of the people of this world,
for the splendour of their wealth takes away the light of your
faith.

Creative Writing

Is it possible to be wealthy, or even comfortable, and still call
yourself a Christian? That would possibly depend on what opportunities came your way for doing good with your money. Imagine
that you were suddenly given £10,000, and that you lived in an
under-developed part of the world. Could you spend all that money
on yourself and still call yourself a Christian? How might you spend
it? Make a list of possible uses of the money, dividing your work
into two columns of activities: those you would consider Christian,
and those you would consider to be unchristian. Which would be
the better column?

28
THE MIRACLES OVER NATURE

Apart from his miracles of healing, Jesus was also reported as having performed certain acts which indicated that he had a special power over the forces of nature. In St John's Gospel, his miracles are known as **signs**, and people were supposed to think about what Jesus had done, and draw conclusions about him. Then, as now, not everyone was able to believe in him, but for those who had eyes to see, the actions of Jesus would indicate the wonder and the power of God. Nowhere did Jesus state that his signs *proved* that he was a divine being, but they did reveal God's power and love.

Jesus pointed out that he was not the only person who could perform wonders – many people had done, and would be able to after he had gone – but all who discovered these gifts would know for certain in their hearts the truth of what they believed.

If we leave out the phenomena associated with the resurrection of Jesus, there are eight recorded miracles over nature in our four gospels. They are the turning of water into wine (John 2:1–11); the stilling of the storm (Mark 4:35–41; Matthew 8:23–27; Luke 8:22–25); the feeding of five thousand (Mark 6:35–44; John 6:5–15; Matthew 14:13–21; Luke 9:11–17); walking on the water (Mark 6:47–52; Matthew 14:22–33; John 6:16–21); feeding four thousand (Mark 8:1–10); withering a fig-tree (Mark 11:12–14, 20–23; Matthew 21:18–19); the miraculous catch of fish (Luke 5:1–11); and the coin in the fish's mouth (Matthew 17:24–27).

An explanation for these narratives is difficult to give in scientific terms, and peoples' reactions vary from scornful disbelief to fanciful credulity; but to reject the miracles makes the temptations of Jesus rather pointless, since it is surely assumed there that Jesus could have turned stones into bread, or jumped unharmed from the Temple pinnacle, had he so wished. If the stories were untrue it would also mean that the people who reported these happenings were either incredibly stupid or gullible, or dreadful liars.

Were the people who witnessed these phenomena all suffering from mass hypnosis? It seems no answer to the problem – one could perhaps convince a wedding party that had already had plenty to drink that water had been changed into wine, or make a crowd of five thousand think that they had been eating, but surely one cannot seriously accept that they continued to gather up the imaginary crumbs into twelve imaginary baskets, still under hypnosis?

The miracles had a stunning effect on those who witnessed them. John 6:15 reports that the crowd was so impressed that they tried to force Jesus to be their king, and he had to get away from them, to the hills. Why should they have been so impressed if he had merely encouraged them to share their picnic baskets? If they had had picnic baskets, where had they hidden them while the disciples, in their concern for them, went to look for food for them? Had they had time to prepare them anyway? The gospels tell us that the people had seen Jesus set off in a boat, and had run round the lakeside to meet him when he beached some distance away. That doesn't suggest that they went off to pack lunch-baskets first!

No local baker's shop in a small village could produce enough bread for even a dozen people at about 5.30 p.m., and in any case, Jesus had deliberately gone to an area where there were no shops. The people would have had to have gone home for provisions, and if they had done so at that late hour, then they wouldn't have come back.

The producing of a quantity of food from a little, and the transforming of water into wine, are miracles which seem to imply a manipulation of atomic forces in a way not shared by even scientists as yet – although wonderful things are going on in the laboratories of our chemists and biologists. However, similar feats have been claimed by other people, not only the supposed incarnations of the Eastern gods or god-heroes, but quite human, if saintly, folk in more recent times.

In 1835, at La Puye near Poitiers, France, it is claimed that 30 bushels of grain blessed in June by St Andrew Hubert Fournet fed about two hundred people for six months. The two heaps, one of wheat and the other of barley, did not diminish. In the convent of the Daughters of the Cross in 1883, a six-week wine ration lasted in the barrels for three months. Similar miracles are said to have occurred for the Curé d'Ars in 1829, St Mary Pelletia in 1845, St Mary Magdalene Postel in 1871, and St John Bosco in 1886. Were all these saintly people lying? Or deluded? That must surely be at least as unlikely as the supposed miracles themselves.

What about Jesus walking on the water? The theory of levitation must be examined more fully by men of science before one can reject Christ's ability to do this. It is all too easy to say that Jesus must have been walking on the shore, or on a sandbank. Surely these Galilean fishermen would not have been taken in by that?

This world is full of odd phenomena that fall into the category of levitation. If you are interested, you can look up facts about yoga, fire-walking, egg-walking, Simon Magus (a famous 'floater') and even mediums like Daniel Dunglas Home, who used to rise from a table, drift out of the window and come in at another, several floors up. Home certainly wasn't claiming to be the Messiah – just an ordinary man who knew a bit more than others about nature's mysterious forces.

Calming the storm on the lake may have been an amazing set of coincidences. Galilee was certainly known for its sudden storms caused by the wind falling down from the heights as if through a funnel. Storms started and broke off as suddenly as the wind itself, and could be quite localised in their effect. The violence of the wind causes these dangerous storms within a certain narrow corridor of water on the lake. On either side of the wind's path, the water remains calm and placid. Many fishermen lost their lives in the sea every year; they treated it with respect.

So, it could be desperately rough where the wind smashed on to the lake, and quite calm a few yards further on. Yet the gospel writers obviously felt that more was implied than Jesus' simply sailing into calm water. Maybe when he said, 'Peace be still,' he was speaking to Peter and the other disciples, who were in such a panic. Or maybe he really did have a power that could break up clouds and deflect winds.

It has been claimed that the case of the miraculous catch of fish was possibly no more than Jesus, on the shore of the lake, seeing a shoal of fish in the clear waters of Galilee that the disciples had not seen for some reason. This particular miracle is interesting because it is one of the narratives with many points of comparison to a similar story in St John's Gospel. In the fourth gospel, the event took place not at the beginning of Jesus' ministry, but right at the end, after his resurrection (see John 21:1–8).

St Luke's version indicated how what happened completely changed Peter's life. The miracle revealed something much deeper than Jesus simply spotting fish. Peter had been reluctant to waste his time; he had tried all night to catch fish, and taken nothing. Why bother to go on? Yet when he was prepared to keep on trying in obedience to Jesus' will, his catch overflowed the nets. One can imagine Jesus grinning as Peter fell to his knees, declaring that he was a sinful man and not worthy to be a disciple of Jesus – and Jesus cheering him up with the wonderful promise that he would become a 'fisher of men'.

The story of the fish that had the coin in its mouth sounds like a typical oriental tale of wonder. And yet the Sea of Galilee contains a remarkable fish, the musht, that does pick up glittering objects and carry them in its mouth – so the story was not impossible, even though it would have been an amazing coincidence.

The last nature miracle is most interesting as it is the only example we have of Christ's power to destroy. Jesus went up to a fig-tree when it was not the season for figs, found nothing on it, and cursed it. According to St Mark it died overnight, and according to St Matthew it simply withered on the spot. It places Christians in an awkward position when it comes to explaining *why* Christ did what appears to be an unreasonable action. He must have known that he would not find figs on it, unless he was incredibly obtuse, or content to be satisfied with the shrivelled remains of a previous year's crop. Was he being bad-tempered? Was he being cruel to the tree? Perhaps Christ somehow knew that the tree would never produce more figs, having become too worn out. Maybe he was merely speeding up the natural processes that would lead to the tree's decay.

Some people think that the miracle never happened at all, that it was merely a parable about the failure of Israel to produce fruit, and their coming destruction. St Luke, indeed, leaves out the incident altogether, and has a parable about a fig-tree elsewhere in his gospel with precisely that message.

Be that as it may, it is useful to observe that if Jesus *did* have this power (and presumably he used it to destroy sickness, germs, growths and so on), it shows what tremendous love and self-control he must have had *not* to have used it for his own benefit at his arrest, torture and crucifixion. He could have paralysed or withered the arms of the soldiers who approached him with their nails. A careful reading of St John's version of the arrest reveals that they were frightened of arresting him. However, instead of striking them down he suffered, and prayed that they might be forgiven. Perhaps this odd miracle of the fig-tree shows us Christ's love and compassion more than any other.

Questions and Research

1. How many nature miracles are there recounted in the gospels?
2. What were these signs supposed to prove?
3. Find John 3:2. What did Nicodemus say there about the signs?
4. Find John 14:10–14.
(a) Copy out verse 11.
(b) What did Jesus say about other people doing works?

5. Give two examples of modern miracles of feeding.
6. What is meant by levitation?
7. Which of Jesus' miracles implied that he could levitate?

8. Which of Jesus' miracles implied that he had the power to destroy?

9. Find Mark 6:30–46. This is the only miracle to be mentioned in *all four gospels*.

(a) How do we know that the disciples were tired?

(b) Where did they go to get away from the crowds?

(c) Why didn't they manage to get away?

(d) Would the crowds have had time to prepare picnic lunches?

(e) When did they begin to think about food?

(f) If the word pence is taken to mean the Roman denarius, which was the equivalent of a labourer's day's pay, how much would it have cost to have fed them?

(g) How much food did they actually have between them?

(h) How much was left over afterwards?

(i) How many people were involved?

(j) What is wrong with the following attempts to explain the miracle:
    (i) The people brought their own food with them.
    (ii) The people shared the picnics of those who had brought them with them.
    (iii) The people went off and bought food from the shops.
    (iv) The people caught fish in the lake.

(k) Find John 6:9. What extra details does this version mention?

10. Find Mark 6:47–56.

(a) At what time of day did this miracle occur?

(b) Briefly tell the story in your own words.

(c) What is added to the story in the version given in Matthew 14:22–36?

11. Find Mark 4:35–40.

(a) What happened on this occasion?

(b) Where was Jesus when the storm blew up?

(c) What was the cause of the storm?

(d) How did Jesus calm the storm?

(e) Would Galilean sailors have been familiar with wind storms?

12. Find Mark 8:1–21.

(a) How many loaves and fishes did they have this time?

(b) How many baskets of leftovers were taken?

(c) How many people were fed?

(d) Why do you think Jesus was disappointed and angry with them in the boat afterwards?

(e) What did the Pharisees want, in verses 11–12?

(f) Look up Matthew 16:1–4. What sign did Jesus say *would* be given to them?

(g) Find Jonah 1:17 (in the Old Testament). How long was Jonah in the belly of the fish? Could this have been referring to Jesus' death and resurrection?

13. Find Matthew 17:24–27.
(a) Did Jesus pay his taxes or not?
(b) Where did Peter find the shekel to pay with?
(c) What sort of fish in Galilee carries shiny objects in its mouth?

(Work on the miraculous catch of fish can be found on p. 64; work on the cursing of the fig-tree can be found on pp. 171–3.)

Creative Writing

Many modern scholars try to convince people that this sort of miracle is simply impossible – nothing but a legend created by simple and rather stupid people. Yet the descriptions are full of little circumstantial details that do not look as if they were made up. There are many mysterious things that still happen in the world today. Science is a long way from knowing all the answers, and in fact this present generation is seeing a new humility and open-mindedness.

Pretend you are a witness of one of these nature miracles. Describe in your own words what happened, and try to think out what this implied about the powers of Jesus.

29
THE CLIMAX OF THE MINISTRY

As soon as Jesus felt the time was ripe, he organised the disciples to go on practice missions. He no doubt realised that the amount of time that he would be left in freedom to continue his ministry would be very limited, and wanted to prepare them so that they would be able to carry on when he had gone. He decided that they should each go out with one companion, to preach and explain about the Kingdom of God to anyone who would listen. They were also given the ability to heal and cast out demons, and their usual method of healing seems to have been to anoint the sick with oil.

They were not to take any provisions for their journey, such as money or food or extra clothing, but to rely absolutely on other people's generosity for their needs. In any village that received them, they were to stay at the first house that offered hospitality, and not to choose out the most comfortable or luxurious, and thereby give offence to others. If it so happened that a village was not willing to receive them, then they were simply to leave, and not linger where they were not wanted. The time was too short.

In St Matthew's version, Jesus restricted the mission to the Jews only, and told them to bypass Gentile and Samaritan settlements. He also added a great deal of advice which some scholars believe to be instructions to the early Church that belong to a much later date, when Christians were really suffering from persecution.

They were to be like sheep in the midst of wolves; to live blameless lives so that their accusers might not have a case against them. They were warned that they could run into a great deal of trouble, but the Holy Spirit would put into their heads what they were to say, when the time came. God knew everything that would happen – He saw the whole picture. Not a sparrow fell to the ground without Him knowing. It was most important that they should take His kingdom seriously, and not be afraid of the people trying to hurt them.

St Luke's Gospel mentions another practice mission, this time involving seventy or seventy-two disciples, not just the twelve. This mission is reported only in St Luke's Gospel, and one wonders whether it is perhaps just another version of the first one – but then, why should he have included both stories in his book? Some scholars think that St Luke wanted to tell about a mission to the Gentiles as well as the Jews, and that the number 'seventy-two' gives us the clue. 'Twelve' was supposed to represent the twelve tribes of Israel, and 'seventy-two' the number of Gentile nations of the world – as they thought then. Certainly the instructions given are virtually the same. St Luke's account ends with the disciples returning in great excitement over their success, and Jesus being pleased on their behalf.

Some time after these missions, Jesus took his disciples to the region of Caesarea Philippi, in the area governed by Antipas' brother Philip. He felt that his Galilean ministry was drawing to a close and the time had come to try out the opinions of his disciples. What conclusions had they formed about him, after all that they had seen and done? He asked them what the general opinion of the people was, and they replied that there was some confusion. Some thought he was a prophet, perhaps Elijah, or even John the Baptist come back again from the dead. Then Jesus asked for their opinion, and Peter, as the spokesman for the group, admitted for the first time in public that they thought Jesus really was the Messiah.

Jesus was delighted, and gave Peter the instructions to be the founder of his Church – according to St Matthew's version. There is a difference of opinion over what was to be the 'rock' on which the Church was to be founded. Jesus may have meant Peter, or he may have meant the truth about himself that Peter had just stated – in which case, the rock would be Jesus himself. Crossed keys have become the symbol of St Peter – the symbol of rule and authority over a household.

However, the moment of joy was short-lived. Jesus immediately began to shatter any high hopes the disciples might have had about a glorious future. He was not going to ride into Jerusalem as a military leader and tackle the Romans; on the contrary, he was to be betrayed and arrested, and put to death by the priests – the very people who should have supported him. Peter was horrified. He could not believe that this could really be true after all that he had expected and worked for. He tried to reason with Jesus, and Jesus suddenly knew that he was once more facing the third temptation all over again – to be ambitious and successful, and to rule the world. He rounded sharply on Peter and said, 'Get thee behind me, Satan!' He put the temptation behind him again.

Six days later, he took Peter, James and John up a high mountain, where they were allowed a brief glimpse of his true glory and radiance. Six days was the length of time often taken by Jews for

158

strict ritual purification before an important spiritual event. The high mountain concerned has not been identified for certain. There is a strong tradition that it was Mount Tabor, but it seems more likely that it was Mount Hermon, just to the north of Caesarea Philippi.

On the mountain a mysterious event took place that is known as the **transfiguration**. As the disciples watched, Jesus' clothes began to shine with brilliant light, and the figures of Moses and Elijah appeared and talked with him.

It has been suggested that Moses and Elijah appeared at this important moment because they, of all people, represented the Old Testament – the Law and the prophets. According to ancient traditions, neither of them had experienced normal human death. Both had had exciting confrontations with God on a mountain in their own times.

Peter then spoke, and suggested making three tabernacles or shelters, and St Mark's Gospel reveals that the watching disciples were overcome with fear and did not really know what to say. Finally, a cloud overshadowed them and they heard a voice speaking to them. The cloud was no ordinary one, but the cloud of God's presence that had guided Israel through its times of wandering. The voice was very similar to the one that had been heard at Jesus' baptism, but this time the disciples heard it. It said, 'This is my beloved son; listen to him.' It reassured Jesus, and gave the divine approval to the course of action he was about to take.

After the voice, the vision faded as suddenly as it had begun, and they were alone upon the mountain. Jesus advised them to keep what they had seen to themselves, until he had risen from the dead. Twice more he predicted the certainty of his having to suffer and die, and the third time he described his fate in great detail. Some scholars think that this prediction is so detailed that it must have been written by the Church fathers after the events had actually happened; but others believe that Jesus really did have this foreknowledge, and set out to go to Jerusalem *knowing* what it would mean for him.

Questions and Research

1. Find Matthew 10:5–33.
(a) What were the disciples told to do?
(b) What instructions were they given in verses 9–13?
(c) Why do you think Jesus wanted the twelve to have this practice?
(d) What did Jesus say about the people who would not listen?
(e) What did Jesus warn might happen to the disciples?
(f) How did Jesus encourage them, in verses 26–33?

Mount Tabor *This mountain is the traditional site of the Transfiguration of Jesus, although many authorities would place the event on the slopes of Mount Hermon. Mount Tabor was a wooded slope rising out of the vast plain near Nazareth.*

(g) Copy out verse 39.
(h) Find Luke 10:1–12. How many people were sent out this time?
(i) Why is it suggested that St Luke included this mission?
(j) Make a chart to compare the instructions given to the disciples in Matthew 10 and Luke 10.
(k) What was the result of the mission, as recorded in Luke 10:17–20?

2. Find Mark 8:28–9:1.
(a) What did Jesus ask his disciples at Caesarea Philippi?
(b) What answers was he given?
(c) What conclusion had the disciples formed about him?
(d) Who was the spokesman for the group?
(e) Find Matthew 16:16–19. What did Jesus say to Peter?
(f) Go back to Mark 8:31. What did Jesus say would happen to himself?
(g) Why did Peter rebuke him?
(h) Why did Jesus called Peter 'Satan'?
(i) What two promises did Jesus make in Mark 8:35–39?

3. Find Mark 9:1–7.
(a) Which three disciples went with Jesus?
(b) Which mountains have been suggested for this event?

160

(c) What happened to Jesus' clothing?
(d) Which two figures did they see?
(e) What did those persons represent?
(f) Which disciple tried to speak to them?
(g) What was the reaction of the disciples to what they could see?
(h) What other strange thing did they see?
(i) What did they hear?
(j) There are two mentions in the gospels about a voice from heaven. When was the voice heard the first time?
(k) Find these passages in the Old Testament, and report what it says there about the Shekinah, the cloud of God's presence: Exodus 13:22; 24:15–16; 40:34. Also look at Acts 1:9 in the New Testament.
(l) What does it say about Moses in Exodus 34:29–35?
(m) What did Elijah discover about God in I Kings 19:11–12?

4. Find Mark 8:31; 9:30–31; 10:32–34.
(a) What exactly did Jesus predict in Mark 8:31?
(b) Are the words any different in Mark 9:30–31?
(c) What details were given in the prediction as it occurs in Mark 10:32–34?
(d) Which of the predictions is the most detailed?
(e) What do some scholars think about this prediction?
(i) If Jesus really knew these things in advance, what does it indicate about his character?

Creative Writing

Either: Imagine that you are one of the disciples setting out on the practice mission. Describe how you feel about starting your work, and the instructions you have been given.
Or: Imagine that you are one of the three disciples who saw the transfiguration of Jesus. Describe what you saw then, and what effect this strange event had on you.

30

CAUSES OF OPPOSITION

During Christ's lifetime he did not always meet with unqualified success. Because he was always so forthright and honest, he inevitably made enemies; and, far from being a meek and mild milksop, desperate to placate them, his uncompromising actions led him into the attack as he challenged peoples' ideals and principles.

Jesus met his opposition in the main from three directions: the Pharisees, the Sadducees and the priests. He met with very little opposition from the ordinary people (with the exception of his neighbours at Nazareth at the start of his ministry), because, on the whole, they were delighted with his preaching and appreciated his healings, and probably enjoyed his attacks on the pompous and hypocritical village worthies. Don't think that all Pharisees disliked Jesus – many of them loved him and agreed with all he had to say.

The people who opposed Jesus were those who had reason to fear him – either because he was showing them up for what they were, proving that they were not really living up to the standards they set for themselves and for others; or because they could see that he posed a threat to their most treasured beliefs and customs. Some feared him for purely political reasons. They knew that people who claimed falsely to be the Messiah would not be able to defeat the Romans, and would only bring terrible reprisals upon their nation.

The Sanhedrin, the ruling council of the Jews, took the matter very seriously indeed. They were frightened that if Jesus started rousing the crowds, the Romans would take ruthless action and destroy the whole nation. They were also very worried that, if not the whole nation, then the Romans would become impatient with the national religion which had given birth to these fanatics and destroy the Temple and wipe out the priests.

The priests, except when they were off duty, lived and worked near the Temple of Jerusalem, the only place where sacrifices were allowed to be made. And only priests were allowed to offer these sacrifices – it was not like the old days of Abraham, when anyone could make a sacrifice if he felt like it. Moreover, the priests had

Herod's Temple, Jerusalem *This reconstruction of what the Temple may have looked like can be seen in the grounds of a Jerusalem hotel. The innermost court could only be entered by priests. The castle in the background was the Roman barracks, the Antonia fortress, where Jesus may have been taken for trial.*

the right to decide whether or not an animal was suitable for sacrifice, and made life easier for the general public by breeding and raising their own sheep and oxen especially for the Temple. These special animals were actually sold in the Temple premises, in the Court of the Gentiles, and fetched a high price. Since money with the image of the Roman Emperor on it was not allowed in the Temple, they even made a profit out of a coin exchange, before their special animals could be bought! This system had gone on for years, but Jesus had very definite views about it.

Questions and Research

1. Find Mark 11:11, 15–19.
(a) What did Jesus do on his first visit to the Temple?
(b) Describe what happened on his second appearance there.
(c) What do you think the reaction of the priests in charge would be to all this?

2. Find Mark 11: 27–33.
(a) What did the priests ask Jesus?
(b) How did Jesus avoid giving them a straight answer?
(c) If the priests had admitted that John was a genuine prophet of

God – and since John had identified Jesus as Messiah when he baptised him – what would the priests have had to admit about Jesus?

3. Find Mark 12:1–12.
(a) Write out the parable of the vineyard carefully.
(b) Make the following list:
    Farmer = God.
    Vineyard = God's Kingdom, His people.
    Tenants = those in charge of it, the priests.
    Servants = those 'checking up', the prophets.
    The son = Jesus himself.
    The others = God's new people, the Christians.
(c) Was Jesus being polite to the priests, or critical?
(d) How had the priests treated God's prophets in the past?
(e) What did Jesus think the priests would do to him?
(f) What would happen to the priests, the supposed guardians of God's Kingdom?
(g) Who would the new people of God be?
(h) Do you think the priests would have liked Jesus stirring up feeling against them in this way?

4. Find Mark 12:28–34.
(a) What did the scribe ask?
(b) What did Jesus answer?
(c) What was the scribe's reaction to the answer?
(d) Do you think the other priests would have agreed with verse 33?

5. Find John 11:47–54.
(a) Why was the council worried about Jesus?
(b) Who was Caiaphas?
(c) What did Caiaphas think should be done?
(d) What was Jesus' reaction when he heard of the plots to destroy him?

*

Jesus was once picked up for a 'party-political' question. Most of the priests were also Sadducees, and one of their main disagreements with the Pharisees was on the question of life after death. The Pharisees accepted that there was such a thing, with rewards or punishments according to what one deserved. They thought that an after-life was necessary since so many of the good died young, which would have been most unfair of a God of justice! Persons after death could become forces either for good or for evil, and when they managed to make anyone on earth see them or notice them, they were known as either angels or demons. The Sadducees believed none of this – as far as they were concerned, once you were dead you were dead. There was no evidence in the Old Testament for purposeful life after death. Any place for the de-parted was the dread shadow-land under the earth called **Sheol**. Pharisees and Sadducees were always arguing about their beliefs – and because Jesus accepted life after death, angels and demons, the Sadducees assumed that he was a Pharisee, and attempted to make fun of him.

However, since Jesus spent most of his ministry far away from Jerusalem in the north country of Galilee, most of his opposition came from the Galilean Pharisees. They started off by welcoming him with open arms as one of themselves, but pretty soon realised that Jesus had ideas of his own. He kept doing the wrong things and outraging them. He mixed with the despised tax-collectors, and street women, and Gentiles and Samaritans – people that the Pharisees thought made you unclean if no more than their shadow fell across you in the street.

Secondly, the thing that was dearest to the hearts of the Pharisees was their tradition. Jesus took no notice of it if he thought it was wrong or if it had missed the point. Local Pharisees were very offended when he tried to show them that they were wrong. They considered him to be an upstart. Jesus argued that sometimes, in their efforts to keep the letter of the Law, they broke with the spirit of it. Two examples he gave were the practice of regarding contact with 'unclean' persons and things as defilement, without realising that real defilement came from evil thoughts and practices within; and the noble practice of **corban**, making a gift to God, was being used to deprive certain parents of their rightful due.

Questions and Research

1. Find Mark 12:18–27.
(a) What was the question the Sadducees asked him?
(b) What were they really trying to prove by their question?
(c) What did Jesus say about marriage in the after-life?
(d) What do you think he meant by the 'angels'?
(e) If Abraham, Isaac and Jacob all died at different times, with many years in between their deaths, what does verse 26 imply about the after-life?

2. Find Mark 2:23–26. What tradition did Jesus' disciples break on this occasion?
3. Find Mark 7:1–6. What did they do wrong this time?

4. Find Mark 7:21–23. What did Jesus say were the things that really made people unclean?
5. Find Mark 7:9–13. Something *corban* was promised under oath for God's use. Sometimes people made their money *corban* so that they did not have to look after their aged parents. What did Jesus say about the practice in this passage?
6. Healings were not allowed on the sabbath, unless it was a matter of life or death. We are told of four healings that Jesus performed quite openly on the sabbath, and in each case the Pharisees were very annoyed indeed. The first time it took them by surprise, for it was one of Jesus' very first healings; but the second time they were ready and waiting for him.
(a) Find Mark 1:21–28. Describe what happened very briefly in your own words.
(b) Find Mark 3:1–6. Describe very briefly what happened on this occasion.
(c) Find Luke 13:10–17. What was wrong with the woman? How did Jesus heal her? How did Jesus justify doing it on the sabbath? Notice in verse 17 how Jesus 'put to shame' those who did not think as he did, and how the people around him 'rejoiced'. That must have annoyed the Pharisees.
(d) Find Luke 14:1–6. What was wrong with the man? With what direct question did Jesus challenge his critics? Why shouldn't a Jew have pulled an ox out of a well on a sabbath day? Why would he have done?

7. Another of Jesus' healings upset the Pharisees for quite a different reason. Jesus claimed that he could forgive sins, and as far as the Pharisees were concerned, that was blasphemy. Only God could forgive sins – was Jesus claiming to be God? Or as powerful as God? Jesus challenged them by asking whether the miracle itself was not a proof of the validity of what he had just done.
Find Luke 5:17–26. Write the story briefly in your own words.

*

Occasionally Jesus wanted so much to puncture the Pharisees' false composure that he deliberately said things against them. He forgave the sins of a prostitute while a guest in the house of a Pharisee, and also put his host to shame for not treating him with the proper courtesies.

The Pharisees also came in for criticism in the most famous of all parables: the prodigal son. Jesus had eaten with the publicans and sinners, and outraged the Pharisaic sense of propriety by making himself unclean, in their view. The Pharisees thought that one should remain clean in order to help the brethren who deserved their help. Their unwillingness to forgive a sinner who turned back was criticised sharply. The Pharisees were already safe and happy and prosperous in God's love, so they should have been willing to open their arms to receive back the sinner. They should have been glad to see tax-men being converted, not grumbling because Jesus was mixing with them.

The whole question of Jesus' relationships with the unclean can be seen when Jesus called the tax-man Matthew to be one of his closest disciples. The Pharisees found it impossible to understand Jesus accepting an unclean man among his friends and helpers.

In St Matthew, Chapter 23, there is a stern and terrible condemnation of the hypocritical Pharisees. These may not be the actual words of Jesus, but if they reflect the gist of his opinions, one can see why the Pharisees felt affronted and indignant. Not all Pharisees were hypocrites. Some were very holy men indeed, and Jesus recognised this and gave them credit in Matthew 5:20. Many of them loved and accepted Jesus, and agreed with what he was teaching. But the majority were suspicious and resentful of him.

At one point they had asked Jesus to give them a special sign to prove that he really was the Messiah, but he refused to oblige them and referred them back to the scriptures. It was up to them to make their minds up from what they saw and heard, like everyone else. Jesus was angry with them, and referred to them as being the evil influence in Israel, like yeast spreading through a loaf.

Although they loathed the Sadducees, and the luxurious pro-Roman living of the priests, they were prepared to join forces with them in order to do away with the menace that threatened them all – Jesus of Nazareth.

Questions and Research

1. Find Luke 7:36–50.
(a) What happened when Jesus was dining at a Pharisee's house?
(b) How had the Pharisee offended Jesus?
(c) What was the parable of the two debtors?
(d) What did it mean?
(e) Which of the two debtors meant the woman, and which the Pharisee?

2. Find Luke 15:1–2, 11–32.
(a) Why were the Pharisees upset by Jesus?
(b) Which of the farmer's sons was supposed to represent the tax-man and which the Pharisees?

(c) When the prodigal son returned, what was the reaction of the eldest brother?

(d) What should it have been?

3. Find Matthew 9:9–13.

(a) What was Matthew's profession?

(b) What was the Pharisees' reaction to Jesus' actions?

(c) What did Jesus say in verses 12–13?

4. Find Matthew 23.

(a) In what way did the hypocritical Pharisees do their good deeds?

(b) What sort of things did they love?

(c) What did Jesus call them in verse 16?

(d) Copy out verse 23.

(e) How did Jesus compare them to graves or dead people?

5. Find Matthew 16:1–4.

(a) What did the Pharisees want Jesus to do?

(b) What sign did Jesus say would be the only one given to them?

(c) Find Jonah 1:17, in the Old Testament. How long had Jonah been in the belly of the fish?

(d) What do you think Jesus could have been referring to by this sign?

Creative Writing

Either: Imagine that you are a tax-collector in Capernaum, one of the guests dining with Jesus. How would you defend Jesus' action in befriending you to an angry and critical Pharisee?

Or: Imagine that you are a Galilean Pharisee writing to a friend in Jerusalem. Tell him what you think about this new prophet and his attitude to people and the Law. (You could either agree or disagree with Jesus' campaign.)

31

THE TRIUMPHAL ENTRY INTO JERUSALEM

According to the gospels, Jesus went up to Jerusalem to celebrate the Feast of the Passover on a Sunday, and within one week he had been tried, executed and buried, and his body had disappeared. His followers' emotions had changed swiftly from wild excitement and joy to horror and disbelief, and finally bewilderment with a ray of hope. This final week of Christ's earthly life is known as **Holy Week**.

It divides up into three main sections: (a) the events of each day from the Sunday to the Thursday; (b) the arrest, trials and execution of Jesus; (c) the resurrection appearances of Jesus (resurrection meaning the rising again of Jesus' body, which vanished from the tomb).

As with the birth narratives, each gospel varies in the events it picks out and the emphasis it places on those events. For example, Matthew and Luke suggest that Jesus overturned the tables of the money-changers in the Temple immediately he went there, on the Sunday, whereas Mark has him going out to Bethany and coming back again on the Monday to do it. In Mark's version, when Jesus curses a fig-tree, it dies overnight, but Matthew has it withering away on the spot as they watch. Luke leaves this incident out altogether. Mark and Luke tell of the offering of the poor widow, but Matthew leaves that out. Matthew has a collection of parables not found in the other gospels. Mark and Matthew record the anointing of Jesus at Bethany, but Luke omits it entirely.

Palm Sunday

When Jesus arrived at Bethphage on the Mount of Olives, he sent two of his disciples on ahead with instructions to fetch him an ass. He intended to ride into Jerusalem. Now, it is very unlikely that Jesus was suffering from exhaustion, or that he would have ridden so selfishly while his followers stumbled on with their blistered feet. It seems obvious that Jesus had a very specific purpose in wanting to ride the animal. The whole business of Jesus knowing about the animal waiting for him, and the reaction of the ass's owner, is somewhat amazing.

The disciples were told that they would see a colt tied at a door out in the open street, and they were simply to untie it and take it away. If anyone spoke to them or tried to stop them, they were to say, 'The Lord has need of it.' How did Jesus know that this ass would be there waiting for him, and that the owner would let it go so willingly? It looks rather as if the whole transaction had been arranged in advance by Jesus himself. The disciples were obviously in the dark about what was going on, but Jesus seems to have been instructing them to give the unnamed owner a password.

Sure enough, when they went to the village, presumably Bethany, they found everything happened exactly as Jesus had said that it would. Jesus must have had friends in Bethany. If we read further on into the story of Holy Week, we discover that he actually spent the nights of Sunday to Wednesday with friends there, who are identified in Mark 14:3 as the household of Simon the leper. If we look at John 12:1–8 we see that Simon was possibly another name for Lazarus (which means 'leper'), or he may possibly have been his father. This Lazarus was the brother of the two sisters Mary and Martha, who are mentioned in Luke 10:38–42. These were possibly the friends with whom Jesus had made the arrangements for the ass.

But *why* did Jesus make his entry into Jerusalem in this fashion? Why did the crowd go wild with enthusiasm and cheer him into the city? Why should the crowd be so excited, and the Pharisees so alarmed? Luke's version reports that the Pharisees were very worried, and tried to stop the people shouting out. Jesus, however, did not stop them. He said if they were silent, then the very stones would cry out. The hour had come!

Was what Jesus was doing a special sign? If we turn to the Old Testament, we find a prophecy that suggests that it *was*. Jesus was deliberately and publicly claiming, at long last, that he was the Messiah they were waiting for. Matthew's version actually gives the prophecy, from Zechariah, that their king would enter Jerusalem in triumph, riding on an ass. A horse would have signified that a battle was about to take place, but the ass was the animal of peace, and signified that the battle had already been fought and won. Jesus was fulfilling this sign: he rode into Jerusalem as the Messiah-king, in triumph.

The people realised this and cheered him in, placing garments and palm branches down for him to ride over. They shouted, 'Hosanna to the Son of David! Blessed is he who comes in the name of the Lord!' The people of Jerusalem were astounded, and rushed to find out what was going on. The crowd informed them that the Messianic claimant was the prophet Jesus from Nazareth in Galilee.

Questions and Research

Find Mark 11:1–10.
(a) Where did Jesus stop and wait?
(b) What did Jesus ask his disciples to do?
(c) What were they to say when questioned?
(d) Where did they find the colt?
(e) Do you think the owner of the ass would have let the animal go so easily if it had not been arranged?
(f) Find Luke 19:39–40. What did the Pharisees say to Jesus?
(g) What did Jesus reply to this?
(h) Find Matthew 21:4–5. What prophecy was Jesus fulfilling?
(i) Find Zechariah 9:9 (in the Old Testament). Read through to the end of the chapter. Copy out verses 14 and 16.
(j) Turn back to Matthew 21:2–7. Matthew seems to have taken the prophecy rather literally. What rather odd detail does he add to the story?

Jesus and the fig tree

The next event is one that poses several problems, of all kinds. According to St Mark's Gospel, Jesus went straight to the Temple after his entry into Jerusalem on the Sunday, but as it was then evening, and getting dark, he turned back to Bethany with his twelve disciples, presumably to stay with his friends. It would take about half an hour to walk from the Temple to Bethany.

Then, on the Monday, as Jesus was going back to Jerusalem, he noticed a fig-tree. Feeling hungry, he went to see if it had any figs on it, although it was not the season for them. When he found nothing, he cursed the tree. According to Matthew, the tree withered immediately; but according to Mark, they saw that it had died when they went along the same road the next day.

It has been suggested that if the story of the miracle was true, then the action of Jesus was most unreasonable. The figs were not in season, so Jesus shouldn't have expected to find any – and he certainly shouldn't then have indulged in what looked like a fit of temper. Some have tried to make allowances for his un-Christlike tantrum by saying that old figs might still reasonably be left on the tree from the previous year. Others have suggested that perhaps the tree was dying anyway, and that Jesus knew this, and simply speeded up the natural process. One feels a need to make excuses for Jesus. Certainly the tradition behind the story must have been

171

exceedingly strong, for it was hardly the sort of thing that one of the Church fathers would have invented.

Jesus cursed the tree and it died. If this story is true, it is of vital importance – for it is the only recorded miracle that suggests that Jesus had the power to destroy. It might explain why the soldiers who came to arrest him, according to St John's version, were so reluctant to lay hands on him, and when they did so, trussed him up with heavy thongs. They were possibly afraid of what he might do to *them*!

The miracle makes the events that follow so much more moving. Jesus was to submit to extreme physical torture culminating in his death, without resisting. To add salt to his wounds, the priests had convinced themselves that this form of death proved that Jesus could not possibly have been the Messiah – it was a death cursed by the Law of God. They challenged him to prove himself by resisting and overcoming this brutal end – yet he refused to do so. He fulfilled his own words of Luke 6:27–28, to love his enemies and pray for those who were tormenting him. What incredible self-control, and what tremendous generosity and compassion for his enemies!

Yet the cursing of the fig-tree obviously caused embarrassment. St Luke's Gospel omitted the miracle altogether. However, he did have in his gospel a parable about a fig-tree which was not in the other gospels, and it has been suggested that this was his version of the occurrence. In it the farmer represented God, and the fig-tree was the Jewish people. Instead of being loyal and true to God, they had 'borne no fruit' – their religion had become hypocritical. The vine-dresser represented someone who pleaded to God not to cast them off without waiting till the last possible moment. Tragically, for them, the last moment had come.

If this parable was connected with the incident, it could well be that the cursing of the fig-tree in Holy Week was a **symbolic act** of Jesus, intended to underline the very point made in St Luke's parable. This kind of 'acted parable' was not unknown among the Old Testament prophets; the tree was a fairly frequent symbol for a nation. The point Jesus was making could have been that Israel was making a great show of being vigorous and healthy in spiritual growth, and a healthy crop of good fruit might reasonably have been expected. Sadly, when one looked closely, this was not seen to be the case: the fig-tree was barren. Israel was pretending to be what she was not. She would be judged. The time had come, the Kingdom of Heaven was in their midst, the moment of judgement was there. For those on the wrong side, it was already too late. Like the fruitless fig-tree, they would be cut down.

172

Questions and Research

1. Acted parables.
(a) Find Jeremiah 13:1–11. What was this strange acted parable all about?
(b) Find Jeremiah 18:1–10. What did Jeremiah learn from watching the potter at work?
(c) Ezekiel 4:1–3. What lesson did Ezekiel teach with his brick?
(d) Ezekiel 5:1–4. What acted parable was used here to indicate the fate of the people?

2. Find Jeremiah 11:16. Israel was here compared to a tree about to be destroyed. Copy out this verse.
3. Find Mark 11:12–14, 20–24.
(a) What was wrong with the fig-tree?
(b) What did Jesus say to it?
(c) What was the result, as observed the next morning?
(d) Copy out verses 23–24.
(e) Find Matthew 21:18–22. What was different about the miracle in this version?

4. Find Luke 13:6–9.
(a) Write out the parable of the fig-tree.
(b) Why did the farmer want to cut it down?
(c) Who were the people 'not bearing fruit' with whom God was disappointed?

Creative Writing

Imagine that you are one of those approaching the Temple with Jesus. Describe how you felt and what you saw, and what the atmosphere was like among the crowd.

32

THE CLEANSING OF THE TEMPLE

The great Temple at Jerusalem was the only place, in the time of Jesus, where the Jews were allowed to offer sacrifices, although in Old Testament times any high place would have sufficed. After the reign of King Josiah, worship had been centralised at Jerusalem, and only the priests there could perform the sacrifices.

The site of the Temple was the old threshing floor of a man called Araunah the Jebusite, from whom King David had bought it for 600 shekels of gold (II Samuel 24:18–25). It was on this spot that the Lord had stayed His hand after a serious outbreak of plague. The site itself may have been the very spot where Abraham prepared to offer up his son Isaac (Genesis 22). David did not actually build a Temple, but contented himself with bringing to Jerusalem the Ark of God in its holy tent, the Tabernacle – and organising priests, Levites, singers and an orchestra (II Samuel 6). The task of building the Temple was taken on by his son Solomon, who achieved this during the fourth to eleventh years of his reign (I Kings 5–6). It was a small building, obviously designed not to admit worshippers but to act as an inner sanctum for God.

In 597 B.C. it was burnt to the ground by Nebuchadrezzar, the conquering Babylonian king (Jeremiah 52:13). During the reign of Zerubbabel, after the exile, in about 516 B.C., it was rebuilt. A vast amount of repair work was done (Ezra 6:15). But the Ark had disappeared and never came back to the Temple. What happened to it remains a subject of much speculation, but ancient tradition suggests that it was hidden by the priests, and the secret guarded too well by too few until finally it became lost altogether.

The Temple never regained its former glory until the reign of Herod the Great. He began rebuilding and enlarging it in about the year 20 B.C. and the work was not finished until long after his death. Only five years after its completion in A.D. 65, it was burnt to the ground by the invading Roman troops.

Herod had enlarged the sacred area to about thirty-five acres, with many auxiliary buildings. It was made of white limestone, and there was a lavish use of gold. It was divided into four courts: one for anybody, including Gentile visitors; one for Jews of either sex, provided they had no physical imperfections; one for all Jewish males over the age of twelve; and one for priests alone. As the Temple was built on the hill of Zion, the courts ascended through different levels, the most sacred enclosure being at the very top.

The only part of Herod's vast building to survive to this day is a wall of massive stones which originally formed part of the Temple substructure.

Animals for sacrifice had to satisfy all sorts of regulations, and to save people from being disappointed at having their own livestock rejected as not good enough, the priests used to provide suitable animals for sale. Naturally, they took a profit on their sales. Since they sold these animals in the Temple itself, another problem arose. The ordinary money used by the people was Roman coin, which always had the Caesar's head on it, and because Caesar was supposed to be a god, it was an insult to the True God to bring the image of a rival deity into the Temple. Therefore the priests used a special coinage, and before people could buy animals they had to buy the special Temple money. Again, a profit was taken, and it was these business practices in a place of worship that Jesus really objected to.

Any payments made in the Temple had to be in Tyrian currency. The Temple had become one of the chief banking centres of the Near East, and business was at its height at the feasts of Passover, Pentecost and Tabernacles. The court of the Gentiles was occupied by money-changers for the three weeks before the Temple tax fell due. Each changer sat at a table, which may have been covered in glass, and when uncertain of the genuineness of a coin would drop it and listen carefully to the sound, to see if it 'rang true' (see I Thessalonians 5:21).

All this activity took place in the Court of the Gentiles, which was divided from the main part of the Temple by a barrier. Gentiles and invalids were not allowed past this barrier, on pain of death (see Acts 21:29). Nothing imperfect could be allowed to draw nigh to God's presence (Leviticus 21:17–21).

The Treasury Chests for the offerings, where Jesus saw the poor widow put in her two little coins, were in the Court of Women, the area in which the women and children were obliged to wait while their menfolk went through to the inner court. Only a Jew without blemish was allowed to make an offering here at all. There were thirteen chests, known as 'trumpets', because they were narrow at the mouth and wide at the bottom, and each was for a set purpose.

The great Altar was in the open air, in full view of the men. It was built of unhewn blocks of stone, and stood 48 feet square and 15 feet high. A circuit ran round it for the priests, who approached

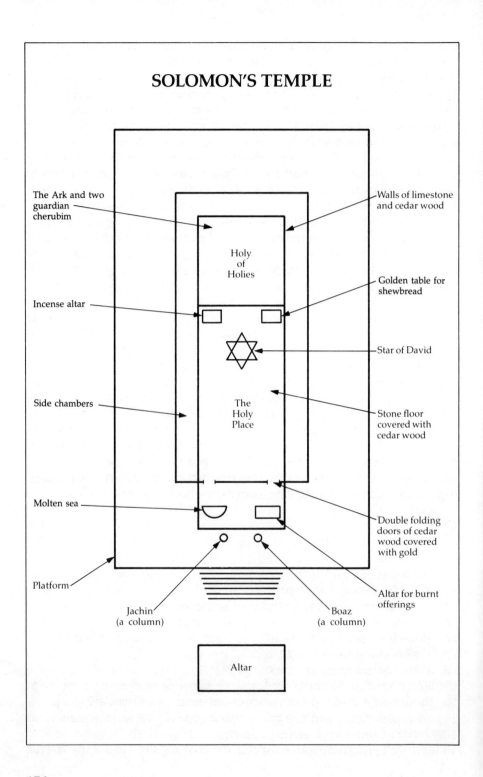

SOLOMON'S TEMPLE

The Ark and two guardian cherubim

Walls of limestone and cedar wood

Holy of Holies

Incense altar

Golden table for shewbread

Star of David

Side chambers

The Holy Place

Stone floor covered with cedar wood

Molten sea

Double folding doors of cedar wood covered with gold

Platform

Altar for burnt offerings

Jachin (a column)

Boaz (a column)

Altar

it from the right and retired by the left. This circuit was raised 9 feet from the ground, and a ramp 48 feet long merged with it from the south. Close by was a great heap of salt which was regularly thrown on to the ramp to stop the barefoot priests from slipping. The Altar was in the open air for very practical reasons. Large quantities of blood were shed there daily, and three fires burnt on it all day. It is very hard for us to visualise fully what exactly the sacrificial ritual must have involved – the smell and the flies were said to be overpowering at times. There was an elaborate system of drains beneath the Temple, so that it could be easily sluiced down.

Near the Altar were the necessary requisites for the sacrifices: six rows of four rings to fasten the sacrifices to while they were waiting to be slaughtered; eight marble tables for dealing with the flesh and fat, and cleaning the animals' insides; eight low columns set with three hooks each, for hanging up the pieces of meat once they had been butchered; another marble table for laying them out; and a silver table for the gold and silver vessels of the service.

Apart from their own sacrifices, two lambs and a bull were slaughtered every day with prayers for the well-being of the Roman emperor. It was the stopping of this sacrifice in A.D. 66 that in fact signalled the start of the famous Jewish Revolt.

Presumably Jesus did not object to the sacrifices – he and his family must have made many themselves. Yet his reply to the question asked of him by a scribe indicates his real feelings about those ancient ceremonies. The scribe said that to love God with all one's heart, mind, soul and strength, and to love one's neighbour as oneself, was worth more to God than all the burnt offerings and sacrifices. When Jesus saw that he answered wisely, he commended him, and said that he was not far from the Kingdom of God.

Questions

1. Where was the great Temple?
2. Who bought the original site?
3. Who built the first Temple?
4. Who burnt the first Temple to the ground?
5. In whose reign was the second Temple built?
6. Who rebuilt and enlarged the Temple at the time of Jesus?
7. What was it largely made of?
8. Who were the main courts for?
9. What part of Herod's building works still remains?
10. Why could Roman coins not be used in the Temple?
11. In which court did the money-changers have their tables?
12. Where were the Treasury chests?
13. Give a brief description of the Great Altar.

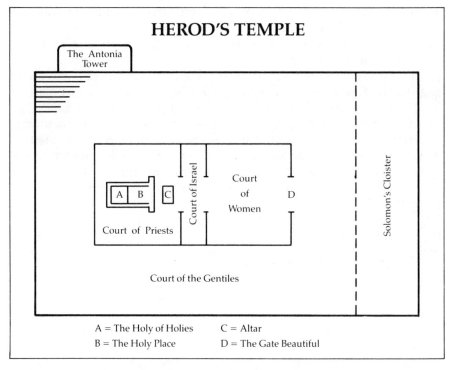

HEROD'S TEMPLE

The Antonia Tower

A = The Holy of Holies
B = The Holy Place
C = Altar
D = The Gate Beautiful

Court of Israel

Court of Women

Court of Priests

Court of the Gentiles

Solomon's Cloister

A B C

D

14. What act signalled the start of the Jewish Revolt?

Research

1. Find Mark 11:15–19.
(a) How did Jesus cause chaos in the Temple?
(b) Which courtyard would this have been in?
(c) What did Jesus say to them?
(d) Find John 2:13–22. What details are added in verses 15–16?
(e) What did Jesus say when asked for a sign?
(f) What was he really talking about?

2. Find Mark 11:27–33.
(a) Who came and asked the first question?
(b) What was Jesus asked?
(c) What event had just taken place in the Temple that probably 'sparked off' that question?
(d) Did Jesus give them a straight answer?
(e) What did he in turn ask them about?
(f) Copy out the following reasons why the priests would have been reluctant to admit that John the Baptist was acting 'on his own authority':

(i) By the way he dressed and the things he said, he was deliberately claiming to be the forerunner of the Messiah. If he wasn't really, he must have either been a lunatic or a fraud.

(ii) John's parents were a respectable priest and a Levite woman.

(iii) The priests should have put John 'in care' if he had become a lunatic.

(g) If John had been a genuine prophet, acting on God's authority, what did this imply about his choice of Jesus as the Messiah?

(h) If the priests had admitted John's claim to be a genuine prophet, what would they have had to admit about Jesus?

3. Find Mark 12:13–17.

(a) Who asked Jesus the second question?

(b) What did they ask?

(c) What reply did Jesus give?

(d) What did the Romans want their tax-money for?

(e) Why did the Jews not use Roman money in the Temple?

(f) What would have happened to Jesus if he had refused to pay his taxes?

(g) Why would his followers have turned against him if he had been enthusiastic about paying Roman taxes?

(h) What do you think the 'things of God' could be?

(i) Make a note that some scholars have seen Jesus' reply as being very ambiguous. He might have meant that the loyalty and service and even the money of the Jews really belonged to God, not the Romans, and therefore Caesar had no right to them.

4. Find Mark 12:18–27.

(a) Who asked the third question?

(b) Briefly, what was it?

(c) Why should a Sadducee ask about resurrection or life after death?

(d) Which religious party did believe in it?

(e) What did Jesus' answer tell us about life after death?

5. Find Mark 12:28–34.

(a) Who asked the last question?

(b) What was it?

(c) Write out Jesus' answer in verses 29–30.

(d) What was the second greatest commandment?

(e) Why did Jesus say that the scribe was close to the Kingdom of Heaven?

(f) The answer Jesus gave was a quotation from the Old Testament known as the **Shema**, a passage which Jews recited daily. The word *shema* means 'listen' or 'hear'. Find Deuteronomy 6:4–9,

179

and copy it out. The Jews did keep copies of the Law in little boxes which they fastened round the arm or round the forehead when they went to the synagogue. These were called **phylacteries**. They also kept the Law in a little box fixed to the side of the door to the house, and touched it or kissed it every time they went in or out. These were called **Mezuzahs**.

Creative Writing

Either: Write a short play or dialogue summing up the argument between Jesus and the Pharisees and Sadducees.

Or: Pretend you are a bystander in the Court of the Gentiles on the occasion when Jesus drove out the money-changers. Give a description of what happened, and what your feelings were about Jesus' action.

33

WHAT DID JESUS PREDICT ABOUT THE END OF JERUSALEM?

Chapter 13 of St Mark's Gospel is unique in his book. It is a long, continuous section of Jesus' teachings in a literary form known at that time as an **Apocalypse**. The word 'apocalyptic' means to bring something out of hiding, to reveal secrets about some unknown thing or event. A great deal of apocalyptic teaching was also 'eschatological', another Greek word, referring to a study of 'the last things' (*ta eschata*), or the end of the world.

Many scholars find it hard to believe that this long speech was really made by Jesus, and think that it came from a writer living after the fall of Jerusalem. The suggestion is that someone who had lived through the destruction of Jerusalem in A.D. 70 was able to put references to those events into the mouth of Jesus. Possibly St Mark found the speech as a written document, and added it to his gospel. However, we have no concrete evidence that these are *not* the words of Jesus. The imagery used in the speech was fairly common among other apocalyptic writers, both before and after the time of Jesus, so there is no reason to suppose that Jesus could not also have used these expressions. In any case, there is no reason why Jesus should not have been able to prophesy future events in the same way that other prophets had done.

Apocalyptic literature often described visions that revealed future events, using symbolic language rather than plain speech. In the Old Testament, there are many examples of this kind of writing: Isaiah 13:9–11; 24:21–23; Chapters 25–27; Daniel Chapters 7–12; Joel 2; Ezekiel 32:7–10; Zechariah Chapters 9–14.

Jesus' speech opens when his attention is drawn to the huge stones Herod used in building his Temple. Jesus foretold that, in spite of their immensity and solidity, there would not be left one stone upon another. In similar fashion, Micah and Jeremiah had predicted the destruction of Solomon's Temple (see Micah 3:12; Jeremiah 26:6). Jesus' words were to come true in A.D. 70.

After this prophecy, the disciples asked him privately what the signs would be that the end was approaching. Jesus had previously warned them that they could expect sufferings and persecutions.

Now he warned them of false prophets, wars, earthquakes and famines. (Earthquakes and famines were not unknown in the Mediterranean, of course. Acts 11:28 refers to a terrible famine, and there were serious earthquakes in several places between A.D. 61 and 62.) The disciples would be arrested and delivered up to courts of law and be made to stand trial – but they were not to be afraid. God would inspire them with what they were to say when the time came. The hatred engendered by those against their message would even cause families to split up, and the terrible situation would arise of children informing on their parents and vice versa.

By the time that St Mark wrote his gospel, much of this prophecy had actually come true. The Christians in Rome were suffering fearful persecution – partly stemming from Nero as he tried to deflect the blame for causing the Great Fire of Rome on to the Christians in A.D. 64, and partly because many Romans naturally regarded the Christians as being a sect of Jewish extremists, and hated enemies – following the Zealot Revolution and the war against Rome. The Roman historian Tacitus recorded that Nero put many Christians to gruesome deaths in his arena, and even tied some of them to posts and set fire to them in order to use them as illuminations for his night-time shows. Many were crucified on low crosses, and wild beasts were let loose in the arena to feed on them while they were hanging there, still alive.

The details given in St Luke's Gospel about the collapse of Jerusalem were even more specific, and certainly looked as if St Luke was actually recalling the siege of Jerusalem.

Apocalyptic writing was intended to be a means of sustaining hope among an oppressed people, and was especially used during periods when any direct reference to the oppressors or their coming downfall would have been extremely dangerous. It was to encourage the persecuted that, no matter how black things might seem, God was still in control, and would soon put everything right for them. An Old Testament example of this is the Book of Daniel, written in the second century B.C. to bring comfort to faithful Jews who were suffering persecutions then, but pretending to be the life of a Jew who was a captive in Babylon in the sixth century B.C.

If the passage in St Mark's Gospel did come from a document, which was written perhaps around A.D. 40, the reference to the 'desolating sacrilege' in verse 14 might well refer to a statue of the Emperor Caliilgula in the guise of the Greek god Zeus that was very nearly set up in the Temple in 38. Only the emperor's timely assassination thwarted his sacrilegious plan. Alternatively, the phrase might refer to the profanation of the Temple by Antiochus Epiphanes, the king who was persecuting the Jews in the second century B.C. and who *did* manage to set up a statue of Zeus in the

Temple. There is a third possibility, and that is that the desolating sacrilege was in fact a person – Titus, the destroyer of Jerusalem, who captured the Temple, set fire to it, and burnt it to the ground. If this last alternative is the true one, then it certainly suggests that the passage was composed after the fall of Jerusalem.

The Christians were warned to flee for their lives. They were not to rush inside the walls of the city, as was the practice in a time of siege, for this would be no protection to them. The city would fall. Instead, they were to get away into open country. If they were on the housetops, then they should not stop to pack possessions, or try to come down and force a way through the narrow streets, which would be full of panicking people – but to make straight for the hills. Those stripped for work in the fields should likewise not hesitate, but get away. It would be a hard thing for those women who were pregnant or carrying infants – for speed was vital. It would be hard if it happened in the winter months.

Not only an earthly chaos, but a cosmic overthrow would take place. 'The sun will be darkened and the moon not give its light; the stars will be falling from heaven, and the powers in the heavens shake.' Then the heavenly figure of the Son of Man would come to earth, Jesus returning in his glory as a supernatural figure, and would gather together all those who had survived faithful throughout these terrible trials and tribulations.

The Book of Daniel mentioned this strange 'Son of Man', who the Christians identified as Jesus at his second coming. It says in Daniel 7:13–14: 'I saw in the night visions, and behold, with the clouds of heaven there came one like unto a Son of Man; and he came to the Ancient of Days and was presented before Him. And to him was given dominion and glory and kingdom; that all peoples, nations and languages should serve him. His dominion is an everlasting one which shall not pass away, and his kingdom one that shall not be destroyed.'

The faithful Christians were all to watch, and be ready – for no one would know exactly when this moment would come. They were to be like servants left in charge of a house in the absence of their master – to remain alert, if they were sensible, so that the master would not return and catch them sleeping.

Questions

1. What does the word 'apocalyptic' mean?
2. What does the word 'eschatological' mean?
3. What does apocalyptic literature do?
4. Name three Old Testament prophets that used this kind of writing.

The Temple Wall, Jerusalem *The 'Wailing Wall' is the western wall of the Temple erected by Herod the Great. The smaller stones at the top are from a later period. Jesus himself commented on the large stones of Herod's walls, and how his wonderful building would soon be destroyed.*

184

5. What was Jesus' first prediction?
6. What were the earthly signs of the end to be?
7. Why do some scholars think this passage was written after A.D. 64?
8. Why was apocalyptic symbolism used?
9. What are the suggestions made about the desolating sacrilege?
10. What would be the heavenly signs of the end?
11. What was the supernatural figure coming to earth called?
12. Which Old Testament prophet also mentioned this?
13. Why were the Christians to 'be prepared'?

Research

1. Find Isaiah 13:9–11.
(a) What would happen on the 'Day of the Lord'?
(b) Copy out verse 10.
(c) What sort of people would be punished?

2. Find Joel 2: 1–11.
(a) What sort of things are prophesied here?
(b) Copy out verse 5.

3. Find Zechariah 14. What was prophesied in verse 4?
4. Find Daniel 7.
(a) How did he describe the Ancient of Days in verses 9–10?
(b) What happened in verses 13–14?

5. Find Mark 13:1–21.
(a) What did Jesus say about the Temple?
(b) What earthly signs are mentioned in verses 5–8?
(c) Why were the Christians not to be anxious over their defences in court?
(d) What examples of fleeing in haste are given in verses 14–18?

6. Find Luke 21:20–24. Copy out verses 20 and 24.
7. Find Mark 13:22–37.
(a) Copy out verses 22–23.
(b) What heavenly signs were mentioned in verses 24–27?
(c) Could Jesus say exactly when these things would happen?
(d) What was the parable of the watchful servants?

8. Find Matthew 24: 36–51.
(a) Why did Jesus mention Noah?
(b) What was the parable of the thief in the night?
(c) What was the parable of the good and bad servants?
(d) Copy out verse 44.

34

THE ANOINTING AT BETHANY

In the four versions of the anointing of Jesus by a woman, St John's Gospel states that it was done by Mary the sister of Martha in Lazarus' house in Bethany on the day before Christ's entry into Jerusalem (John 12:1–8); St Mark and St Matthew say that it was an unnamed woman in the house of Simon the Leper in Bethany, on the Wednesday of Holy Week (Mark 14:3–9; Matthew 26:6–13); and St Luke has a version of an anointing of Jesus by a sinful woman in the house of Simon the Pharisee in Galilee, much earlier in Jesus' ministry (Luke 7:36–50).

Anointing, or pouring a special scented oil on to a person, was significant to the Jews in three different ways. Kings were anointed before their coronations, the Messiah was supposed to be the Anointed or Chosen One, and bodies were anointed for burial.

The woman who anointed Jesus presumably gave her precious ointment to him as an act of homage, but Jesus saw it as a sign of his impending death and burial. Some scholars have suggested that Jesus really did claim to be the King of the Jews, and that this anointing took place as a kind of coronation ceremony. However, our gospel records draw no such conclusions – rather they hint that there was some disapproval at what appeared to be a waste of a valuable asset which could have raised much money for the care of the poor.

The ointment that was used was a very special one. St Mark says that it was pure nard, and worth more than 300 denarii. A denarius was a day's wage for a Jewish labourer. In St John's Gospel it reveals that it was a pound in weight, and that it was Judas who complained about the woman's wasteful action. He also stated that Judas was a thief, and would probably have stolen part of the money for himself.

In the different versions there seems to be some confusion as to whether it was Jesus' head or feet which received the attention, and the differences between St Luke's account and the others are really so great as to suggest a completely separate occasion. And yet, the idea of two anointings seems far-fetched. Some people think there is quite a strong case for the theory that Mary Magdalene was the same person as Mary the sister of Martha and Lazarus of Bethany, although the case does not amount to a proof.

Magdala was a seaside resort near Antipas' new city of Tiberias where the Roman troops often went, their superiors favouring Tiberias itself. It was well served with prostitutes. It was also, incidentally, the place where the doves for the Temple sacrifices were bred. The fact that one of Jesus' lady disciples was known as 'the Magdalene' has been taken to mean that she may have been a prostitute. We are told in Luke 8:2 that this Mary had been possessed by demons and that Jesus had cured her. It is not improbable that she was the sinful, wealthy and very grateful lady who came to Jesus in Galilee, as reported in Luke 7.

The suggested theory is that Mary, the sister of Martha and Lazarus, had been troubled with evil demons (however one may interpret these), and had become a prostitute working in Magdala. At some point in her career she had met Jesus and been cured of her demon possession. Then, while he was in Galilee, she went to him in gratitude and anointed him, and had her sins forgiven, as St Luke records. Then, presumably, she continued to stay with him during his ministry (one of the women who followed him from Galilee), but later she appeared with Martha at a dinner party (Luke 10:38–42). There Martha fussed and treated Jesus as an honoured guest, but Mary, who seemed more familiar with him, sat lovingly at his feet. Possibly she had travelled there with Jesus and his party, and expected to be treated as a guest too. Maybe she had returned earlier to Bethany when her brother became ill.

We do not know what his illness was, but the word 'lazarus' implies 'leprosy'. It is possible that Lazarus was only a nick-name, which would be highly significant if it was used to identify him *after* he had been cured of leprosy. If his real name was Simon, we would have a man called Simon Lazarus, or Simon the Leper. It is quite certain that the Simon the Leper of St Mark and St Matthew's Gospels would not have been living in a house in Bethany entertaining guests unless he was an ex-leper, since all lepers were regarded as unclean, and were obliged to live outside the city walls.

Another theory is that Simon of Bethany was the father of Mary, Martha and Lazarus. Alas, we shall never know for sure. In St Luke's version, Jesus' host at the meal is Simon *the Pharisee*. Lazarus no doubt was a Pharisee, because we know that his sisters believed in the resurrection from the dead, a key Pharisaic belief (John 11).

Jesus raised Lazarus from the tomb shortly before Holy Week, and during the last week of his life spent much time in Bethany when he was not in Jerusalem. He may well have stayed there with the family of Lazarus, a friend he is said to have loved. We know of no other friends of Jesus in Bethany, although this is by no means to suggest that he had no other friends there. It may well have been on his last evening there that Mary anointed him, and Jesus interpreted this as a sign of his coming death and burial.

The traditional timing of the events in Holy Week places this anointing on the Wednesday night (Mark 14:1–9). On Thursday night he was dining with his disciples in an upper room in Jerusalem, and was arrested the same night – and by three o'clock on Friday afternoon he was dead. After the publicity and wrangling with the authorities on Monday and Tuesday, it seems as if Jesus spent a quiet day with his friends in Bethany on Wednesday before going to his death.

It is certainly odd that Mary, who sat at his feet and loved him, is not mentioned among the women followers who were witnesses to Jesus' last moments and subsequent burial, whereas little-known ladies such as Joanna and Salome are mentioned. Did the Mary that loved Jesus desert him in his hour of need? Or could she have been the same person as Mary Magdalene, who played such an important role in these last events? It was Mary Magdalene who stayed mourning at the tomb when all Jesus' other friends had gone away, and Mary Magdalene who first saw the risen body of Christ. We shall never know for certain, but it seems not impossible to suppose that Mary Magdalene and Mary the sister of Martha were one and the same person.

Questions

1. Where do the different gospels say the anointing took place?
2. What is anointing?
3. Give three occasions when persons were anointed.
4. How did Jesus interpret his anointing?
5. What kind of ointment was used?
6. What does the name Lazarus mean?

Research

1. Find Mark 14:3–12.
(a) In which village did the incident take place?
(b) In whose house did the incident take place?
(c) What did the woman do?
(d) What sort of ointment did she use?
(e) How valuable was it?
(f) Why were some people indignant?
(g) What was Jesus' reaction to their criticism?
(h) What ominous note was struck in verse 8?

2. Find John 12:1–8.
(a) In whose house did the supper party take place?
(b) Who anointed Jesus?
(c) Where did she pour the ointment in this version?
(d) What suggestion was made about Judas?

3. Find Luke 7:36–50.
(a) Where was Jesus on this occasion?
(b) Verse 40. What was his host's name?
(c) What suggestion was made about the woman's character?
(d) What was usually meant by 'sinner' when referring to a woman?
(e) What parable did Jesus tell in verses 41–42?
(f) Copy out verse 47.
(g) What was the reaction of the people at the table to these events?

4. Find Luke 8:1–3.
(a) Which women are named here?
(b) Why were they very useful to Jesus?
(c) What had been the matter with Mary Magdalene?

5. Find Luke 10:38–42.
(a) Who entertained Jesus on this occasion?
(b) Why was Martha cross with Mary?
(c) Why do you think Jesus was not cross with Mary?

6. Find these references to the women at the cross and at the tomb and make a list of the ladies mentioned in each gospel: Luke 23:55; 24:10; Mark 15:40, 47; Matthew 27:56, 61; John 19:25.

Mary the mother of James and Joses was presumably the same person as the wife of Cleophas. Tradition reveals that Cleophas was the brother of St Joseph, Jesus' 'father', so this lady was really the Virgin Mary's sister-in-law and Jesus' aunt. Salome was probably the mother of James and John, the disciples. Joanna was mentioned in Luke 8:1–3 as being the wife of Herod Antipas' steward Chuza.

Creative Writing

Jesus never married, and yet he was loved by a considerable number of ladies. He was obviously attractive and kind. What qualities do you think Jesus had that made him inspire particular devotion from the women?

35

THE LAST SUPPER

Jewish days went from 6 p.m. to 6 p.m. The date from 6 p.m. Friday to 6 p.m. Saturday in the year of Christ's death was Nisan 15th, the day of the Feast of the Passover. Therefore 6 p.m. Thursday to 6 p.m. Friday would have been Nisan 14th, the 'Day of the Preparation'. It was during the afternoon of Preparation Day that the sacrificial lambs were killed ready for the feast that took place during the night of Nisan 15th (Friday night). During this Thursday evening Jesus entertained his disciples and friends to a farewell meal.

Some people have wondered if the meal that we call the Last Supper was actually supposed to be a Passover Meal, but St John's Gospel makes it perfectly clear that Jesus was executed on the Friday afternoon, on the day before the feast, at the very time when the passover lamb was being sacrificed in the Temple.

Backing up St John's version of the dating, scholars have pointed out that Matthew 26:5 says that Caiaphas wanted to arrest Jesus by stealth and kill him, but 'not during the feast, lest there be a tumult among the people'. The disciples carried weapons to the garden of Gethsemane, which would not have been allowed on a feast day (Luke 22:38). Jesus carried the cross, which would not have been allowed on a feast day, and in any case, it would be highly unlikely that crucifixions would take place on a Passover. Simon of Cyrene, who carried the cross, was coming 'up from the country', which may have meant from work. Work was not done on any sabbath, let alone this one. Also, one was limited in the amount of travelling one could do on the sabbath. Joseph of Arimathea and Nicodemus brought linen and a hundred pounds of spices, breaking the sabbath by carrying more than the weight of one dried fig, by intending to do work, and by defiling themselves through contact with a dead body. In any case, very early Christian tradition identifies Jesus with the lamb, and that was sacrificed on the afternoon of the 14th.

Mark 15:42 actually mentions that it was still the Day of Preparation when they took Jesus down from the cross. The accompanying chart should make this clearer. This would mean that the Last

Supper was not a Passover meal at all, but a private family meal that took place before the great festival. Certainly no lamb was mentioned on the menu, and lamb was the chief part of a Passover meal.

Thursday, Nisan 13	Friday, Nisan 14	Saturday, Nisan 15	Sunday, Nisan 16
6 p.m. The disciples prepare the upper room	The Crucifixion	The Sabbath and the Passover	The women go to the tomb at dawn
The Last Supper	The Preparation	Passover meal eaten	
	Passover lamb sacrificed		
Night in Gethsemane	Body of Jesus taken down from the cross	Day of rest until 6 p.m.	
Arrest			
Trials	Burial before sunset		
	6 p.m. Passover began		

Just as, when Jesus entered Jerusalem, the ass was ready for him, so in this instance the room was also ready. One presumes the arrangements had been made in advance. Tradition states that the scene of the Last Supper was in the upper room or guest room in the house of John Mark's mother, and that Mark himself was the young man carrying the pitcher of water, whom the disciples were to follow. This presumably meant that the disciples themselves did not at that stage know where Mark lived, or such a procedure would have been unnecessary. (The tradition of the early Church also suggested that the mother of Mark was related to Peter's wife, hence a possible previous connection.)

Jesus must have been very aware of how dangerous it was for him to go back into Jerusalem, where the warrant was out for his arrest. So he only made his way there after darkness had fallen.

As they sat at table, Jesus stated that he knew that one of them was going to betray him. In the Synoptic Gospels he did not reveal the identity of the man, but in St John's version it is indicated that he told Peter and the beloved disciple; but he did not allow them to stop Judas from carrying out his course of action.

Then came the meal itself, of which only the bread and wine was mentioned. Jesus used the breaking and handing over of the bread and wine as symbols of his approaching self-sacrifice, and spoke of a New Covenant which he was making with them through the pouring out of his blood.

The Old Covenant was precisely what the Feast of the Passover was all about – when a lamb had been sacrificed so that the eldest Israelite in every family might live. It referred back to the time of Moses, when the Israelites were slaves in Egypt. The last of the terrible plagues that were sent to smite Pharaoh so that he would let the slaves go, was the death of the first-born in every house not marked with the blood of the lamb. Later, on Mount Sinai, Moses made a contract between the Israelites and God. The blood of a sacrificed lamb was drained off, and half of it sprinkled on the altar and half on the people. God promised to be with them and protect them, if they would obey His Laws. Sadly, the Israelites had not kept their part of the bargain, and the prophets (especially Jeremiah in 31:31) had warned that a new covenant would have to be made. The Christians saw this as the sacrifice of Jesus himself.

The Last Supper ended on a very sombre note. Jesus knew that all his disciples would desert him, even his loyal friend Peter. Peter was horrified that Jesus should think this, and declared that he would never leave him, even if it meant his death. Jesus sadly told him that before the cock crowed at dawn the next day, Peter would have denied knowing him three times.

Questions

1. When did a Jewish day start?
2. What was the date of the Passover?
3. When were the lambs for the sacrifice killed?
4. Give a list of reasons why scholars think that Jesus cannot have been killed on Nisan 15th.
5. What was the Old Covenant?
6. Why was the blood of the lamb important?
7. What did Christians see as being the New Covenant?

Research

1. Find Mark 14:10–21.
(a) Who plotted to betray Jesus?
(b) Why do verses 12–16 look like another example of Jesus having arranged events in advance?
(c) Look at Acts 12:12. Whose house in Jerusalem was used as a headquarters by the Christians after the death of Jesus?

(d) Mark 14:17. When did Jesus himself go to the house?
(e) What did Jesus say in verse 18?
(f) Did he betray the traitor?

2. Find Mark 14:22–25.
(a) What did Jesus do with the bread at the meal?
(b) What did he say the bread was?
(c) What did he say about the wine?

3. Find Luke 22:14–21.
(a) What did Jesus say when he took the cup in verses 17–18?
(b) What command did he give in verse 19? (Look at the footnote.)
(c) What did he say about the second cup in verse 20?

4. Find Luke 22:31–38.
(a) What did Jesus say about Peter?
(b) What was Peter's reaction to this?
(c) What did Jesus predict about Peter?
(d) What did the disciples have with them as they set out for Gethsemane?

Creative Writing

Imagine you are one of the guests at the Last Supper. Describe what took place then, and what Jesus' actions meant to you. How did you feel when Jesus made it clear that he knew he was about to be arrested and killed? How do you think Jesus felt at this time?

36

THE SIGNIFICANCE OF THE LAST SUPPER MEAL

This meal, which represented Christ's giving of his body and blood, became very important in the Christian Church, being an act which symbolised the complete union of all the church members with their Lord. Some Christians think that the meal, which we call Holy Communion, or Mass, or the Eucharist, is a kind of remembrance service in which we think about Jesus and what he did for us; other Christians believe it is far more than that – they believe that, in some mystical way, to 'eat Christ's body and drink his blood' makes the Church into one real body, the body of Christ.

Strangely enough, the giving of the bread and wine at the Last Supper was not even mentioned in St John's Gospel. His version included the example Jesus gave to them of acting the role of a servant by washing their feet, and some wonderful teachings as Jesus prepared his Apostles for the time when they would shortly have to continue their work without him.

The fourth gospel put its teaching about the body and blood of Jesus after the miracle of the feeding of the five thousand. Here the gospel writer gave an explanation of what the Last Supper was all about. Jesus warned his disciples not to spend their lives working for ordinary food, which would soon perish, but for the Bread of Life that came from God. This Bread of Life was Jesus himself; those who were hungry for the real meaning of life would be satisfied when they at last found God, through Jesus. Those who believed in Him would never hunger or thirst, for he was the living bread that came down from heaven. Jesus told them that they must eat his flesh and drink his blood, for, 'He who eats my flesh and drinks my blood abides in me, and I in him. As the living Father sent me, and I live because of the Father, so he who eats me will live because of me' (John 6:56–57).

Many people listening to Jesus could not understand this saying and began to leave him, but Jesus insisted that the act of belief in God was absolutely necessary in order for a person to 'have life'. His speech went on to state that, 'It is the spirit that gives life, the flesh is of no avail; the words that I have spoken to you are spirit and life. But there are some of you that do not believe' (verses 63–64).

As in the parable of the sower, the seed was sown but fell on all sorts of soils, some of which were barren or choked with thorns, or so hard-baked that the seed never even penetrated beneath the surface.

St John's version of the Last Supper includes several chapters of teachings that Jesus may have given on his last night on earth. It is very moving to read them through, and to visualise the scene as Jesus sat with his dearest friends, knowing that this was his last meal with them, and that in a very short while he would be arrested and executed.

He taught them that if they were truly his disciples, then they would love one another and help each other, and even lay down their lives for each other if need be.

The most important thing was that they were to be one, as Jesus and his Father were one. What would Jesus think of all the different branches of the Church today, and all the different teachings of the various denominations? It is hard to believe that he would not be disappointed by such lack of unity. Nevertheless, in real terms, Christians are one, for even though they may worship in different ways, they all believe in God and His son Jesus, and the activity of the Holy Spirit; and they are all working to see God's will done on earth, in acts of kindness and forgiveness and good living. Different sorts of Churches are only not one with the others when they start being un-Christian; when they start being selfish and conceited and lazy and unkind.

The Holy Communion reminds Christians of what they stand for and who they believe in. It draws them together in a fellowship with God, with all God's children who live now, and all who have gone before. Many Christians feel particularly moved by the thought of the communion of saints, especially of those who have died but who can still draw near and be close to their loved ones. In a rather wonderful way, the Holy Communion makes all the Christians into one body, the body of Christ on Earth. Just as Jesus was in the father and the Father in him, so God may also be in us. Whether the Communion is interpreted as a symbolic action or a miraculous action, the aim is the same: to draw us nearer to God and nearer to each other.

Questions and Research

1. Find John 6. What did Jesus say about himself in verses 35 and 51?

2. Find I Corinthians 10:16–17 and 11:23–26.

(a) Copy out 10:16–17.

(b) Which gospel writer's words are closest to the version of the Last Supper given in I Corinthians 11:23–26?

3. Find John, Chapters 13–17.

(a) What example of love and service did Jesus give to his disciples (13:2–11)?

(b) What sort of thing do you think Jesus meant when he commanded the disciples to wash one another's feet? Did he mean it literally? What sort of things could we do to obey that commandment?

(c) What commandment did Jesus give in 13:34? (These are actually the only two direct commandments that Jesus ever gave to us, and that makes them supremely important!)

(d) What did Jesus suggest about the things we would be able to do in 14:12–13?

(e) What promise did Jesus make in 14:18?

(f) What did Jesus say was the greatest expression of a person's love (15:13)?

(g) What did Jesus pray in 17:11 and 17:20–21?

37

THE ARREST IN THE GARDEN OF GETHSEMANE

After the Last Supper, Jesus went to the Garden of Gethsemane instead of going back to stay in Bethany. His disciples seem to have been unprepared for a night of watching and prayer, for we are told that while Jesus suffered his agonies of mind they slumbered and slept, an unreasonable and callous desertion of their lord if they had known in advance what was about to happen.

This garden was a quiet, peaceful place not far outside Jerusalem, full of olive trees, and with a cave where people could shelter. It stood in the triangle between the two mountain tracks and the main road that all led to Bethany. The name 'Gethsemane' has been said to mean 'oil-press' or 'perfume-press'.

When they arrived in Gethsemane, Jesus began to face in his mind the task that lay ahead of him. He asked his disciples to support him with their prayers while he went on alone to speak to God.

Jesus asked God if it was really necessary for him to drink the 'cup of suffering'? Was there not some other way that he could do God's will? This was the moment when all Christ's agony of mind was poured out, and he had to decide whether he was willing to go through with whatever was in store for him in Jerusalem, and submit to it without resistance, or choose some other way.

After Jesus .had died, many of the Jews who had hoped that he really was the Messiah could no longer believe in him, for they thought that the fact of his death proved that his claim must be false. God had abandoned him and not saved him – he was no better than all the other people who had claimed falsely to be the Messiah and who had suffered the ultimate penalty. However, those who believed that Jesus had risen from the dead saw his submission to the experience of death as his greatest triumph. Jesus had not held back from any of the things that ordinary men have to go through – he had shared everything with them, even death itself.

When he described Jesus praying in the garden, St Luke added two facts that were not in the other versions. He said that Jesus was in such agony that his sweat became like great drops of blood. The actual sweating of blood is a phenomenon that is certainly rare, but it is not unknown in cases of extreme anguish. There is a possibility that this phenomenon was what St Luke, the doctor, recorded. St Luke also stated that an angel appeared and gave Jesus the strength to make his decision to go forward.

As soon as Jesus had reconciled himself to his fate, the betrayer and 'a mob' arrived in the garden. Peter had a sword and made a show of resistance, cutting off the ear of one of the High Priest's servants. Jesus stopped the fighting and healed the man. Then, as predicted, all the disciples ran away. St Mark's Gospel alone records how there was a certain young man hiding behind a tree wearing only a sheet. The soldiers caught him, but he managed to slip out of the sheet and make his escape. It is thought that this person was St Mark himself, who had followed them from his house after the Last Supper, and had heard everything that went on in the garden – while the other disciples slept!

In St John's Gospel, it indicates that the arrest of Jesus was carried out by a posse from the Temple Sanhedrin accompanied by a 'speira' with a 'chiliarch' in command. The Greek word *speira* meant a force with a possible strength of 760 infantry and 240 cavalry! The chiliarch would have been their military tribune. (Acts 21:31 and 23:26 mentions one Claudius Lysias as the military tribune in charge of the Antonia tower in A.D. 57, when St Paul was arrested.) This suggests that a large force of Roman troops was actually responsible for Jesus' arrest – but it presents us with a problem, for the accounts specify that Jesus was not taken into Roman custody, but to a series of trials before the priestly hierarchy.

A more plausible suggestion is that the people arresting Jesus were not Roman troops at all, but the Temple guard, and the chiliarch was the Captain of the Temple. The Levitical guard on duty at night at the outer gates and in the Court of the Gentiles was a force of twenty-one men – enough to deal with opposition from eleven disciples, and not so many as to make movement impossible in the Garden of Gethsemane and the ways leading from it. St Luke actually mentions the captains of the Temple when Judas made his pact with the priests, and at the arrest (Luke 22:4, 52).

There is a mystery about the role that Judas played in the arrest. The disciples had not been prepared for Gethsemane, but Judas knew exactly where to lead the soldiers. Also, from St John's Gospel, we know that Jesus knew he was going to be betrayed, and who his betrayer would be (John 13:26), yet made no move to stop him. It also appears that Judas was aware that Jesus knew what was going on, yet still went ahead with his task (John 13:27–30). Why? And why did he kiss Judas in the garden, according to the

The Garden of Gethsemane *Here Jesus prayed alone before his arrest. The ancient olive trees protected in this garden are centuries old, and are probably offshoots of the very ones Jesus sheltered under.*

Synoptic Gospels, when surely everyone would know which of the men was Jesus, and particularly when, according to St John, Jesus deliberately stood forth and identified himself?

The miserable sum of thirty pieces of silver, the price of a slave, would hardly tempt a man who was treasurer of the group, who would profit far more from keeping Jesus alive. Why, in any case, did he return the money? And why did he kill himself afterwards?

The name 'Iscariot' has provoked speculation. It could indicate that Judas simply came from the town of Kerioth. The word *ish* just means 'man'. A second theory is based on the group of Zealot resistance fighters known as Sicarii from the Latin *sica* meaning 'dagger'. In this case, 'Ish-sicarii' would mark Judas as a member of that militant group. A third theory suggests that 'dagger-man' was a bitter and ironic nickname for Judas, the man who 'put the dagger in' for his master by betraying him.

It looks suspiciously as if the whole mission of Judas was arranged beforehand, by Jesus himself, in the same way that providing the ass and preparing the room for the Last Supper had been arranged. Jesus knew that he would die, and took no steps to avoid capture, or to defend himself by a display of his powers once he had been captured. During his trials there were several occasions when he could have avoided sentence simply by defending himself legally – for example, if two witnesses did not agree, a defendant was legally innocent.

Could the strange passage from Zechariah 11 have been in his mind, Jesus deliberately organising his death so that, through it, men might be brought to true belief? Jesus was certainly familiar with the book of Zechariah. As the officials found it so difficult to arrest Jesus because of his following, the simple expedient of letting one of his disciples bring the enemy to a prearranged place where he would be waiting for them could well have been the easiest answer, with the least trouble and bloodshed.

Maybe Judas, instead of being a villain, was the one chosen secretly to act this role, perhaps thinking that, at the last moment, when Christ had been brought to the cross, he would reveal himself publicly as the Messiah for all to see, without any shadow of doubt. When his hopes were not realised, maybe that is why he was overcome with grief and killed himself.

Whatever the secret behind the man Judas, the only southerner in the group of Christ's twelve chief disciples, we must keep an open mind and not condemn him too readily. It is inconceivable that Jesus, with all his insight into human nature, should have had a man working alongside him, performing healings and receiving intimate instruction with the rest of the twelve, and not have re-alised that he was likely to betray him.

Questions

1. Where did Jesus go after the Last Supper?
2. What decision did Jesus have to make on this last night?
3. Why did many Jews think Jesus could not have been the Messiah?
4. What special things did St Luke mention as happening to Jesus in Gethsemane?
5. Who witnessed the arrest, and escaped in the nude?
6. What do the use of the words *speira* and *chiliarch* suggest about the people who arrested Jesus?
7. What is a more likely suggestion about the guards?
8. What suggestions have been made about the name 'Is-cariot'?
9. Was Kerioth in the north or south of Israel?

Research

1. Find Mark 14:32–42.
(a) Where did Jesus take the disicples?
(b) What did Jesus want to do?
(c) Who did he take with him?
(d) Put the prayer of Jesus in verse 36 into your own words.

(e) How did his three friends let him down?
(f) How many times did Jesus go away on his own to pray?

2. Find Luke 22:43–44. What details does St Luke add in his version?
3. Find Mark 14:43–52.
(a) Who came to arrest Jesus?
(b) Who had betrayed him?
(c) What sign had he arranged to use to betray Jesus?
(d) Who got injured, and how?
(e) What did the disciples do?
(f) Who nearly got captured by the guards?
(g) How did he escape?

4. Find Matthew 26:46–56.
(a) What does this version add in verses 52–53?
(b) What does it leave out at the end of the story?
5. Find John 13:21–30. Why does it look as if Jesus already knew that Judas was going to betray him?
6. Find John 18:1–12.
(a) Had Jesus been to Gethsemane before?
(b) Who did Judas fetch to arrest Jesus?
(c) Was the kiss of Judas mentioned?
(d) How did the troops know which man was Jesus?
(e) Who had his ear cut off?
(f) Who cut the ear off?
(g) Which ear was it?
(h) What did they do to Jesus?

Creative Writing

Either: Imagine that you are the mother of John Mark. Describe how you discover that he has gone out after Jesus and his disciples. What did he tell you after he returned home?
Or: How do you think you would have reacted to the arrest of Jesus? Why do you think Jesus would not allow his followers to fight for him?

38

THE TRIALS BEFORE THE PRIESTS

An old flight of steps descended from the Upper City to the gate leading to the Pool of Siloam at the south-east angle of the city wall. From the Garden of Gethsemane, the party that arrested Jesus followed the course of the Kidron Valley to the foot of these steps, and then climbed up into Jerusalem.

According to St John's Gospel, the band of soldiers and their captain took Jesus, bound securely, to the house of Annas, the father-in-law of Caiaphas the High Priest. Annas had been the High Priest himself, from the years A.D. 6 to 15, and still had enormous authority in the city. Apparently the Beloved disciple knew him personally, and he and Peter followed the crowd into the courtyard of his house. It was the middle of the night, and cold, and the servants had made a charcoal fire. They were warming themselves at it with the soldiers of the guard. Peter went and stood with them.

Annas questioned Jesus about his disciples and his teachings, but Jesus refused to give him direct answers. He pointed out that he had always taught openly – there were plenty of witnesses to what he had said; he had no need to make any statement about himself. One of the officers was infuriated by the manner in which Jesus spoke to Annas, and punched him. Annas decided that he was getting nowhere with his prisoner, and sent him, still bound, to Caiaphas. Only St John's Gospel mentions this first interview of Jesus with the priestly hierarchy.

According to St John, it was while Jesus was with Caiaphas that Peter was challenged. He had been recognised as one of the disciples. Terrified, Peter denied knowing anything about Jesus, especially when confronted by a kinsman of the person whose ear he had cut off after Jesus' arrest in Gethsemane.

St Mark's version dwells on the trial of Jesus before Caiaphas. All the chief priests, elders and scribes were assembled, even though it was the middle of the night. These persons constituted the ruling body of the Jews, a council known as the **Sanhedrin**. A considerable time was spent in hearing the evidence of witnesses

The Pool of Siloam *Hezekiah's water tunnel under Jerusalem comes out in this pool, which used to be a lake surrounded by trees. The man who carried a pitcher of water and led the disciples to the place where they held the Last Supper probably drew his water from this pool at the foot of Mount Zion.*

about a threat Jesus was supposed to have made on the Temple itself. These witnesses had obviously been gathered up some time during the previous day, in expectation of the arrest of Jesus. Some said that he had threatened to destroy the Temple and rebuild it again in three days. Others must have known that Jesus had not meant this at all. St John's Gospel makes it quite clear that Jesus had been talking about himself, his death and rising again. As the witnesses simply did not agree, a clear enough case on which to have Jesus condemned was not presented. Incidentally, the fact that the witnesses did not agree proves that they had not been 'fixed' by Caiaphas, as some have tried to suggest.

Caiaphas next tried to force Jesus to make a statement by which he might incriminate himself, but he stood silent. Then, according to St Matthew's version, Caiaphas in desperation used the Sacred Oath which all Jews were bound to answer. He asked Jesus under oath whether or not he really was the Messiah. Jesus admitted that he was. At this point Caiaphas tore his robes as a gesture that he believed what Jesus had said was blasphemy. Jesus was instantly condemned to death. The meeting broke up with persons spitting at him contemptuously, and blindfolding him so that they could hit him and try to make him guess who had touched him. He was handed back to the guards, a condemned man. The guards beat him up.

It is at this point that St Mark mentions Peter's denial, and the sequence ends with cock-crow as dawn broke, presumably around 5 a.m. Peter realised what he had done, and broke down weeping. Jesus was kept under guard, pending the judgement of Pilate, the Roman Governor of Judaea.

It is often claimed that the trials of Jesus before the priestly authorities were completely illegal, a travesty of justice. These claims are based on the study of Pharisaic laws as laid out in the Mishnah, Jewish teachings which were not written down for at least a century after the death of Christ. However, the procedures laid down there were based on rules which must have been practised during the period when capital punishment was actually exercised by the Sanhedrin, before Jerusalem fell in A.D. 70.

According to these rules, no Sanhedrin was allowed to sit as a criminal court and try criminal cases outside the Temple precincts in any private house; they could not put a man on trial for his life at night – only trials for trivial reasons could be conducted after sunset; a criminal charge could not be tried on festival days or on the eve of a festival. No person could be convicted on his own testimony, or on the strength of his own confession. Two lawfully qualified witnesses had to agree conclusively, and it was illegal for a judge to cross-examine the prisoner after testimony of witnesses had broken down. Incidentally, if the witnesses could have been proved false, then *they* were liable to sentence of death by stoning. The capital offence of blasphemy consisted in pronouncing the actual name of God (which was a closely guarded secret) and the criminality of the act and the penalty prescribed for it had first to be pointed out to the accused. The judge of a case might not also be the prosecutor.

The fact that Caiaphas did not get his own way over the witnesses proves two things: first, how seriously the witnesses took a trial 'for life', because their own lives were in the balance if they could be proved false; and secondly, that there must have been very strong influences in the council to see justice prevail, and make sure that Jesus was given an adequate defence. No doubt such men as Nicodemus and Joseph of Arimathea made sure that Jesus got a fair hearing, so far as it was possible for them to do so.

When Jesus replied 'I am' to Caiaphas' question, this would not have been counted as blasphemy – the pronunciation of the name of God was the capital offence, at which point *all* those present should have torn their garments.

Some scholars have wondered whether the priests have been misjudged in their representation as the bitter enemies of Jesus. Was their meeting by night an attempt to *save* him, to dissuade him from admitting his guilt in front of a Roman tribunal, which would automatically condemn him? The rending of garments was also a sign of grief and despair, so was the High Priest giving him up after Jesus made it obvious that he would not back down from his belief that he really *was* the Messiah, the King of the Jews?

Other scholars, however, are impressed with the weight of evidence that suggests that the priests were the motive force behind the execution of Jesus.

If Jesus was being quizzed about his disciples and his teaching, it was probably leading towards a condemnation for the crime of apostasy – leading the Jews astray from their religion. It was quite in order for the High Priest to investigate the nature of his teachings and the extent of his following (see Deuteronomy 13:1–11 and 21:22).

One of the Tractates in the Babylonian Talmud (Sanhedrin) states that, 'Jesus was hanged on the Eve of the Passover. A herald went before him for forty days saying, "He is going to be stoned because he practised sorcery, and enticed and led astray Israel. Let anyone knowing anything in his defence come and plead for him." But nothing was found in his defence, so he was hanged on the Eve of the Passover.'

It is interesting to note that, in Acts 10:39 and 5:30, it mentions that Jesus was put to death by 'hanging on a gibbet'; and in Galatians 3:13, St Paul actually quotes Deuteronomy 21:23: 'Cursed be everyone who hangs on a gibbet.' However, there is no attempt to deny that Jesus was crucified and no hint in any of the Christian sources suggests that Jesus was stoned to death. The blame for Christ's death was outlined in Acts 2:23, where Peter stated that the Jews killed him by fastening him to a cross 'through the agency of heathen men'. The Roman crucifixion carried out the intent of the Jewish authorities.

So far as the early Christians were concerned, Jesus was the martyred Messiah of Israel, killed by the Romans and their Jewish collaborators. The Roman law would have taken little notice of threats to destroy the Temple, or claims to be the Son of God – but a political charge was something completely different. That is why Jesus was next accused of conspiracy against Caesar.

Questions

1. When was Annas the High Priest?
2. Why would Jesus not answer any questions?
3. What was the Sanhedrin?
4. How did Caiaphas get Jesus to admit that he was the Messiah?
5. What is the Mishnah?
6. What rules in the Mishnah suggest that Jesus' trial before the priests was illegal?
7. What was the penalty for false witnesses?
8. Name two Sanhedrin members who were sympathetic to Jesus.
9. What penalty was normally given for those who had 'led Israel astray'?
10. What did the Talmud say about the condemnation of Jesus?

Research

1. Find John 7:45–52.
(a) Why did the officers not arrest Jesus on this occasion?
(b) Who defended Jesus?
(c) What did he say?

2. Find John 11:45–53.
(a) Why did the council meet on this occasion?
(b) Who was Caiaphas?
(c) What did Caiaphas have to say?

3. Find John 18:12–24.
(a) What did the soldiers do to Jesus?
(b) Who was Annas?
(c) What had Caiaphas said about Jesus?

(d) Where did Peter wait while the trial was on?
(e) What did Annas question Jesus about?
(f) Why did the soldier hit Jesus?
(g) What did Annas do with Jesus?

4. Find Matthew 26:57–68.
(a) Where was Jesus taken next?
(b) What did the false witnesses say about Jesus?
(c) Why couldn't Jesus be convicted on this evidence?
(d) What did the High Priest finally ask Jesus?
(e) What did the High Priest do when he heard Jesus 'blaspheme'?
(f) Copy out verses 67–68.

5. Find Mark 14: 66–72.
(a) Who was waiting in the courtyard?
(b) Who challenged Peter about his connection with Jesus?
(c) What happened when the cock crew?

6. Find Matthew 27:1–10.
(a) What happened to Jesus at dawn?
(b) Who had betrayed Jesus?
(c) How much money had he received for betraying him?
(d) What did he do with the money?
(e) What did the priests do with it?
(f) How did Judas die?

7. Find Acts 1:15–26.
(a) According to this version, written by St Luke, what did Judas
    do with the money?
(b) How did Judas die?
(c) Who was chosen to take his place?

Creative Writing

Either: Imagine that you are the maid at the house of the High
    Priest. Write to a friend describing what happened.
Or: Imagine that you are one of the priests called to the Sanhedrin
    in the middle of the night. Describe the events that took place,
    and what the feelings of the Sanhedrin were towards the pris-
    oner. Did they all condemn him? Were they all happy about the
    way in which the trial was conducted?

THE TRIALS BEFORE PILATE

In spite of the statement in John 18:31 that it was 'not lawful for us to put any man to death', it seems that the death penalty *was* sometimes passed by the Sanhedrin, the Jewish court. The usual Jewish death sentences were by stoning or burning – and the Pharisees favoured burning by having molten lead poured down the throat, so that one's body would still be available for resurrection later! However, the right to give the death penalty without the stamp of the Roman Governor was only given as a reward for loyalty to Rome, and it seems unlikely that turbulent Judaea should have received such a concession.

The fact that Jesus was crucified, the Roman death penalty, suggests that Jesus was tried and found guilty on a Roman capital charge – the *Lex Julia Majestatis* – which included causing the friends of Rome to become her enemies. The Jews presumably wanted Jesus to die in this fashion, not to make a nationalistic hero out of him, but because of the Levitical law which declared a hanged man to be accursed by God. The hanging of Christ's crucified body would prove to all spectators that God had cursed him publicly, and therefore he could not possibly be the Messiah and need not be regarded as a martyr.

Pontius Pilate was a Roman official, possibly a Spaniard by birth. In his early manhood he became a member of the Ordo Equester, the Knights of the Cavalry, a company of gentlemen who could afford the minimum property qualification of 400,000 sesterces. He had served for a time under Germanicus in Germany, and had married Claudia Procula, a lady having connections with the imperial family. Tradition reveals that she was the illegitimate daughter of the third wife of the future emperor Claudius.

In A.D. 26, Pilate was made the sixth procurator, or governor, of Judaea by Tiberius' evil friend Sejanus, a man noted for his dislike of the Jews. Once in Judaea, Pilate distinguished himself mainly for his lack of tact and diplomacy in dealing with this difficult job. On one occasion he deliberately sent Roman insignia into Jerusalem by night, knowing full well that other governors had not done so, and that the act would be considered as blasphemy. The furious Jews besieged him in Caesarea for six days, demanding the removal of the offensive ensigns. He surrounded the deputation sent to him with an armed force and threatened to kill them, but when he discovered that they would rather die than give in, he weakened and removed the ensigns.

He then tried to install votive shields dedicated to the emperor in the Herodian palace, and this time only gave way after a letter from Herod Antipas was sent to Tiberius himself. Another example of his lack of tact was when he used money from the sacred Temple treasury to finance a building project, an aqueduct from Solomon's Pools, many miles from Jerusalem, to the interior of the Temple. Although a water supply for the Temple was immensely beneficial, and could be interpreted as for the service of the Lord, his high-handed taking of the money resulted in a tumult that was only settled by soldiers disguised as civilians surprising and attacking the mob, with many deaths resulting. The gospels mention briefly a further occasion, shrouded in mystery, on which he 'mingled the blood of Galileans with the sacrifices'. This veiled hint suggests a cruel reprisal taken against another party of Jews.

All this background to his character makes his part in the trials of Jesus the more extraordinary. He arose in the early hours of the morning, left his quarters, and came out of the Praetorium to meet the Jews – because they refused to be defiled on their holy day by entering a Gentile area. The accounts of the trials suggest that he was more than casually interested in the affair. Presumably he had prior knowledge of Jesus, certainly from Caiaphas, to prepare him for his role in giving judgement, and perhaps through his own official channels. The curing of the centurion's servant may have called forth a report from Galilee.

St John's account of the trials suggests that his attitude to Jesus was one of curiosity and fear. All the gospels portray him as being exceedingly reluctant to execute Jesus – strange behaviour in such a cold and tactless Roman official!

Charges of threatening to destroy the Temple and blasphemy would have little meaning to one who had shown such scant respect to Judaism as had Pilate, so the priests altered their case to one of treason. According to St Luke, Jesus was accused of 'perverting the nation, forbidding to pay tribute to Caesar, and claiming to be the king of the Jews', all instances of the *Lex Majestatis*, and carrying the death penalty – the *Jus Gladii*.

Pilate then asked Jesus if he was claiming to be a king, and Jesus replied that he was. Pilate, however, had little evidence to go on, and did not take the charge seriously. In Jerusalem at this particular time there was someone with far more claim to be the king of the

Jews – none other than Herod Antipas, the uncrowned son of Herod the Great. As soon as Pilate found out that Jesus was a Galilean, he sent Jesus to Antipas and invited him to give judgement.

Herod was quite pleased to have the opportunity of questioning Jesus, and hoped to see him perform some miracle. He cannot have regarded Jesus as a serious claimant for the throne, or he would surely have arrested Jesus himself. Some scholars have interpreted the sudden movements of Jesus around Galilee and out into the neighbouring regions as attempts to keep out of Herod Antipas' clutches, which may well be true. Nevertheless, if Herod had been aware of claims made by Jesus to be a king, he would have been in serious trouble had he not arrested him! Jesus disappointed him. He just stood quietly and would neither defend himself nor do a wondrous deed. Herod seems to have used this opportunity to heal his enmity with Pilate. He dressed Jesus up as a mock-king and sent him back.

Pilate then called together the Sanhedrin and informed them that he could not find Jesus guilty of a capital crime. Matthew's version even suggests that Pilate's wife, Claudia, intervened on Jesus' behalf because she had suffered a nightmare about him. Some scholars have thought this intervention highly unlikely, but there are many known instances of important wives taking just this sort of action, even dealing with cases in their husband's absence on occasion. Calpurnia's message to Julius Caesar, Livia's use of the seal of Augustus, Fulvia's activities on behalf of Mark Antony, and Munatia Plancina's on behalf of Calpurnius Piso are notable examples.

The gospels suggest that there was a Passover custom at that time that a prisoner could be released by the governor and handed over to the people. Evidence for this custom is not conclusive, but there is enough to allow for its possibility. Pilate decided to avail himself of this custom in order to release Jesus, but the priests demanded to have, instead, one Barabbas, a 'notable prisoner', who had been condemned for rebellion and murder. He was presumably a leader in the Zealot resistance movement, and was under sentence of death for having killed Roman soldiers. As far as the Jews were concerned, he had been doing exactly what the Messiah ought to have been doing – trying to drive out the hated enemy. Ironically enough, his first name was probably Jesus (see Matthew 27:16 footnote).

St Matthew's version then recounts how Pilate called for water and washed his hands of the whole business, declaring that he was 'innocent of this man's blood'. St Luke records that Pilate had decided to sentence Jesus to a scourging but not to death. St John's version backs up this tradition, and adds that after the vicious scourging was carried out, Jesus was brought back out to the priests – dressed in a purple robe and wearing a cap of thorns on his head to see if they would now be satisfied. At this point the priests realised that unless they put pressure on Pilate Jesus would soon be back, causing them more problems, and with the added reputation of being a martyr. They threatened Pilate that if he released Jesus they would report *him* to Tiberius for treason.

Throughout St John's version we are given details of the conversations between Jesus and Pilate which are not in the Synoptics. In them, Jesus revealed to Pilate that his kingship was not of this world, and that he had come to bear witness to the truth. He told Pilate that he really had no authority over him at all – he was merely acting out the part required of him by God. Pilate had been told by the priests that Jesus had claimed to be the Son of God, and appeared almost to be acting as Jesus' champion against the Jewish authorities, a point that many scholars find very hard to accept.

Even at the end of the trial, the wording of the so-called accusation that Pilate ordered to be placed on Christ's cross looked like another attempt to placate the man he was executing. Instead of giving the customary summary of the victim's crime, 'he dies for being a thief', or 'here hangs a traitor and a murderer', or even – in Jesus' case – 'here hangs a blasphemer who called himself the king of the Jews', it was a simple statement, leaving those who saw it to make up their own minds – 'The King of the Jews'.

In A.D. 36, after hunting down and killing another 'messiah', this time a Samaritan with considerable influence and backing, Pilate was removed from office by Vitellius, the Prefect of Syria, and banished by the emperor Caligula to Gaul. The traditions concerning his death are that he either commited suicide – the only honourable death for a disgraced Roman – or died a Christian martyr. (One legend told that his body was dumped in a lake near Lausanne in Switzerland, which is reputedly haunted by him to this day!) The Coptic and Ethiopian Churches accept him as a martyr, and his festival is celebrated on 25 June. The Greek Church makes his wife Claudia a saint also, with her festival on 27 October.

The place where Pilate gave his infamous judgement was the Gabbatha (John 19:13) or Lithostrotos, a paved court in the governor's headquarters. According to the Jewish historian Josephus, the governor Florus had his headquarters, or praetorium, in the palace of Herod in the year 65, but no pavement has been found there to date. In the 1930s, Father L. H. Vincent disclosed a pavement 2,500 yards square at the site of the Antonia fortress adjoining the Temple. This may well have been the Gabbatha, since it is set on a rocky height, and the name in Hebrew implies a ridge or elevation.

From this austere pavement, Jesus set out carrying the beam of his cross, to face his hardest trial of all.

Questions

1. What were the death penalties given by Jewish courts?
2. Why didn't the Pharisees agree with burning peoples' bodies?
3. What would the hanging of Jesus' body prove?
4. When was Pontius Pilate made Governor of Judaea?
5. What was the 'insignia affair'?
6. How did Pilate's building of an aqueduct offend the Jews?
7. What were the charges against Jesus that he put on trial?
8. What was the treason law called?
9. What was the death penalty called?
10. Who was Claudia Procula?
11. Who was Barabbas?
12. When was Pontius Pilate removed from office?
13. Where did Pilate pass judgement on Jesus?
14. What has modern archaeology revealed about his spot?

Research

1. Find Luke 23:1–5.
(a) Blasphemy against the Jewish God was not a crime worthy of death in Roman law, so the priests laid different charges against Jesus. What were those charges?
(b) Had Jesus ever refused to pay taxes? (See Luke 20:22–25.)
(c) Did Jesus have any claim at all to the Jewish throne?
(d) How did Pilate discover Jesus was a Galilean?
(e) Who was the Governor of Galilee?

2. Find Luke 23:6–12.
(a) Where was Herod Antipas at this time?
(b) Why was he pleased to see Jesus?
(c) What did he want Jesus to do?
(d) Who was 'vehemently accusing' Jesus while he was with Herod?
(e) Did Jesus perform any miracles?
(f) In what way did Herod then treat Jesus with contempt?

3. Find Mark 15:6–15.
(a) What was the Passover custom that Pilate allowed?
(b) Why was Barabbas in prison?
(c) Who did the crowd choose? Why, do you think?
(d) What was the death penalty given to people in the poorer classes? (A gentleman would have been beheaded with a sword, or invited to poison himself, or to cut his own wrists.)

4. Find Matthew 27:15–26.
(a) Why did Pilate's wife interrupt the trial?
(b) What happened in verses 24–25?
(c) What was the name of the Roman area outside the Temple (verse 27)?
(d) What did they do to Jesus in verses 27–31?

5. Find John 18:28–40.
(a) Why wouldn't the priests enter the Praetorium?
(b) Why did the Jews want Pilate to judge the case?
(c) What did Jesus say about his kingship?
(d) Copy out Jesus' speech in verse 37.

6. Find John 19:1–16.
(a) What did the soldiers do to Jesus?
(b) What did the Jews say in verse 7?
(c) What was Pilate's reaction to this information?
(d) Was Jesus afraid of Pilate?
(e) What charge did the Jews intend to bring against Pilate if he did not do what they wanted?
(f) What was the place of judgement called?

Creative Writing

Either: Choose one of the trial sequences and create a short play-script about what happened.
Or: Give as many reasons as you can why you think Pilate may have been reluctant to execute Jesus. Was it because he thought he was innocent? Or a harmless lunatic? Did he really admire Jesus? Did he think Jesus was a Roman sympathiser, unlike the Zealot Barabbas? Outline the possible thoughts that might have gone through Pilate's mind as he considered the famous prisoner.

40
THE CRUCIFIXION

Jesus was condemned to be crucified. Crucifixion, after scourging, was the common method of Roman execution reserved for subject peoples. Even in those cruel times, everyone accepted that it was one of the most horrifying tortures ever invented by man. Roman citizens were killed by the 'kinder' method of beheading. Tradition claims that St Paul, being a Roman citizen, was beheaded, whereas St Peter was crucified.

Every condemned man was scourged first. A Roman scourging was a barbarous punishment. The condemned person was stripped naked and bound to a post or pillar, or occasionally hung by the wrists from a beam, and beaten by several torturers until his flesh hung in shreds. The beating could be with rods, or with the flagrum, an implement with a short handle to which were attached two thongs, at the ends of which were inserted *tali* – the anklebones of sheep. Sometimes a spike, or several sharp pieces of bone, or lead nails were used instead. In Hebrew law, the number of strokes was limited to forty, and the Pharisees insisted that the punishment should not exceed thirty-nine. The Romans, however, imposed no such limitation – they stipulated only that a man condemned to die by crucifixion should still be alive when he was fastened to his cross. Many people *did* die of scourging – Josephus the historian had some of his enemies scourged until their entrails were visible (*War*, ii, 21, 5, 612). In one sense, it was almost a kindness, since the more severe the scourging the shorter the time one would suffer the agony of crucifixion.

After the soldiers had scourged Jesus, they put on his badly wounded shoulders a red cloak, and taking a handful of thorny branches, formed a cap and pressed it down on his head as a mockery of a crown. The thorny bushes, which grew profusely around Jerusalem, had spikes an inch long and were probably kept in a heap in the Praetorium, waiting to be burnt on the fires. We are told in Mark 15:19 that Jesus was also cudgelled about the head, and that they spat on him and mocked him. Then he was led out,

Golgotha, the Skull Face *Just outside Jerusalem, this rocky face was once a quarry lying alongside a main road. Some people think it was here that Jesus was crucified, in the open space at the foot of the hill. (A modern Arab graveyard lies at the top.)*

still having enough strength to stand and carry his cross-beam, to the place of crucifixion.

The crosses were usually a simple affair: just one beam of wood to lay across another in the shape of the letter 'T'. Because wood was scarce, they were often used again and again. Usually prisoners were obliged to carry their own cross-beam, known as a *patibulum* (a barricade bar), to the place of execution, but if they were too weak, a bystander could be forced to do this for them. Simon of Cyrene, an African, whose sons Rufus and Alexander became leading Christians in the early Church, did this task for Jesus.

Prisoners were allowed to take myrrh to deaden the pain and stupefy the senses. Charitable woman lined the road on the way to the execution ground and gave it to the prisoners. St Luke's Gospel records a conversation that Jesus had with some women, who may have been offering Jesus this last act of kindness. We are not told, however, that Jesus took the myrrh.

Golgotha, the Place of the Skull, was on the hill of Calvary outside Jerusalem, and may have been so named because it was a skull-shaped hill, or because the sparse, scrubby grass at the execution ground had been deliberately removed, leaving the white limestone gleaming like a buried skull, or simply because bones and skulls were to be found there. Just outside Jerusalem there is a rocky escarpment in which there are deep caves that give the rock face the impression of looking like a skull; some people think this was where Jesus was executed, but there is no guarantee that those caves were there in the time of Christ.

Crucifixion was carried out in various ways, according to the sentence or the whim of the executioner. By far the most normal procedure was for the person to be stripped and his outstretched arms nailed to the cross-beam he had carried, as he lay on the ground. The beam would then be lifted with his body on it, and fastened over the vertical post. The feet were then nailed to the post, one on either side, or by one huge nail through both feet. Sometimes criminals were only tied to the cross, which involved less acute physical torture and loss of blood, but made for a much slower death.

Opinions vary as to the actual cause of death during crucifixion, but it seems reasonable to suppose that the main causes would be heart-failure and traumatic shock, or progressive suffocation brought about by the gradual contraction and rigidity of the muscles and lack of oxygenation of the blood. It was a vicious circle of agony that led inevitably to death. How soon that death came would depend on the strength of the individual. Josephus the historian once discovered that three of his friends had been crucified by mistake. He had them cut down, still alive, but only one of them survived his injuries. If the Romans wished to hasten death, they gave the victim's legs a blow with an iron club and broke them – the *crurifragium*. Death then followed swiftly, because they could no longer push themselves up. The two thieves crucified with Jesus had their legs broken because it was approaching nightfall and they were still alive.

The nails from crucified men were highly valued for use in magical rituals and there was a great demand for them throughout the Roman Empire. Jewish texts reveal that they were used to reduce swellings and inflammations and as a cure for fever; Pliny, the Roman historian, said that they were used to check the spread of epidemic diseases, and as a cure for epilepsy. These nails, incidentally, were not inserted through the palm of the hand, because this fleshy part would not sustain the weight of a body – the nails would just tear through. They were inserted through the wrist. The skeleton of a crucified man was found in 1968 in a cemetery near Jerusalem. He had been nailed through the wrists, and by one huge nail through both heels, after his legs had been broken and doubled up beneath him.

The guards who carried out the executions were entitled to the prisoners' effects as part of their wages, and these were divided equally. We are told that they cast lots for Jesus' tunic so as not to have to divide it. This casting of lots may well have made Jesus think of Psalm 22, and to quote it aloud to show how truly it was being fulfilled. To quote the passage as he did was not necessarily a cry of despair and abandonment – the psalm ends on a note of triumph. The other things that Jesus said on the cross do not suggest that he was cringing in darkness and desolation – on the contrary, they suggest that he was exceedingly composed, and gave up his spirit willingly, with a prayer.

For Jesus to die so quickly was unusual, and to make certain that he was dead, according to St John's Gospel, a soldier pierced him in the side with a spear.

The fact that Christ's body was being allowed burial was unusual, but there is evidence that it was permissible for a corpse to be handed over once it had been dealt a blow that opened up the heart. In other texts, for example Cicero's *De Suppliciis*, certain governors were reproached for refusing to give this authorisation. In Cicero's case, he reproached a certain Verres for only handing over corpses after exacting an enormous payment from the relatives. Quintilian, a first-century lawyer, insisted that it was permissible to bury the bodies of executed people once they had been pierced. As the executioner was usually a soldier, this blow would be inflicted with his lance or a short javelin – a blow studied in the fencing schools of the Roman army throughout the world.

The fact that Jesus met his death by crucifixion was seen as being highly significant, as the cross had long been an established religious symbol, and meant far more to the early worshipper than a mere gibbet. For St John's Gospel in particular, the cross was the very symbol of life. In 3:14–15 he said that, even as Moses had lifted up the serpent nailed to the post in the wilderness to cure people of snakebite and thus give them back their earthly life, so Christ would be lifted up (upon the cross) to redeem them for eternal life. The Egyptian symbol of the cross, the Ankh, represented the male and female elements in nature in the very act of creation itself, and therefore it signified the constant renewal of life.

Visitors to Jerusalem today can visit the Church of the Holy Sepulchre, which holds within its walls both the supposed site of the crucifixion and the place where Jesus was buried. Is there any guarantee that these sites are genuine? First, one might well ask how the tomb was so close to the place of execution. Burials, and executions, had to take place outside the city walls, and the richer a man was the nearer to the gate of the city his tomb would be situated. Jesus was said to have been buried in the tomb of a rich man, possibly Joseph of Arimathea. Tradition makes him a relative of Jesus, the brother of the Virgin Mary's father Joachim. It would be in keeping with Jewish practice for a body to be handed to the senior male relative.

Eusebius of Caesarea visited Mount Zion in A.D. 135 and a church was certainly in existence then. In 212, when Bishop Alexander founded a library in the city, regular pilgrimages to the site began. One famous visitor to this library was the learned Origen of Alexandria, who came searching for old manuscripts, and also to investigate the origins of the holy places. The search for the true sites was ironically made much easier by the destructive activities of the Roman Emperor Hadrian, who had tried to undermine Christianity. He had erected a temple of Venus over what he understood to be the tomb of Jesus; a statue of Jupiter at the site of Calvary; and a grove of trees sacred to Adonis round the cave at Bethlehem which was said to be the birthplace of Christ.

Following the conversion of the Emperor Constantine, in 326 the Bishop Makarios of Aelia (Jerusalem's new name) got permission to dismantle the Temple of Venus, and rediscovered the tomb. Constantine's mother, Helena – who had been converted at the age of sixty-five, and who then became the patroness of many great buildings – visited the site to search for the cross on which Jesus had died. According to tradition, there was a cistern between the tomb, Calvary, and the old wall, and among the debris in it three crosses were found. Nobody knew which one was the cross of Christ, so a dying woman was made to lie down on each of them, and the one which cured her was declared to be the true cross. This cross became a relic of the utmost importance.

Under the Temple of Venus, a tomb *was* found, surprisingly intact, a double chamber hewn out of the rock, with a rolling-stone to cover the entrance. The rock was cut away carefully all round it, and the church lovingly built over and around the site. To this day, the place where our Lord was hurriedly laid to rest can still be seen, protected now by a marble slab. The Romans had done with him – the rebel king was dead.

Questions

1. How were Roman citizens executed?
2. What was scourging?
3. What was a flagrum?
4. What was the difference between Hebrew and Roman law on scourging?
5. Where did the soldiers probably find the thorns for Jesus' crown?
6. What was a patibulum?
7. Why were prisoners given myrrh?

8. How were prisoners fixed to crosses?
9. What are the most likely causes of death in crucifixion?
10. What was the *crurifragium*?
11. Why is it unlikely that people were nailed through the hand (unless they were tied well)?
12. What were the guards entitled to as part of their wages?
13. Why were crucified men speared in the side?
14. What was the cross seen as the symbol of?
15. What was erected over the tomb of Jesus by the Emperor Hadrian?
16. When was Jesus' tomb rediscovered?

Research

1. Find Mark 15:21–28.
(a) Who carried Jesus' cross?
(b) Where was Jesus crucified?
(c) What did this name mean?
(d) What did they offer him as a pain-killer?
(e) Did Jesus drink it?
(f) What did they do with Jesus' clothes?
(g) What inscription was placed over him?
(h) Who was crucified with Jesus?
(i) What did the bystanders challenge Jesus to do?
(j) When did darkness descend on them?
(k) What Aramaic words did Jesus cry out?
(l) Who did they think he was calling for?
(m) What final kindness was offered him? (Vinegar was the sour wine mixed with raw egg and honey that was issued to the troops, and known as *posca*.)
(n) What happened when Jesus died?
(o) What did the centurion in charge say?

2. Find Luke 23:26–49.
(a) Who wept for Jesus as he was led to execution?
(b) What did Jesus say to them in verse 28?
(c) What prayer did Jesus make for the soldiers who nailed him to the cross?
(d) Why did one of the thieves defend Jesus?
(e) What did he ask Jesus?
(f) What did Jesus say to him?
(g) What were Jesus' last words? (This was the 'good-night prayer' of a Jewish child.)
(h) What, according to St Luke, did the centurion say?

3. Find John 19:23–30.

(a) Why did the soldiers cast lots for Jesus' tunic?

(b) What scripture did this fulfil?

(c) Find Psalm 22, and read verses 1–2, 6–8, 16–18. How does this psalm fit the crucifixion of Jesus? (The saying, 'Eli, Eli, lama sabacthani?' has caused a lot of difficulty to scholars. It seems to indicate that Jesus thought he had been deserted by God. The other sayings from the cross do not back this idea. Was it really a cry of despair and desolation? Maybe Jesus was deliberately quoting from Psalm 22 because it fitted his circumstances so closely. That psalm ends not in despair but in triumph. Read verses 23–51!)

(d) What arrangements did Jesus make for his mother?

(e) What did Jesus say in verse 28?

(f) Did Jesus taste the vinegar?

(g) What were his last words in this version? (This last saying was probably the 'loud cry' that we are told about in the Synoptic Gospels.)

4. Find Matthew 27:50–54. What does St Matthew add about the things that happened when Christ died?

Creative Writing

Imagine that you are either one of the lady disciples at the foot of the cross, or one of the soldiers on duty. Describe how you felt as the prisoners were crucified, and what your reaction was to the words Jesus spoke from the cross.

41

WHAT WAS THE SIGNIFICANCE OF THE DEATH OF JESUS?

The fact that Jesus died on a cross is an accepted part of history. Scholars still argue as to whether it was the Jewish priests or the Roman authorities who were really responsible for his execution. Perhaps Jesus was, after all, a leading member of the Zealot resistance movement, making a claim to be the King of the Jews in the literal sense. We cannot tell on the small amount of evidence available, but the general tenor of his teachings and mission do not seem to back that theory.

The Christian Church has concentrated more on the deeper meaning of why Christ died. Jesus did not have to die because of either the Romans or the Jews, but because of us – because of the world. This is the real message of the gospels.

St John's version states quite openly that 'these things are written that you may believe that Jesus is the Christ, the Son of God, and that believing, you may have life in his name' (John 20:31). The writer hoped very much that the things he recounted in his gospel would convince people that Jesus was more than just a man, just a brilliant teacher or compassionate friend. If a person believes that Jesus was a living revelation of God, indeed the Son of God, then he is starting to learn something very important about God.

For God allowed His son to die. Every time a person thinks he hates God, or cannot understand why such a tragedy had to happen, or wonders why they or their loved ones have to suffer, and wonders how people can believe in a God of love who apparently allows dreadful things to happen – he must consider the meaning of the cross. For God *did not intervene for Jesus*, his agony was not spared. God let his own son die.

Religious thinkers, including Jews and Christians, have been aware that, although the universe was supposedly God's creation and good, yet it was riddled with evil and sin. The Jews worked out a system whereby a person could put his relationship with God right from time to time, using the symbolic act of a sacrifice, usually of the blood of an animal. The Day of Atonement, one of the chief Jewish festivals, was the annual occasion when the High Priest sacrificed on behalf of all the people. At the Feast of Passover each family made fresh religious vows and sacrificed a lamb – in memory of when God delivered the Hebrew slaves from Egypt.

To the Christian, the death of Jesus was seen as the greatest of all sacrifices, the means whereby God and Man could be united, and Man forgiven for his sins. St John's Gospel suggested that Jesus, the 'Lamb of God', was actually killed at the precise moment when the Passover lambs were being ritually slaughtered (cf. I Corinthians 5:7). But why was the sacrifice of Jesus necessary at all?

Over the centuries, the Church gradually worked out rather a mechanical answer to this question. Man was basically supposed to be sinful and selfish; he was trapped in a web of sin and evil from which he could not escape. No matter how hard he tried, he could never repay God for his own sins and the sins of the world. God was Eternal Justice, and therefore could never just simply let Man off for his sins – a price would somehow have to be paid or God's justice would be at fault. But God could not bear to see Man, whom he loved, condemned for ever and helpless. Therefore it was necessary for God to take on human form so that He could Himself in this miraculous way put everything right. Man had the price to pay, but only God could pay it; to get out of this legalistic tangle God became Man, a Man that was born to die.

However, this scheme has the defect that it also gives the idea that somehow God needed to be persuaded to forgive us – which really does seem very artificial and strange. It makes it look as if somehow Jesus was more merciful or compassionate than God Himself; as if Man desperately wanted to be forgiven, but God could not bring Himself to do this freely without this odd legalistic charade. There was also the problem of how the death of Jesus could possibly be of any benefit to anybody. How could the death of the innocent God-Man affect *me*? Would it not mean that I could then commit whatever sins I liked, since the price for me had been paid anyway?

All this seems to miss the point. What matters very much is a study of who and what Jesus was, and what really happened at the cross. Jesus was not just Jesus, a man from Galilee, but a manifestation of God Himself. To see Jesus was to see the Father (John 14:9). The concept of God as an offended and irate Being needing to be appeased is wrong; the delivery that Man needs is not from the punishment he deserves for his sins, but from the grip of sin itself. God's love for us is without limit, boundless. He is always ready to receive back the lost son or the lost sheep. His love works by sacrifice in a way that we will probably never understand fully, but may understand a little when we think about the death of Jesus.

222

There is a beautiful line in one of the new communion services which reads: 'Father, we thank Thee, that while we were yet (still) sinners, you met us on the way and brought us home.' There is the clue. God comes to us in love anyway – not if and when we promise to do this or that, or be reformed characters, and so on. He comes while we are still sinners. There are no conditions. It is just a question of whether or not we can understand that and accept it in our hearts. God loves Man beyond what he deserves, beyond what he has any right to expect. He sacrifices Himself, and all we can do is to realise that although we owe God something we can never pay, He has remitted our debt as though it were paid already. The sacrifice is not the appeasing of God's anger, but the very outcome of His love.

Jesus on the cross showed us how God loves us, even though we have not yet loved Him or perhaps even realised He is there. 'When he was reviled, he reviled not again. When he suffered, he threatened not' (I Peter 2:23). His prayer for those who were still torturing him was, 'Father, forgive them, they know not what they do.'

What Jesus did can perhaps be illustrated by the story of Schamyl, a Circassian chieftain who died in the Caucasus in 1871. Bribery and corruption were so rife in his kingdom that he ordered that anyone caught at it should be sentenced to a hundred lashes. To his horror, one culprit soon caught was his own mother. Schamyl spent two days in agony not knowing what to do. How could he order this dreadful punishment for his own mother? Yet how could he set aside his own laws against corruption? There was no way out, but one. Schamyl's mother was brought out and tied to the post, and given five lashes. Schamyl himself took the other ninety-five. Imagine the effect this must have had on Schamyl's mother, who had been the one who had done the wrong, and who had to watch her son suffer so much because he could not bear the punishment to fall on her.

Christ pays our price in an existential way. We have somehow to cross the barrier of understanding. We do this best by considering the cross, and how Jesus died. So we must see that Jesus was not suffering because of God's anger, or satisfying God's honour, or even accepting God's punishment. He was actually meeting sin head on and suffering its consequences, in an act of voluntary obedience, in such a way as to call out our love and loyalty and devotion.

That is why a Christian can never regard Christ's death as in any way a failure or a defeat. It was Jesus' greatest triumph, and an act of pure love and faith.

Questions

1. Can you think of any of Jesus' teachings or actions that might make us think that Jesus was not a Zealot revolutionary leader?
2. What benefit were the symbolic actions of sacrifices for the Jews?
3. Name two occasions in the Jewish year when sacrifices were made.
4. What did the fourth gospel indicate about the significance of the time of Jesus' death?
5. What answer was traditionally given by the Christian Church as to why God had to become Man?
6. Find Luke 15:20–24. What was the reaction of the father in the parable to the returning son? Did the father wait for the boy to make his apologies and explanations? What does this tell us about God's love?
7. How does Jesus' prayer on the cross reveal God's love for us?
8. Why was the death of Jesus in no way a defeat?

42
THE BURIAL OF JESUS

Standing at the foot of the cross were several people who loved Jesus dearly: his mother; his aunt Mary, the wife of Cleophas, St Joseph's brother; Mary Magdalene; and Salome the mother of James and John.

As evening drew near, and the hour for the Passover meal to be eaten approached, Pilate was asked for permission to break the legs of the crucified men so that they might die quickly and their bodies be removed. Pilate gave his authority, and the two thieves' legs were smashed with the iron bar. When the soldier came to Jesus, he saw that he was already dead. Meanwhile, Joseph of Arimathea and Nicodemus, two important Pharisees and members of the Sanhedrin, applied for permission to take away Christ's body for burial. Pilate agreed.

The soldier at the cross was duly informed, and gave Christ's body the customary stab with his javelin, to make certain officially that he was dead. The beloved disciple, who was at the cross throughout the crucifixion, saw that blood and water flowed from the wound this made. Then the cross-beam was lifted down, and Jesus was carried to Joseph of Arimathea's own tomb, which was apparently near the place of execution.

Usually the corpses of executed criminals were left on the crosses for the beasts and birds of prey to tear to pieces, but they could be asked for by their families, and the law allowed the bodies to be taken, unless there had been other instructions issued. It was also apparently quite in order for the ashes of those who had been burnt to be returned to relatives. Notable prisoners, however, were sometimes refused burial. Ulpian, the law-giver, stated quite clearly in his *Digest* that the bodies of those who had been executed were not buried, except when permission had been asked and granted. Sometimes it was refused, especially in regard to the bodies of those who had been condemned for high treason.

The tomb in which Jesus was buried was said to be 'a new tomb, in which no man had yet been laid', and St Matthew's Gospel stated that it was Joseph of Arimathea's own sepulchre. Tradition identifies this Joseph as the senior member of the Holy Family – in fact, as the brother of the Virgin Mary's father. If this were so, it would explain why he, of all people, was present to take away the body of our Lord.

Jesus was laid on a linen cloth that Joseph had bought, which had been placed carefully over several linen strips. Spices were placed around his body. A bandage would then have been tied around his face, passing under his chin. Then the linen cloth was brought down over the top of his body, and the linen strips were brought up from beneath and fastened round his ankles, knees and chest.

The Jews did not practise embalming or cremation, but attached the highest importance to a proper and decent burial. The body was normally washed and anointed before being wrapped in its shroud. In Jesus' case, this washing and careful preparation was not carried out, because the funeral party was so pressed for time. They simply packed the spices round his body as a temporary measure, and planned to return to the tomb at the earliest opportunity, when the sabbath was past, to complete their task.

The tomb of Jesus was described as a rock-hewn tomb with a rolling-stone. Sometimes Jews were buried in common graves, or hill-side caves. Simple wayside graves were just burials in the ground, with the earth heaped over in a little mound. These had to be limewashed every year after the rains, so that people did not defile themselves by walking over them accidentally. The ideal was for a man to be 'gathered to his fathers' in the literal sense of being buried in a family vault.

Inevitably, archaeology can tell us more about the elaborate tombs than it can about the simple ones. Generally, these consisted of a series of underground chambers dug out of the limestock rock. One entered by a low door and went down a slope or a few steps to a central room from which other chambers led off. These were provided with rock benches, on which the bodies were laid. The outer door was sealed by a thick slab of stone fitted to the opening. At the time of Jesus, a rolling stone boulder was sometimes used – a wheel-shaped stone, possibly from an oil-press, which was rolled down a groove. These stones were extremely difficult to get out once they had rolled down into position. Many tombs had been in use for centuries, and were simply entered and cleared from time to time. Old bones would be collected up and placed in chests, called ossuaries, or buried in pits. One grave, found in an old cemetery just outside Jerusalem in 1968, contained the bones of thirty-five persons packed into fifteen ossuaries, including the remains of a man who had been crucified!

According to St Matthew, after Jesus had been buried, the priests

The Garden Tomb *Jesus was buried in the rock tomb of a wealthy man. Claims have been made that this garden tomb was where Jesus lay – although most authorities accept that his tomb is the one shown in the Church of the Resurrection in Jerusalem. This tomb still preserves the atmosphere of what Jesus' tomb may have been like.*

approached Pilate and asked him to place a guard on the tomb. Apparently, Caiaphas knew of the rumours that Jesus was expected to rise again from the dead. He was obviously quite convinced that Jesus *was* dead, and that the only way he could 'rise' was if the disciples managed to steal his body and hide it, and fake a miracle. By Roman law, the body of a crucified criminal was state property, and if it was stolen, the guards on duty at the time would have paid for their negligence with their own lives. But Pilate refused to set Roman guards to the task, and Caiaphas was obliged to use his own Temple guards. The stone was duly sealed, and the guards were ordered to keep watch.

When, however, the women arrived at dawn on the Sunday morning with their spices, intent on giving Christ's body its proper washing and anointing, they were worried about how they would roll the stone away from the tomb. They may not have known that Caiaphas had set this guard there – or surely their worries would have been not only whether the guard would get the stone out for them, but whether they would have been given permission to go in at all!

As they arrived, it was obvious that something very unexpected had happened. There were no guards to be seen at the tomb, and the great stone had been rolled away. When they looked inside the black opening, they saw that Christ's body had gone, and there was a young man sitting there who tried to speak to them – but they were too shaken and afraid. They ran away.

Questions

1. Who watched Christ's execution?
2. How did the Romans speed up the death of their victims?
3. Who asked Pilate for Jesus' body?
4. What did the soldiers do before handing over a body for burial?
5. Were crucified persons normally buried?
6. Where was Jesus buried?
7. Why were wayside graves whitewashed?
8. What was a rolling-stone for?
9. What was an ossuary?
10. What practice was not performed at Jesus' burial?
11. Why were guards set at Jesus' tomb?

The approximate timings of the last events

The Last Supper	*c.* 6–10 p.m. Thursday
In Gethsemane	*c.* 11 p.m.–*c.* 3 a.m. Friday
The arrest	*c.* 3 a.m.
Trial before Annas	*c.* 3–4 a.m. (A preliminary investigation)
Trial before Caiaphas	*c.* 4–5 a.m. (A preliminary hearing)
Trial before the Sanhedrin	*c.* 5–6 a.m. (to give official approval of sentence passed)
Trial before Pilate	*c.* 6 a.m. – 7 a.m.
Trial before Antipas	*c.* 7 a.m. – 8 a.m.
Before Pilate again, scourging, etc.	*c.* 8 a.m. – 9 a.m.
Crucifixion	9 a.m. (Mark 15:25)
Darkness	12 noon
Death of Jesus	3 p.m.
Burial of Jesus	3 – 6 p.m.
Passover Day	6 p.m. Friday – 6 p.m. Saturday
Women at the tomb	4 – 6 a.m. Sunday

Research

1. Find Mark 15:40–47.
(a) Which three women are mentioned as being witnesses to Christ's death?
(b) When was permission sought to bury Jesus?

(c) Who asked Pilate for Jesus' body?
(d) What does verse 43 tell us about Joseph of Arimathea?
(e) Why was Pilate surprised?
(f) What did Pilate want to know before he gave permission for Jesus' burial?
(g) What did Joseph do?
(h) Who saw where Jesus was buried?

2. Find Matthew 27:55–61.
(a) Which women does St Matthew say were witnesses to Christ's death?
(b) What does St Matthew tell us about Joseph of Arimathea in verse 57?
(c) What details are revealed in verses 59–60?

3. Find Luke 23:50–53.
(a) Is anything new revealed about Joseph or the tomb?
(b) What did the women do after Joseph had buried Jesus?

4. Find John 19:38–42.
(a) Why was Joseph of Arimathea a *secret* disciple of Jesus?
(b) Who helped him to bury Jesus?
(c) Find these passages, and write out what it tells us about Nicodemus: John 3:1–2; 7:45–52.
(d) Back to John 19:38–42. How much spice did Nicodemus bring?
(e) What are we told about the tomb of Jesus?
(f) Does St John's version mention that the women were going to come back with spices?

5. Find Matthew 27:62–66.
(a) When did the priests go back to Pilate?
(b) What did they want him to do?
(c) Why did they want this?
(d) Did Pilate let them have a Roman guard?
(e) How did the priests 'secure' the grave?

Creative Writing

Either: Write a poem expressing your feelings about the events that took place at dawn on Easter Sunday.
Or: Imagine that you are one of the guards at the tomb. Write your official report to Pilate, describing what happened at the tomb of Jesus.

43

THE RESURRECTION OF JESUS

According to St Mark's Gospel, the women returned to the tomb at dawn on the Sunday morning, where, to their great amazement, they found that the body of Jesus had gone. They had not expected any such thing – they had gone to the tomb for the express reason that they wanted to wash and anoint Jesus' corpse with spices. They found an unknown young man in the tomb, and they fled in fear and astonishment and told no one.

In the two oldest manuscripts of St Mark's Gospel that we have, the text breaks off suddenly at verse 8. Our Bibles usually offer two alternative endings, which are sometimes written in after verse 8, or sometimes given as footnotes in italics at the bottom of the page. It is generally agreed by scholars that neither of these endings was the original one. They first appear in manuscripts round about A.D. 150 and the Greek style and phraseology of either passage is quite different from the rest of the gospel. If neither of these endings is part of the original, we are left with three options. Either the gospel was intended to finish at verse 8, or there was a 'proper' ending but it got lost or torn off, or St Mark was interrupted before he could write the end.

The section we are given as verses 9–20 is an appendix. It briefly mentions several events which are in the other gospels – an appearance to Mary Magdalene, to two disciples in the country, and to the eleven – and it also has a few statements that are only to be found here. It says that the disciples would be able to cast out demons, speak in tongues, be immune to poisons and snakebite, and heal the sick. But it is to the other gospels that we must turn for the resurrection stories.

St John's Gospel gives the very moving story of how Peter and the beloved disciple heard the news and ran back full speed to see the grave. The beloved disciple was a younger man and arrived first, and stooped under the entrance to see that the women's story was indeed true. Christ's body had gone. However, he waited for Peter to arrive and go in first before he also went inside to investigate. Once inside he saw the funeral cloths lying on the slab, and one of the pieces – the napkin which had been round Christ's head – lying rolled up in a place by itself. This piece was possibly a jaw-band of the sort that was traditionally tied under the chin to prevent it from sagging, and not a cloth over the face, as is often thought. This particular cloth, it is claimed, is the relic preserved at Oviedo in Spain. If Jesus' body really had been stolen, then the thief had for some reason taken it out of its funeral wrappings. The 'linen cloths' were presumably the shroud itself and the strips of bandaging that would be tied round it at ankle, knee and chest (see John 19:40). The shroud may be the relic preserved at Turin.

The gospels vary in their accounts of what happened next. According to St John, after telling the disciples about the empty tomb, Mary Magdalene followed them back there. After they had left, she remained behind, heartbroken. She suddenly saw two angels sitting at the head and the feet of where Jesus had lain. Then she heard a voice asking her why she was weeping, and she assumed that the person silhouetted in the doorway of the tomb was the gardener. She assumed that he had removed the body, and begged him to tell her where he had taken it, so that she could fetch it away. When he spoke again, she realised that it was not the gardener at all, but Jesus himself. He would not let her touch him, but told her to tell the disciples that he was ascending to God his Father.

In St Matthew's version, however, it was not just Mary Magdalene who saw Jesus but a group of women. They did not see two angels, but only one. They ran from the tomb, but before they left the area Jesus met them, and they were able to take hold of his feet and worship him. They were given the message that Jesus was going to Galilee, and that the disciples would see him there. The eleven remaining disciples dutifully went to Galilee, where Jesus did appear, and gave them some final instructions before leaving this earth for ever.

St Luke's version stated that the women did not see an angel, but two men in white, and that the disciples did not believe their story. Then Jesus appeared to two persons walking along the road to Emmaus, a village some seven miles away from Jerusalem. These people were completely unknown so far as the gospel narrative is concerned – they appear nowhere else in the account of Christ's life. They were certainly not among Christ's chosen disciples, so who were they? Why did Jesus appear to them?

One of them was identified as a man called Cleophas. The other was unnamed, but it might well have been Cleophas' wife. Her name is given as Mary in John 19:25, assuming that Cleophas was the same person as Clopas. The Synoptic Gospels reveal that this lady stood at the foot of the cross as Jesus died, and she was the mother of James and Joses. According to tradition Cleophas was the younger brother of Jesus' earthly father Joseph and the four persons named in the gospels as the 'brothers' of Jesus – James, Joses, Simeon and Jude – were actually Jesus' cousins. If Joseph died shortly after Jesus was born, leaving Mary a very young widow, it is quite possible that she may have gone to live with Cleophas, Joseph's next of kin. This theory would certainly explain why Jesus should have appeared to these people – his aunt and his uncle – who may not have been the complete strangers that the Gospel of Luke seems to suggest.

However, despite his walking with them for some distance, the two people on the road to Emmaus did not recognise Jesus until he had entered their house. He took bread, blessed it and broke it. Then they knew who he was, and were very startled. As soon as they recognised him he vanished. They immediately rushed back to Jerusalem with the news, only to discover that Jesus had just appeared to Peter as well. Could Jesus really have revived and recovered from his wounds and appeared to them in his body that had died? They might well have known from his other healings that Jesus could probably have healed himself too – but how could they explain the fact that he had walked with them for miles, talking with them, and they had not recognised him – and then suddenly they did? Had he somehow been able to change his shape before their very eyes? And how had he just disappeared? And wasn't it ludicrous to think of him rushing away from them up the road towards Jerusalem so fast that not only did they not see him, or his dust, but he was able to get there so long ahead of them that he had time to appear to Peter as well?

While they were discussing the implications of all this, Jesus suddenly appeared again. This time they all saw him, and they were terrified! To prove that he was not just a ghost, he took some broiled fish and ate it. He led them out to Bethany, promised them that they would soon be 'clothed with power from on high', told them they were to stay near the Temple, blessed them, and disappeared.

St John's Gospel mentions two other appearances of Jesus in Jerusalem. In one, which may possibly have been a variant of the one just referred to above, he appeared in the room where ten of the disciples were gathered. The narrative suggests that he made his entry into the room through a locked door. In the second account, he made a special appearance for Thomas, the one disciple who had missed the previous visit. Thomas had said that he would not believe until he had seen Jesus for himself, and actually touched him. Jesus held out his arms and invited him to feel his wounds, and even put his hand into the great hole torn in his side where the spear had entered. Thomas was completely convinced. For the first time, a person acknowledged Jesus as his God.

Finally St John recorded an appearance of Jesus in Galilee, where the disciples had gone fishing. The story is rather similar to that of the miraculous catch of fish when Jesus first called his disciples, in Luke 5:1–11. They had caught nothing. Jesus appeared on the shore and called to them. They tried again, and found that this time the nets were full to bursting. By the time they had beached the boat Jesus had cooked them a breakfast over a charcoal fire. He asked Peter three times if he loved him, presumably giving him the chance to make up for his threefold denial of him during the trials.

St Paul's letter to the Corinthians mentions (15:3–7) other appearances of Jesus – to 500 brethren at one time, and then to James the brother of Jesus. There was a tradition mentioned in the Gospel according to the Hebrews, that James had sworn that he would not eat until he had also seen Jesus. Jesus appeared before him and told him to take his bread and eat. This James then became the leader of the Church in Jerusalem, until his martyrdom at the hands of another High Priest, in A.D. 62.

Questions

1. When did the women return to the tomb?
2. Where does St Mark's Gospel officially end?
3. What suggestions have been made about the end of St Mark's Gospel?
4. What does St John's Gospel mention about the grave-clothes?
5. What did the women do to Jesus in St Matthew's version?
6. What suggestions have been made about the relationship between Cleophas and Jesus?
7. How did Jesus prove he was not just a ghost in St Luke's version?
8. What proof did Thomas require before he would believe in the resurrection?
9. What had Jesus' brother James sworn? What happened?

Research

1. Find Mark 16:1–8.
(a) When did the women return to the tomb?
(b) What was troubling them as they approached the tomb?
(c) What did they find had happened?
(d) What did they see inside the tomb?
(e) What did they *not* see inside the tomb?
(f) What were they told?
(g) What was their reaction to all this?

2. Find Luke 24:1–11.
(a) What did the women see in the tomb according to this version?
(b) What was the reaction of the disciples to their story?
(c) What is added in verse 12? (This may be in a footnote at the bottom of the page.)

3. Find Matthew 28:1–15.
(a) What happened as the women approached the tomb, in this version?
(b) What was the reaction of the guards to this?
(c) Does the angel's message agree with St Mark's or St Luke's version?
(d) What happened in verse 9?
(e) What did the guards do?
(f) What were they bribed to say?

4. Find Matthew 28:16–20.
(a) Where did the disciples see Jesus?
(b) What instructions did he give them?
(c) Copy out the last sentence of the gospel.

5. Find John 20:1–10.
(a) Who first saw the empty tomb in this version?
(b) Who did she tell?
(c) What did they see in the tomb?

6. Find John 20:11–18.
(a) Who remained at the tomb?
(b) What did she see?
(c) What did they ask her?
(d) What did she say to them?
(e) What did she see next?
(f) Who did she think it was?
(g) What did she say to him?
(h) Why didn't Jesus let her touch him?

Creative Writing

Either: Write a short play about one of the appearances of Jesus to his followers.
Or: If Jesus did *not* come back to life, try to consider some of the other possibilities for what happened to his body. Explain why you think these possibilities are either likely or unlikely.

44

THE RISEN LORD

What happened to the body of Jesus is probably the greatest mystery of all time, and the starting-point of the Christian faith. The founders of the Church did not become founders because Jesus had been a good man, or a perfect example of righteous living, or a brilliant teacher, or even a worker of miracles. All those things became past history the moment he died. They became the Church founders because of the tremendous impact on them of what happened to Jesus *after his death*. At his death they were in despair, they were frightened, they thought Jesus had failed. Suddenly, they changed completely into joyful and powerful missionaries, many of whom died rather than admit that it was all a fake, a fraud. They could not stand up and say that Christ had not risen, that his body was rotted away in some hidden grave – because they knew beyond any shadow of a doubt that they had seen him alive again, talked to him and touched him.

Numerous theories have enjoyed being fashionable as explanations of this amazing miracle. First, it has been suggested that the resurrection of Jesus was only a legend. Legends, however, take time to form and grow. How does one explain the fact that the belief in the rising of Jesus sprang into being *immediately* after his death?

Perhaps Jesus had not really been dead when he was buried, and recovered in the cool of the tomb, and got away under cover of the darkness. Was the man dressed in white a friend who helped him escape? If so, where did Jesus hide until his final death? Did his disciples know that he had really been alive all the time? Then why were they later to allow themselves to be tortured and killed, and even worse, to see their families and loved ones put to death? Why did they continue to make hundreds of converts and see them martyred too? Surely they would have been the most evil of criminals if they carried out this fraud? Was it possible that Jesus *was* alive, but managed to hide himself from them so that they honestly did not know about him? How then would one explain the appearance of Jesus to them? It is totally inconceivable.

Crucifixion was a terrible punishment, and was very rarely survived, especially after scourging. The historian Josephus did have some friends who had been crucified by mistake, and they were cut down – but only one survived. And he had certainly not had a spear thrust into his side! The author of St John's Gospel makes special mention of the fact, and the flowing of blood and water from the wound. He actually breaks into his narrative at this point and says: 'He who saw it has borne witness – his testimony is true, and he knows that he tells the truth!'

Although it was not unknown for people to be buried alive – and Jews usually visited a grave for three days after burial and inspected the bodies to make certain they were really dead – it was not known for a crucified man, speared through the heart, to be active enough to push a rolling-stone out of the entrance to his tomb!

What other suggestions have been made to account for the missing body of Jesus? Perhaps the women went to the wrong tomb. This would mean that they had all incredibly forgotten where they were the day before; that there was a choice of new, rich men's tombs hewn out of the rocks; that the guards had been in the wrong place.

Maybe the disciples *did* steal the body, as the guards said they had. If so, why did they then stick to the story when they were being tortured to death, and allow their converts to suffer as well? And surely the priests, with their vested interest in finding that particular body, would have been able to bribe some informer and discover the truth?

Did Joseph of Arimathea remove the body in the night? If so, where did he take it? He went to a great deal of trouble to get the body put in his tomb in the first place – why should he then move it, and keep it a secret?

Did the Roman or the Jewish authorities remove it? Surely not, for then they could easily produce it to squash all those resurrection rumours. One Jewish document, the *Toldoth Yeshu*, claimed that the body *was* found. It had been moved by the gardener, because the crowds of visitors to the spot were trampling on his cabbages! He dumped it down a well. When he realised what the claims being made about Jesus were, he pulled out the bloated corpse, tied it by the feet to a horse, and dragged it round to the authorities. There was probably little left to identify by that time, anyway, even if the story were true. If the Christians knew of this legend, they certainly didn't take it seriously. They stood by a belief in what the disciples *had seen* with their own eyes – not a mangled, bloated corpse, but their living speaking Lord; and for their faith in him they were quite prepared to die.

Jesus' resurrected body had certain extremely physical characteristics. He walked to Emmaus, a distance of some seven miles, talking to people; he picked up bread and broke it; he actually ate some fish; and he cooked a fish breakfast over a charcoal fire. And yet, at the same time, he also seemed to possess various non-physical characteristics. In St John's Gospel, Mary Magdalene did not recognise him at first, and then a few minutes later she did. Does this suggest that it was dark, he was a silhouette, her eyes were too full of tears, or that he could change his shape? On the road to Emmaus, two other people who had presumably known and loved him, and may even have been his uncle and aunt, didn't recognise him either. Again, does this suggest that his shape could be altered at will? It is also worth noting that Mary was told not to touch him. Was this because he was not yet 'solid' enough to be able to touch? The women in St Matthew's version touched his feet. Was that slightly after his command to Mary not to touch him? Could we be justified in using the word 'materialised'?

How did Jesus appear to Peter before the Emmaus disciples got back to Jerusalem? Is it possible that he could have 'dematerialised' in Emmaus and then 'rematerialised' in Jerusalem? How did he suddenly appear in the upper room? We are given to understand that the doors were shut, which probably meant *locked*, for fear of the Jews. Does this not suggest that Jesus just materialised? Or perhaps, like a traditional ghost, he came through the wall.

If we do consider such a psychical theory, we gather up other problems. If his body dematerialised in the tomb, why was it necessary for the stone to be miraculously moved? Was that simply so that the women could get in? They had been intending to roll it out again anyway. Was it shifted by the earthquake only mentioned in St Matthew's version? Alas, we do not know. On another tack, if Jesus dematerialised through his shroud, when his body rematerialised for his appearances, was he also wearing ghostly clothing? Psychic researchers often get asked this sort of question about much less exalted apparitions. The theory that Christ's body did indeed dematerialise or deatomise would probably include the suggestion that he took his substance for his appearances, including his clothes, from the disciples themselves.

The earliest written evidence for the resurrection of Jesus that we have is not in any of the gospels, but in St Paul's letter to the Christians at Corinth. There he recorded the whole reason for his conversion, the supreme factor that had made him turn from being a persecutor of Christians to being a Christian himself. He had been told that after Jesus' death and burial he rose again on the third day; then he appeared to Peter, to the twelve; then to 500 people at one time, most of whom were still alive when Paul wrote the letter. Next he appeared to his brother James, an appearance not mentioned in our four gospels (nor was the appearance to the 500). What mattered most to Paul was that finally he appeared to *Paul also*.

Paul would probably never have become a Christian had he not had his famous experience on the road to Damascus. Jesus' appearance to Paul was described in one text as being a heavenly vision (Acts 26:19). Some modern scholars have argued that all the appearances of Jesus were really visions in the minds of the disciples, and not real evidence for Jesus' resurrection. One should read the accounts through carefully and try to make up one's own mind.

The account of St Paul's dramatic trial before King Agrippa in Caesarea gives plenty of details of his experience. 'At midday, O King, I saw a light from heaven, brighter than the sun, shining round me and those who journeyed with me. And when we had all fallen to the ground, I heard a voice . . .' (Acts 26:12–18). 'Those who were with me saw the light but did not hear the voice of the one who was speaking to me . . . when I was blinded because of the brightness of that light, I was led by the hand into Damascus' (Acts 22:8–11). St Luke's version of what happened to Paul, given in Acts 9:1–9, stated that the fellow travellers did hear the voice, but saw no one – an interesting contradiction!

Some have tried to argue that Paul's blindness was not real, but spiritual or symbolic – ignoring the fact that he became blind *after* seeing Jesus.

Paul was also told by the risen Christ that when he got to Damascus he was to find a man called Ananias. Ananias had also been granted a vision of Jesus, which he took very calmly as if quite used to such things, in which he was told to go to the place where Paul had been taken, and cure him. And so the two men met, despite Ananias' understandable reluctance, and Paul got back his sight.

These appearances do seem to be of a visionary nature, and have no physical details such as the Risen Christ eating fish or being touched.

However, the supreme miracle of the Christian faith is that God became a human being at all. This is the most fundamental and far-reaching of all the miracles recorded in our gospels. The people who lived then were not idiots or easily deceived. They were as capable as we are of making balanced judgements. Was the miracle of the resurrection contrary to the laws of nature? How can we say? We don't know yet what all the laws of nature are. If God did enter the world in the person of Jesus, then the Resurrection is quite logical. Death cannot be stronger than God.

We have arrived at the end of the gospels – yet, in the New Testament, the story was very far from over. Things were just about

The Summit of the Mount of Olives *The disciples saw Jesus for the last time when they were standing at the summit of this hill.*

239

to happen. Exciting things. Things that changed peoples' lives completely. The labourers in the field were just about to stumble on their buried treasure. Has it ever occurred to you that *you* are disciples too? *Good ploughing!*

Questions

1. Why is the resurrection unlikely to be only a legend?
2. Why did Jews visit graves for three days after a burial?
3. Why is it hardly likely that the disciples *did* steal the body?
4. If the authorities had taken Jesus' body, what would they have done to prove the Christians were wrong?
5. Why is the evidence of the *Toldoth Yeshu* not acceptable?
6. List the physical characteristics of Christ's resurrected body.
7. What is the 'materialisation theory'?
8. In what ways does it seem more likely that the appearance of Jesus to St Paul was a vision and not a physical appearance?

Research

1. Find Luke 24:13–35.
(a) Who was walking to Emmaus?
(b) Who walked along with them?
(c) What is revealed in verse 16?
(d) What did they tell the stranger in verses 22–24?
(e) What did Jesus talk to them about?
(f) What happened when they reached Emmaus?
(g) When did they recognise Jesus?
(h) What happened when they recognised him?
(i) What was their immediate next step?
(j) What did they find out had happened when they got back to Jerusalem?

2. Find Luke 24:36–53.
(a) What happened while they were talking?
(b) What was their reaction?
(c) How did Jesus prove he was not 'just' a ghost?
(d) Copy out verse 39.
(e) What did he tell them to do in verse 49?
(f) Where did he leave them?
(g) What did they do?

3. Find John 20:19–29.
(a) Copy out verse 19.
(b) Which disciple was not there on this occasion?
(c) What was his reaction when told of the appearance of Jesus?

(d) When did Jesus appear again?
(e) What did he say to Thomas?
(f) What did Thomas say to him?

4. Find John 21.
(a) Who went fishing?
(b) When did they see Jesus?
(c) What did Peter do when he recognised Jesus?
(e) What had Jesus done by the time they all came ashore?
(f) What question did Jesus ask Peter three times?
(g) Copy out John 20:30–31.

Creative Writing

Either: Pretend that you are one of the disciples who witnessed the Risen Christ. Write your own account of what happened and what you saw.
Or: Why is the truth of the resurrection so important? Would it have made any difference to Christianity if Jesus had *not* risen?

45
SOME THOUGHTS ON FAITH

A sentence from *Alice Through the Looking Glass* states the problem most clearly. 'With a little bit of practice it is possible to believe six impossible things before breakfast.' To have faith in anything, even in God, does not imply of itself that what is believed in is absolutely true. It may not be. The whole problem of faith is that the key element in it is uncertainty. If a thing was absolutely known for certain, then the question of having faith in it would not arise. To have faith does not mean that you are supposed to believe in what you know is not true – but to believe in something when you can never prove that it is true.

Faith requires a commitment to something, whether it is God, or another person, or a course of action. When we get married, we have faith in another person – we believe that we will be able to get on with that person and live happily together, for better or for worse, until the parting at death, or even beyond death. It may not work out like that, as we know – but getting married is an act of faith.

When we climb aboard a plane to go abroad, we have faith that the pilot will get us there safely. He may not, but we trust that he will, so we get in the plane and we go. When we buy a house, it is an act of faith. We take out a mortgage for twenty years, without having the least idea of whether or not the house will still be standing then! When a jury decides a man is guilty and puts him away for years, it is also an act of faith. They did not actually see him murder his rival, but they believe that he did strongly enough to condemn him. The faith is really in our judgement.

We cannot have scientific proof about the existence of God, just as it is highly unlikely that we could have a film record of our criminal committing murder, or foreknowledge as to whether our house will be bombed down or burnt or survive. All we can do is have a good look at such evidence as is available, make a decision, and act on it.

Can we swim? Can we really do it? How can we tell if we don't get into the water? We must have faith and commit ourselves to the water believing that we can swim. The philosopher Kierkegaard thought that faith was like floating on 70,000 fathoms of water, and not being afraid. That's something like belief in God. Belief by itself is neither here nor there. Jesus said that many people might call him 'Lord', but the important thing was to *do* the will of the Father, not just talk. Not even just believe (Matthew 7:21). The doing, the loving, the having compassion, the caring life will show a person whether God is real or not. That's faith.

Can Jesus give us faith in God? Well, look at his life, consider his teachings. They give us a great deal of evidence about something very special, about a standard of loving and compassion that fits the very highest of our ideas. A person who studies Jesus and admires him, and honestly believes that although he was a very great teacher and wonder-worker he was *not* Son of God, is twisting the evidence in front of him. For Jesus knew that he did have a special relationship with God, and made extraordinary claims about himself, and acted as if all his moves were on God's authority – so much so that many of the religious authorities were offended and considered him to be blaspheming.

If Jesus was *no more than* a teacher, he was not that moral and not that wonderful, for some of his words and actions would imply arrogance, fraud, delusion and a desire to mislead. Look carefully at the evidence: if it does not seem to you that Jesus was deliberately trying to mislead people for his own selfish purposes, then we must take on trust that he was either mad, or exactly what he claimed to be. His life and example were certainly not indicators that he was mad. If he really was what he claimed to be, then what he taught about God was true. To believe this is indeed an act of faith, but not an act that lays aside human reason.

Either the Christianity based on the life, death and resurrection of Jesus is the most outrageous and evil mass hoax; or the whole edifice is the product of ridiculously stupid and gullible people suffering from mass delusion and hysteria; or there just could be something in it.

You have now had a good look at the facts as presented in the gospels. What you believe as a result of those facts is up to you.

46
ESSAYS

1. Explain what the term 'Messiah' means. Relate three incidents in the life of Jesus which illustrate his claim to be the Messiah.
2. What were the Jewish expectations concerning the Messiah? How far did Jesus (a) fulfil them, and (b) differ from them?
3. What were the main titles used either by Jesus for himself, or by his followers to describe him? Explain the meanings of these titles.
4. Who was John the Baptist, and why was his mission significant?
5. What was the connection of John the Baptist with the prophet Elijah?
6. What were the significant events concerning the birth of John the Baptist? Make special mention of the speeches in the narrative.
7. Summarise the preaching of John the Baptist, and explain briefly the purpose of his ministry.
8. What happened at the baptism of Jesus? Are there any significant differences in the gospel versions of Christ's baptism?
9. Why did John have a ministry of baptism? Why do you think Jesus agreed to be baptised? What did the signs at Jesus' baptism represent?
10. What is the significance of baptism in the life of a Christian? Why do some people think it is not right to baptise babies of non-churchgoing couples? Why do some people think it is not right to baptise babies at all?
11. What was the significance of the temptations, and where did Jesus face them again in his ministry?
12. Compare the birth narratives as given in St Matthew's Gospel with those in St Luke's.
13. What are the significant details of the various speeches recorded in St Luke's birth narratives?
14. What is the doctrine of the Virgin Birth? Discuss the problems raised by this belief.
15. How does the birth narrative in St Luke's Gospel illustrate his interest in the poor, the lowly, and the point of view of women?

16. How does the birth narrative in St Matthew's Gospel illustrate his interest in proving that Jesus was the expected Jewish Messiah?
17. Outline the story of the temptations as given in the Synoptic Gospels, and explain the answers given to them by Jesus.
18. How did the early ministry of Jesus indicate what sort of Messiah he was going to be?
19. Who were the Twelve Apostles? What is the difference between an apostle and a disciple? What do we know of the 'calls' of the apostles Peter and Matthew?
20. What were the causes for the mounting opposition of the Pharisaic party to the mission and person of Jesus?
21. Which town became the headquarters of Jesus' mission in Galilee? Give a brief account of two events which took place there.
22. What connection did the Jewish religious authorities have with sickness as indicated in the stories of (a) the healing of the leper, (b) the healing of the paralysed man, and (c) the healing of the man with the withered hand?
23. What were the main methods of healing used by Jesus in his ministry. Give a brief example for each method, or choose two of the methods and discuss them in detail.
24. What conclusions about sickness and health can we draw from Christ's ministry of healing?
25. What is meant by healing by 'mechanical means'? Give two synoptic examples of where Christ used this method.
26. Which four synoptic healings were performed on a sabbath day? Give an outline of the arguments that arose from them.
27. Which synoptic invalids were raised from the dead? Describe one of these incidents in detail.
28. Give in detail an example of where Christ cured (a) a Gentile, (b) a Samaritan, (c) a woman, and (d) a child.
29. What were the main beliefs of the Pharisees concerning (a) the creation of the world and God's purpose for it, and (b) the Messianic leader?
30. What teaching is contained in the 'seed parables' of Mark 4?
31. What are the 'seed parables'? Which one is only in St Matthew's Gospel? Give a summary of this parable, and explain its meaning.
32. 'The Kingdom of Heaven refers to a present fact and a future hope.' What does this saying mean? Illustrate it with two parables that deal with these aspects.
33. What did Jesus teach about the future time of Judgement? On what did he say we would be judged?
34. What did Jesus teach about (a) the value of the Kingdom, and (b) the growth of the Kingdom?
35. What are the beatitudes? What types of people would find

'blessedness'? How do St Luke's beatitudes differ from St Matthew's?

36. Complete these beatitudes and state clearly what each one means:
(a) Blessed are the poor in spirit.
(b) Blessed are the meek.
(c) Blessed are they who hunger and thirst after righteousness.
(d) Blessed are the merciful.
Summarise a parable of Jesus which illustrates one of these sayings.

37. Write out carefully the parables that would fit the following summaries: (a) Keep awake! (b) Defer judgement until the last possible moment. (c) Accept and use gifts, or be cast out.

38. What were the main methods used by Jesus in his ministry of teaching? Give a brief example for each one.

39. What is a parable, and why did Jesus teach in parables?

40. Which of Jesus' parables are given as allegories? Write out one of them in full, including its meaning. What do some scholars suggest about the allegorical interpretations given to these parables?

41. From which gospel do the parable *stories* come? Write out two of them concisely. What qualities do they have in common?

42. Can you see any connection between the parable of the prodigal son, and the parable of the labourers in the vineyard?

43. What was the difference between the Law and the Tradition? What was the attitude of Jesus to both?

44. Give three examples in which Jesus contrasted his teaching with that of the Old Law. In what way do these examples justify his statement that he had come not to destroy the Law, but to fulfil it?

45. What difference existed between the teaching of Jesus and that of the Pharisees on (a) the keeping of the sabbath, and (b) fasting?

46. How did Jesus' attitude to the Tradition of the Elders give offence to the Pharisaic party?

47. What teaching about prayer did Jesus give in the Sermon on the Mount? Relate a parable about prayer he told on another occasion, and explain its meaning.

48. What did Jesus teach about (a) prayer and (b) forgiveness? Briefly summarise one parable he told in illustration of each subject.

49. What do the prayers of our Lord himself teach us about the qualities of a Christian life?

50. In what ways did Jesus consider that a person's motives for his religious life should govern his actions?

51. Give in full:

(a) A parable that teaches humility in prayer.

(b) A parable that teaches persistence in prayer.

(c) Two prayers of Jesus himself, from the cross.

52. What did Jesus teach about anxiety? What kind of thing did he have in mind when he said that we should 'take no thought for the morrow'?

53. Give four illustrations from the Sermon on the Mount which indicate the way the followers of Christ should behave towards other people.

54. What did Jesus say in the Sermon on the Mount about (a) anger, (b) retaliation, and (c) adultery? Consider the relevance of one of those topics for the present day.

55. What was the parable of the two foundations? On what should we base our lives? Write out briefly a parable that deals with our progress in life.

56. What did Jesus teach about forgiveness?

57. What was the parable of the two debtors? What connection did this have with the parable of the prodigal son?

58. Illustrate the teaching of Jesus on forgiveness by reference to (a) a parable, (b) a miracle, and (c) an action of his own, and (d) a prayer of his own.

59. What did Jesus regard as true greatness in a person? Write out the parable of the seats at the feast, and that of the Pharisee and the publican.

60. What was the attitude of Jesus to wealth and luxury? Why was the widow's offering worth more to God than that of the wealthy?

61. What was the teaching of Jesus on marriage and divorce? Do you think he would have sympathy with the divorce laws of the present day? Give reasons for your answer.

62. What teaching about life after death was inherent in the parable of the rich man and Lazarus, and the incident of the Transfiguration?

63. What were the main differences in the beliefs of the Pharisees and the Sadducees? Briefly give an incident from Jesus' life connected with each party.

64. In what ways did Jesus agree with the Pharisees, and how did he differ from them?

65. Give an incident from the life of Christ connected with each of the following places: Jericho, Capernaum, Nazareth, Nain, Gerasa.

66. What happened at Caesarea Philippi? What did Jesus then tell his disciples about his mission? In what ways does this incident mark a turning point in the ministry of Jesus?

67. Write a short account of the religious and political parties among the Jews at the time of Christ.

68. Describe what happened when Jesus took three of his disciples 'up into a high mountain apart by themselves'. Comment on the meaning of this incident.
69. How did Jesus prepare his disciples for his death? What was their reaction when they were told?
70. State briefly what you know about the worship connected with the Temple and the synagogue. Allude to one incident in the life of Jesus connected with each.
71. On what occasions did Jesus reveal his power over nature? Describe one of these incidents in detail.
72. Describe in detail how St Matthew's account of Christ's walking on the water differs from St Mark's.
73. 'The Lord appointed seventy others, and sent them two and two before his face.' What instructions did Jesus give to the seventy? What did he say on their return?
74. Which gospel mentions the mission of the seventy disciples? What theories have been suggested about this mission?
75. How does the miracle of the feeding of the four thousand differ from that of the five thousand? What suggestions have been made by scholars concerning this miracle?
76. Why were the priests and Sadducees so affronted by Jesus' mission?
77. Why was Jesus opposed by (a) Pharisees, (b) Sadducees and (c) the priests? Illustrate your answer fully.
78. Why was Jesus rejected at Nazareth? How does St Luke's account of the incident differ from that of St Mark?
79. Who were the Sadducees? What question did they put to Jesus in Holy Week? Which religious party would have agreed with the answer Jesus gave? Explain the answer.
80. What was the priests' question? Why did they ask it? How did Jesus avoid giving a straight answer, and what did his answer imply?
81. Write out the parable of the vineyard. What did it imply about (a) the priests, (b) Jesus himself, and (c) the new faith Jesus was founding?
82. What was the attitude of Jesus towards (a) the Tradition of the Elders, (b) the *corban* ceremony, and (c) tax-collectors and prostitutes?
83. Describe, with full reference to parables and incidents in the life of Jesus, his attitude to Gentiles and Samaritans.
84. Who were the Samaritans? Why was there enmity between Samaritans and Jews? What did Jesus teach in a parable in which a Samaritan was the hero?
85. Write full notes on the following: (a) Essenes, (b) Zealots, (c) Herodians, (d) scribes and (e) Samaritans.

86. Give an account of an incident in which Jesus was referred to as (a) Son of David, (b) Son of Man, and (c) Son of God. Comment on the significance of these titles in the context you have chosen.

87. What may be learnt from the gospels about the strong and the weak qualities in St Peter's character?

88. Describe the events of Palm Sunday. What was significant about the method Jesus used to enter Jerusalem?

89. What was the incident of the fig-tree? How do details differ in the synoptic accounts? What parable does St Luke have in his gospel concerning a fig-tree?

90. Describe the layout of the Temple at Jerusalem. What action did Jesus take there after his dramatic arrival in the city?

91. Why was the Day of Questions so called? Outline in detail one of the questions that Jesus was asked, and his reply to it.

92. What happened on the Wednesday of Holy Week? How is this incident possibly connected with an earlier one in St Luke's Gospel?

93. Comment on the first few verses of St Luke's Gospel, with reference to his accounts of (a) Holy Week, (b) the rejection at Nazareth, (c) the Sermon on the Mount.

94. Make full notes on the following:
(a) The date of the Last Supper.
(b) The role of Judas.
(c) The Holy Communion.

95. Write a brief account of the events that took place from the arrest of Jesus until his death on the cross.

96. How did the events in Gethsemane reveal the true strength of Jesus? What did Jesus teach elsewhere in the gospel about the cost of discipleship?

97. How does St Luke's description of the events in Gethsemane differ from that of the other gospels?

98. Write a careful account of the trial of Jesus before Caiaphas. What happened to Peter during this trial?

99. What parts were played in the story of the Passion by (a) Herod, (b) Pilate, and (c) Joseph of Arimathea?

100. Describe briefly three incidents in the gospels which shed light on the character of Peter.

101. Describe the part played in the Passion of Jesus by (a) the servant of the High Priest, (b) a certain young man, (c) Simon of Cyrene, and (d) the Roman guards at the Tomb.

102. What features are special to St Matthew's account of the trials of Jesus?

103. On what grounds was Jesus put on trial for his life?

104. Give a careful account of the trial of Jesus before the Sanhedrin.

What part did the chief priests later play (a) at the trial before Pilate, (b) at the crucifixion, and (c) after the burial of Jesus?

105. What special features are mentioned only in St Luke's version of the crucifixion of Jesus? What do these reveal about St Luke's understanding of our Lord's character?

106. Write an account of the crucifixion of Jesus, noting the chief differences in the gospel accounts. Did Jesus really die in the depths of despair?

107. How does a knowledge of Psalm 22 illuminate our understanding of the crucifixion narrative?

108. Discuss the endings of the Synoptic Gospels.

109. State briefly the various occasions when Jesus is recorded as having appeared to people after his death. Choose one of these, and explain its particular importance for our understanding of the Resurrection.

110. What evidence do we have in the Synoptic Gospels of (a) the physical nature, and (b) the non-physical nature of Christ's resurrected body?

111. What problems are raised by the disappearance of Christ's body from its tomb? Suggest some of the possible explanations that have been put forward to account for it.

112. What happened on the road to Emmaus? Give a full account of what was said and done (a) on the road, (b) at Emmaus, and (c) afterwards in Jerusalem.

113. How are the following statements shown to be wrong by the accounts given in the gospels of the resurrection and subsequent events? Give one incident for each:
(a) The disciples removed the body of Jesus from the tomb.
(b) The appearances of the risen Christ were only visions of a spirit or ghost.
(c) The fact that Jesus was crucified proves that he cannot have been the Messiah.

114. It has been suggested that Mark obtained much of his information from St Peter. What evidence is there in this gospel to support this theory?

115. What does St Luke tell us about his purpose in writing a gospel, and his qualifications for doing so? What sources do scholars suggest that he used for his gospel? Relate one parable that is only in his gospel, that illustrates his ability as a storyteller.

116. What evidence is there to suggest that St Matthew's Gospel was written for Jewish converts?

117. List three special interests of St Luke, or characteristics of his gospel, and illustrate each with a parable or incident that is only to be found in his gospel.

118. How far do the Christian gospels present the modern person with a guide to life that is worth pursuing?
119. Christians claim that Jesus was not just a perfect man, but was the Son of God. How could this claim be substantiated from the gospels?
120. Are the ideals and beliefs of the Christian Church worth dying for?

Index